Compassion, Inc.

Compassion, Inc.

How Corporate America Blurs the Line
between What We Buy, Who We Are,
and Those We Help

Mara Einstein

UNIVERSITY OF CALIFORNIA PRESS

Berkeley · Los Angeles · London

University of California Press, one of the most
distinguished university presses in the United States,
enriches lives around the world by advancing
scholarship in the humanities, social sciences, and
natural sciences. Its activities are supported by the UC
Press Foundation and by philanthropic contributions
from individuals and institutions. For more
information, visit www.ucpress.edu.

University of California Press
Berkeley and Los Angeles, California

University of California Press, Ltd.
London, England

Library of Congress Cataloging-in-Publication Data

Einstein, Mara.
    Compassion, Inc. : how corporate America blurs the
line between what we buy, who we are, and those we
help / Mara Einstein.
        p. cm.
    Includes bibliographical references and index.
    ISBN 978-0-520-26652-0 (cloth : alk. paper)
    1. Social responsibility of business—United States.
2. Consumer behavior—Moral and ethical aspects—
United States.   I. Title.
    HD60.E38 2012
    381.3—dc23

                                        2011030385

Manufactured in the United States of America

21 20 19 18 17 16 15 14 13 12
10 9 8 7 6 5 4 3 2 1

In keeping with a commitment to support
environmentally responsible and sustainable printing
practices, UC Press has printed this book on Rolland
Enviro100, a 100% post-consumer fiber paper that
is FSC certified, deinked, processed chlorine-free, and
manufactured with renewable biogas energy. It is
acid-free and EcoLogo certified.

*To my mother, Barbara, who taught me to
embrace education, revel in the theatrical, fight
for social justice, and put family first, and to my
daughter, Cayla, who is so very lucky to have a
grandmother who would leave her such a legacy*

Contents

Preface

The inspiration for this book occurred on October 13, 2006. I was watching *The Oprah Winfrey Show*, and on that day Oprah and U2's lead singer, Bono, were launching a new marketing campaign called (RED). What's that? You know what it is—it's the Gap INSPI(RED) T-shirt; it's the red iPod nano, Apple's mini digital media player; it's the American Express Red credit card. "Oh, right, right," is the typical response. (I know this conversation well, because I've had it hundreds of times over the past several years.)

If you really don't know (RED), the way it works is easy: buy an upscale consumer item (like an iPod or a cell phone or a cup of Starbucks) and an often unspecified amount of money will go to the Global Fund to fight AIDS and malaria in Africa. You don't pay more than you would for a non-(RED) product—a (RED) iPod nano is the same price as a green or blue one—so why not buy it and have the money go to charity, especially when Oprah and Bono and a slew of other celebrities think it's a great idea?

When I first saw this campaign, I thought it was a great idea too. My twenty-plus years of experience in the marketing industry taught me (and physics will suggest as well) that it's easiest to move a body in the direction it's already heading. People are already shopping, so why not turn this self-centered act into an act for good? It was genius!

But after a chance to reflect, I felt a sense of unease about Product (RED). Could shopping really be the best way to "change the world"?

Is spending a little extra money on a T-shirt or buying an iPod nano going to make a difference? Even more broadly, if we buy into the idea that caring for others can be easy, then what happens to *real compassion*, to *real change*, to *real lives?*

These questions bothered me, and I wasn't sure how to process them until three months later when I was asked to speak about Martin Luther King Jr. on a panel at the 2007 Media Reform Conference in Memphis. Like most people, I had a general idea about Dr. King and his legacy, but doing the research for that presentation forced me to dig a lot deeper—particularly because I was speaking on the holiday named for Dr. King and in the city where he was murdered.

Dr. King's work was rooted in a Christian, specifically Protestant, movement to improve social conditions for the poor, the sick, and the less fortunate called the Social Gospel, which came into being in the late nineteenth and early twentieth centuries. He was a strong advocate of the Social Gospel, and he widely applied its ideals to his ministry—first in the Civil Rights Movement and later in advocating for the poor.

My talk focused on how Dr. King used the media to promote the Social Gospel, and it led me to consider how people who carry on his legacy are using the media today. This brought me to Bono, a celebrity widely recognized as a social advocate and activist. Like Dr. King, Bono has successfully used the media to promote his causes, many of which preceded the (RED) campaign and gained him such stature that he has regularly met with world leaders, including the late pope John Paul II. Unlike Dr. King, Bono now uses the media to promote products like cell phones or iPods—ultimately, we hope, for a higher purpose, but high-end consumer products nonetheless. It's a long way off from Dr. King, who promoted the idea of equality for human beings, struggled to right the wrongs of an unjust system, and espoused a world vision in which people will be valued for who they are, and not what they are. People who believed in King's words died in the streets. Forty years later, Bono has suggested that we go shopping.

So I had to ask myself: Would Gap wage the "good fight" if it meant not being able to use cheap overseas labor? Would Apple commit to social justice if it meant selling fewer iPods and the plethora of subsequent $1.29 downloads? Would any company take on a politically divisive issue if it might make consumers angry and ultimately have a negative impact on the bottom line?

The answer, of course, is no.

THE PRICE OF COMPASSION

Subsequent to that *Oprah* episode in 2006, I began to review how consumer companies have gone about aligning their products with social causes in an effort to sell more of them and was surprised by how far-flung this practice had become. Sure, we have seen environmental messages on everything from cars to cleaning products, but now marrying product sales to charity exists for causes from child trafficking to heart health to hunger, and it is being used to sell everything from water to weight loss, from puffer jackets to personal care products.

Research for this work was developed through a combination of methodologies. In addition to reviewing cause-related marketing campaigns over numerous product categories, I did content analyses of some of the more notable ones, including a number of more in-depth case studies. These appear throughout the book. To contextualize this work, I reviewed the literature on cause marketing, corporate social responsibility, sustainability, social entrepreneurship, and the debate over the citizen-consumer hybrid, as well as examined the most recent studies released by consumer marketing research firms. I attended the leading conferences related to the field, including the Social Enterprise Conference at Harvard, the Sustainable Brands Conference (virtually), and the Lifestyles of Health and Sustainability (LOHAS) conference in Boulder, Colorado, all in 2010, as well as smaller events, such as the Herbert Rubin Symposium on the Privatization of Development Assistance at the New York University School of Law in 2009, conferences on social entrepreneurship at the Stern School of Business at NYU, and a symposium on microfinancing at the New York Society of Security Analysts (NYSSA).

I gained significant insights coming out of these conferences and seminars, both because of the firsthand experiences that company marketers and CEOs conveyed and also through access to marketing research that was not readily available elsewhere. However, better to comprehend the thinking behind how and why these campaigns have been created and are continuing to gain momentum, I conducted interviews with people from marketing agencies, public relations firms, and product companies, a number of which entailed on-site visits. Finally, in conjunction with this work, I have been teaching a course on this topic for the past two years at New York University. As part of that course, guest speakers from large and small companies have provided their expertise on philanthropy, cause marketing, and social innovation, and have graciously given of their time both in and out of the classroom. In all this, I came to see the intricate dance among corporate motives, consumer demand, and charitable need as it relates to cause-related marketing (CRM), corporate social responsibility (CSR), and social innovation.

I found that nonprofit organizations likely to be funded by CRM or CSR campaigns are those that appeal to valuable consumer audiences, notably middle-to-upper-income women, particularly mothers. Because women represent more than 80 percent of all consumer purchases, marketers tend to support causes of special concern to them, such as breast cancer research, education, children's welfare, and the environment.[1] In addition, corporations favor noncontroversial charities, or ones that enable them to get a foothold in new overseas markets, over charities that are politically charged. Thus, education is a popular cause, and better still causes that support education in Africa. Moreover, celebrity spokespeople—the more, the better—bolster the appeal of one charity over another. This creates a bandwagon effect, attracting more and more corporations to the same social issue, because they see it as an opportunity for extensive free publicity.

At the same time, nonprofits have adopted sophisticated marketing techniques and harnessed the resources of consumer product companies to raise more money for their causes. In particular, there are an increasing number of branded charity campaigns that court consumer product companies. Campaigns like (RED) and Susan G. Komen for the Cure, which gets companies to produce pink products in October for breast cancer awareness, are designed specifically to appeal to manufacturers of branded goods.

This book is a critical examination of the corporate takeover of caring and the price we pay as individuals and as a society for ceding charitable works to the marketplace. It analyzes how charities are becoming commodities via a twofold process: corporations are using charities to sell their products, and charities are branding themselves as products to be marketed to corporations. Concerns exist on both sides of this equation: (1) nonprofits may be forced to change their mission in order to brand themselves to appeal to corporate partners, and (2) CSR, which has traditionally been understood to include, among other things, environmental issues, workers' rights, community impact, and a civic responsibility to all of a corporation's stakeholders both inside and outside the corporation, is being transformed into yet another element of corporate branding.

A "charitable marketplace" has been created, one in which we come to think of shopping as philanthropy and thereby believe we have been relieved of any responsibility to donate through more traditional methods. The problem with this is that, despite one's best intentions, large amounts of the money being contributed in this way are not going to help the poor and the less fortunate. Moreover, issues like poverty, education, and health care are being repackaged in pursuit of corporate profits with little effect on the underlying concern.

SHOPPING AS PHILANTHROPY

Compassion, Inc. begins by examining why we, as consumers, have come to expect that charities and good works will be associated with the brands we buy. In part, this has to do with the importance of brands in identity creation—we may, for example, be Subaru drivers and iPhone users. We imagine these brands to reflect not only our taste in products but also our personal values. The other aspect that has contributed to the combining of causes with products is the changing emphasis from the receiver of charity to the one who is doing the giving. Certainly (RED) does this, but if you have a rubber bracelet on your wrist, regardless of its color, you have bought a badge of charity to show the world you care.

Chapter 2 lays out why corporations have embraced charity as a means to sell more products. This strategy works on a continuum from governmental compliance (doing what regulations require a corporation to do) to social innovation (fundamentally realigning a company to ensure that it works to improve the lives of people and the planet, while creating profit). The most popular step is cause-related marketing. The simplest form of this is when a company asks you to purchase a product and money from the sale of that item goes to a charity. Think of pink ribbons in October to support breast cancer research, or the green magnifying glass for St. Jude's Children's Research Hospital in December (a logo I'm still not sure I understand), or even Milk-Bone dog biscuits, where money goes to train dogs that aid the disabled.

Out of the growing industry of cause marketing arose what I am calling hypercharities, a concept developed in chapter 3. Hypercharities are oversized philanthropic marketing machines that attract so much attention and money that smaller, local institutions and ones that don't appeal to key marketing demographics don't get the support and funding they need. Examples are Susan G. Komen (breast cancer),

Feeding America (hunger relief), and the National Heart Lung and Blood Institute's *The Heart Truth* (heart health for women). This is not to say that these organizations and their campaigns aren't doing some good. They most certainly are. Problems arise when they set the agenda for what society's most pressing concerns are—even when they are wrong. (Hint: breast cancer is not the leading cause of death among women, even though most women think it is.) Tied to these large fund-raising behemoths is their ability to attract A-list celebrity talent. Use of celebrities and the broader use of charity as entertainment, so-called charitainment, are also discussed.

Chapter 4 asks what the consequences of co-opting compassion are, and why now? Bringing philanthropy into a consumer mind-set has a downside both for individuals and for society at large: it depoliticizes issues by putting a pleasant face on complex problems; one charity is favored over another based on its ability to generate corporate tie-ins and celebrity endorsements, rather than on actual need; and charity becomes mediated and depersonalized, inuring us to human suffering.

Corporations exist to serve the best interests of their shareholders. It is rare when those interests include supporting a better education system or improving national healthcare. If social issues are addressed at all, it is typically done through the filter of marketing—a filter that shows you what corporate interests want you to see and hides what they'd rather you didn't see. You'll see happy women walking for three days in pink shirts to raise money for breast cancer, but you won't see the millions of mothers and children who can't afford basic health care. You'll be privy to how much money was raised by a company's campaign, but not to how much was spent in marketing to raise it.

Further, those charities that don't serve the needs of advertisers—ones that can't be made visually appealing or those that seek to benefit the elderly or the poor, for example—will be decidedly underfunded, or worse still, ignored.

These trends have occurred because of cultural ideologies that drive how the market works. First of all, there has been the rise of neoliberalism: the belief that the market can do a better job than government in managing society. As a result of this ideology, corporations are acquiring increasing power to oversee social concerns. Then, just as important, there is our acceptance of the concept of the hybrid "citizen-consumer." We have come to believe that we can "vote with our pocketbooks" and purchase our way to social change through fair trade, green products, and trips to Whole Foods Market. What is true in this scenario is that the needs of the market and the individual consumer far outweigh the concerns of the society.

Decades of consumer culture have taught us that any problem can be solved through the purchase of a product and disposed of just as easily. Now, that formula—with lots of branding money, the Internet, and celebrity bells and whistles attached—is being widely applied to charitable causes. We may hope that these new ways of marketing will bring more people to care about good works, but given marketing's history, it is far more likely that these campaigns will give us just one more reason to feel good about buying overpriced consumer goods. The ultimate consequence of merging profits and purpose is further desensitization to those less fortunate, while doing little to engage people in meaningful altruism, ideas that are explored in chapter 5.

Given all this, it is easy to become cynical. However, what was heartening in my research was to find companies that really are making a difference and fundamentally rethinking the way business is done. Well-known examples are Newman's Own, which donates all profits after taxes to charitable concerns, and MAC's VIVA GLAM Lipstick, which supports HIV/AIDS initiatives. There are also unexpected and even controversial examples like Walmart and General Electric, and finally, corporations that give back while remaining true to the bottom line by creating products and services that serve what is known as Bottom of the Pyramid (BoP), the poorest of the poor who live on less than $2 a day. BoP is rapidly becoming a field unto itself. The most commonly known example of this is microfinancing, where banks lend small amounts of money to people in impoverished communities so that they can create small local businesses. Are some of these corporations still practicing aspects of business that I find offensive? Absolutely. However, what I bear in mind is something that one of my informants said to me while I was working on this book: McDonald's is not going to stop making hamburgers. So isn't it better, rather than simply bashing the company, to support it in doing what it does in a more ethical and environmentally sound way? After all, it is not the mixing of commerce and caring per se that should concern us. Rather, it is turning true human suffering into a sales pitch for a disposable consumer product. It's a matter of emphasis. Corporate social responsibility, implemented in the traditional sense in which it was developed, can be a powerful source for social good.

In the final chapter, I provide ten suggestions for how to make the world a better place both within and outside of the marketplace. This starts by reclaiming our identities as citizens, parents, children, workers, and friends, but not as "consumers," an overused and outdated label. Changing our minds about who we are is the first step toward changing our world.

Because the book is about corporate America, it focuses mainly on the United States. However, associating causes with companies is not just an American phenomenon. Many of the campaigns examined are sponsored by multinational corporations like Procter & Gamble and the Anglo-Dutch conglomerate Unilever, which have instituted similar campaigns and CSR initiatives globally, and a recent study found that in emerging markets like Brazil, Mexico, China, and India, people "are more likely than Americans to purchase and promote brands that support good causes."[2] Wide use of cause marketing, and consumer acceptance thereof, is not found in all jurisdictions, because in many cases it does not need to be; there are countries where governmental regulation manages social issues rather than corporate entities.[3]

I have to thank the many people who so graciously gave of their time and energy in helping me put these ideas on paper. First, I must thank Reed Malcolm at the University of California Press who saw the value in this work from its very easiest stages. Thanks as well to others at the press who have made this book a reality. To my scholarly colleagues: first, at Queens College, thanks to Susan Macmillan, Rick Maxwell, and Joe Rollins for your continuing support, ready ears, and helpful debate, and to those beyond, Sarah Banet-Weiser, Sarah Dadush, Monica Emerich, Matt McAllister, Toby Miller, and Inger Stole, for your inspiration and for leading the way. Finally, support for this project was provided by a PSC-CUNY Award, jointly funded by the Professional Staff Congress and the City University of New York.

In addition, I owe a huge debt of gratitude to the many people who helped me better understand the market for compassion, including Noopur Agarwal, George Alvarez, Raphael Bemporad, Scott Ketchum and the other folks at BBMG, Pam Cohen, Ellen Feeney, Bob Gilbreath, Dan Osheyack, Tim McCollum, John Rooks, Eileen Stempel, and Patrice Tanaka. Most notably, I have to thank Chad Boettcher, who took me behind the scenes of social innovation and renewed my faith in the possibility of a better world.

Personally, I could not have made it through this process without my coffee and my "coffee girls," Karyn Slutsky and Roni Caryn Rabin (without whom this book might never have been published). It is a blessing to have such smart friends, and, more important, ones that are so giving on every level. It is you who remind me daily what caring and giving is all about. To my sisters, Dari Bookamer and Jan Dannenberg, now you don't have to hear about "the book" anymore. And, to my daughter, Cayla, thanks for giving mommy time to work when you wanted to play.

Let me end this preface with some thought-provoking research. In the mid-1990s, Yankelovich—a consumer research company—conducted interviews with Harvard Business School's class of 1949, admittedly one of the most successful in its history. What they found was "a powerful set of ethical principles." An astounding 97 percent of those interviewed said that "personal integrity—being straight with people and avoiding the quick buck if it means cutting corners" was one of their most important business norms. Living with integrity was more important than corporate allegiance, even when faced with the difficult position of being asked to "cut corners" by a higher-up. Said one respondent: "There comes a time when the organization demands that you do something and there's no way you can do this and still live with yourself. I was the vice president of the organization, and it demanded that I do certain things that I considered not appropriate, and I walked out. I walked away."[4]

When I read this, I couldn't help but think about the mortgage meltdown. How many mortgage brokers or Wall Street traders could have—no, should have—said no to selling loans to people who could never pay them back? Parents with children, older people, and a significant number of people of color were being forced out of their homes for profit's sake. Where were the bankers who should have walked out, walked away?

Do I believe that business people sixty years ago were fundamentally more altruistic? No, I don't. I do believe, however, that there were social structures in place that enabled businesspeople to act more ethically. While something like the Harvard Business School's "MBA Oath," a pledge for the business manager to "serve the greater good," is a nice gesture, it does not have the teeth necessary to make real change. Nor do the many ethics classes being taught in business schools help alleviate the problem. They obviously didn't help when I was in business school twenty years ago, and they won't help now.

Real change will come with new structures. Those structures need to serve business and the people who work for it; that's the only real sustainability. Thankfully, an increasing number of people—both inside and outside of corporations—want companies that not only say they are ethical, but actually walk the walk. Given the people I've met, I have real hope that this will happen. But we're not there yet.

1

Value Brands . . . They Ain't What They Used to Be

Do you have a yellow Livestrong bracelet on your wrist? Okay, probably not on your wrist anymore, but maybe hidden in a drawer somewhere? And maybe it's not a yellow bracelet. Maybe it's a pink one for breast cancer or a red one for AIDS. You probably donated a buck or two to get it.[1]

Acquiring something in return for a donation has been a staple of philanthropic giving for decades, be it personalized address labels or a red ribbon with a safety pin. But in 2004, Livestrong bracelets changed the charitable fund-raising game in two fundamental ways. First, Livestrong combined a charity with a superstar athlete—Lance Armstrong—and a marketing powerhouse—Nike—to promote a cause based on Armstrong's personal experience.[2] Nike created the yellow band, and subsequently a full line of related yellow products; Livestrong takes the spotlight and reaps the profits (tens of millions of bracelets were sold in the first year alone). Notably, Nike loses money on this ongoing campaign, but continues to support the cause because of the goodwill it confers. Second, and more important for our discussion, this was the first step in moving donations from charitable giving to charitable purchasing—a subtle shift in emphasis from receiver to giver.

This change occurred because Livestrong is not simply a charity; it's a marketing program. Marketing, at its base, is the act of understanding consumers' wants and needs. Once marketers understand these underlying desires, they create products that fill those needs. The need being filled might be simple—I'm thirsty, so I buy a bottle of water—or it may be more complex, as in the case of Livestrong—I am a caring person and I want to show that to people I meet. To serve that need, Livestrong's marketers created a readily recognizable symbol that not only communicates "I care" but is highly visible—it's bright yellow, much like the yellow shirt Armstrong got for winning the Tour de France. Thus you aren't just supporting a charity and you aren't just buying a bracelet; you are buying a bracelet with a benefit. For just a dollar you get to wear the latest fashion accessory *and* show the world your philanthropic nature.

This is very different, then, from writing a check at the end of the year in the privacy of your home or donating money via the Internet. Making a purchase and wearing a product, particularly on a daily basis, is a very public act. That bright yellow band broadcasts to the world that you are concerned enough about cancer to do something about it. And, in doing this, Livestrong is as much about you as it is about cancer.

For sure, the Lance Armstrong Foundation benefits from this exchange. Millions of people happily put down a buck to buy a band, and those individually inexpensive purchases added up to serious money. On top of that, everyone who buys the bracelet—something that unlike a T-shirt or a lapel pin can be worn day in and day out— acts as a walking billboard for the charity, providing Livestrong with priceless free publicity.

In the end, though, this campaign did far more than raise money and awareness for charity through the use of sophisticated marketing techniques. It initiated social marketing's march into the world of consumer product branding.

Two years later, another shift occurred that moved social causes fully into the realm of a branded consumer venture—the launch of the (RED) campaign. (RED) amassed numerous upscale consumer product companies and asked them to use the (RED) parentheses to connote to consumers that a percentage of a product's sales price—be it a cup of Starbucks or a red iPod or a Motorola phone—would go to the Global Fund, which works to assuage AIDS in Africa.

From a consumer culture perspective, (RED) created a seismic shift in how we perceive philanthropy and social justice. (RED) is not a product or a company or even a charity. It's a brand—a name, a logo (the parentheses), and a mythology (it was begun by Bono to save the world). That's it. A brand like McDonald's golden arches or Nike's swoosh, slapped onto a number of high-end consumer products so that "companies [can] expand their customer base and bottom-line by combining their products with a brand that is both culturally significant and compassionate," according to Richard Feachem, executive director of the Global Fund.[3] There's just one problem with that sentiment. A brand cannot be compassionate, only people can.

So why did raising money for charity move from appealing to individual altruism to selling consumer products branded as a charitable good? There are three reasons: one consumer-based, discussed here, one based on changes in corporate responsibility, and one based on new methods of charitable fund-raising; the last two are discussed in the next two chapters.

From a marketing perspective, the first thing to consider is that our consumer environment has become increasingly noisy, and it is exceedingly difficult for any one message—charitable or otherwise—to be heard above any other. Americans are exposed on average to 3,000 marketing messages a day, and we have access to tens of thousands of product options in our supermarkets, drugstores, and the nearest Walmart. Because of this, organizations of any type that are trying to get our attention must do something to make themselves stand out. Branding has become the primary means of doing that.

The second consideration is that the proliferation of a personalized economy has contributed to the commercialization of charity. A personalized economy is one where it is assumed that every individual person's needs can be met by a consumer product customized or nearly customized to individual expectations. This specialization in conjunction with ubiquitous media and concomitant advertising has us socialized to expect immediate gratification in an increasing number of areas: "we want what we want when we want it." We take it for granted that there is a product to fulfill any need, from love (online dating is a $1 billion annual industry) to weight loss (a $60 billion business annually). This expectation is rapidly being transferred to social causes—we begin to look for short-term fixes for long-term social ills, not because we believe this can be achieved but because the immediate gratification of consumer culture leads us to think that way.

In a competitive environment where consumers have limited disposable income, charities are compelled to present themselves as valuable commodities, products (not only services) that are worthy of people's dollars, because they meet personal needs. To do this, charities are being packaged and promoted. They are associating themselves with consumer products and celebrities. They need to break through the media clutter, and for that to happen, a charity needs to establish a brand identity.

A QUICK HISTORY OF ADVERTISING AND MARKETING

Criers—young boys crying their wares—are widely considered the earliest form of advertising. It was the invention of the printing press by Johannes Gutenberg around 1440, however, that led to the broad dissemination of advertising. Early ads (handbills really) were used to sell books of religious verse, and sales messages were straightforward— "This is a book, this is how much it costs, and this is where you can buy one." These clear-cut messages remained the promotional standard for hundreds of years.

The Industrial Revolution of the eighteenth and nineteenth centuries ushered in mass production. The goal of marketers, then, was to sell the vast quantity of products coming out of the factories to anyone who would buy them. By the end of the nineteenth century, a few manufacturers began attaching brand names to their wares; it was hoped that consumers would purchase a specific brand-named product over something that was nameless and generic. This strategy was so successful that by the turn of the twentieth century, branding was becoming standard industry practice.[4] The twentieth century also ushered in what the historian T.J. Jackson Lears calls the "therapeutic ethos," which suggested that product purchases could provide not only gratification through having bought a product but also fulfillment and peace of mind for having done so.[5] The advertising spotlight thus shifted from product attributes (physical features) to user benefits (what the customer gets). So, for example, in the 1920s, mouthwash was no longer only about making your mouth healthy, but rather about relieving halitosis, and therefore about making you more appealing to other people. This idea continued into the 1950s, when Marlboro cigarettes were not only about smoking, but about rugged individualism and a way to escape the grind of corporate America. Today, light bulbs aren't only about illuminating a room, but about helping save the planet. Selling through the psyche has prevailed as the dominant marketing method as mass-produced commodity products differentiated by branding proliferated.

There were, however, competing schools of advertising in the 1950s and 1960s when mass marketing was driven by television. One group used a rational sell to get consumers to buy; this was the so-called hard sell or head sell. It was an approach based on the concept of the unique selling proposition (USP), devised by Rosser Reeves of the Ted Bates agency. A good example of a USP is "Melts in your mouth, not in your hands" for M&Ms. This simple line told consumers the most important and distinct thing about the brand—I can have chocolate, and it won't make a mess—implying that no other candy brand could make that claim.

The problem with the rational sell, however, is that advertising becomes based on having something new to say: what the industry calls "new news." If the brand isn't "new and improved," for instance, what can marketers talk about in their advertising? Companies that invest in significant research and development, like the mega-brander Procter & Gamble, have most successfully used this method. Moreover, this approach is most effective when a consumer is in search of information about which product to buy. What medicine is best for my child's asthma? What kind of car needs less maintenance? How many vitamins and minerals are in my cereal? Most brands have a rational component, which needs to be communicated, but most marketers today would agree that this is not the only information that should be conveyed.

The other school of advertising promoted the soft sell, also called the emotional sell, which was advocated by David Ogilvy and the Chicago ad man Leo Burnett. Ogilvy, the founder of Ogilvy & Mather and a leader in the world of advertising, is famous for creating iconic brands with memorable copy like "the man in the Hathaway shirt" and "Dove is one-quarter moisturizing cream," a line still in use today. Leo Burnett is known for creating characters around his brands, notably the Pillsbury Doughboy, the Jolly Green Giant, and the Marlboro Man. These famous admen were influenced by motivational research suggesting that archetypal images would unconsciously attract consumers to brands. Attracting consumers to the brand through image and emotion was at the heart of the soft sell.[6]

Advertising evolved through the late 1960s and into the 1970s during what was called the creative revolution, a period driven by the copywriters and artists of Madison Avenue. Sophisticated, humorous messages were conceived to sell to a more educated population. Notable work from that time includes Volkswagen's "Ever wonder how the guy who drives the snow plow gets to the snow plow?" and Alka-Seltzer's "I can't believe I ate the whole thing." Urbane humor, emotional imagery, and lifestyle benefits became mainstays of the trade, and behavioral psychologists were ever more involved in industry practices. "Advertising agencies started to talk about 'end end benefits' as opposed to just 'end benefits,' meaning the final consumer satisfaction in emotional terms rather than the physical satisfaction to be gained on the way there," according to the Saatchi & Saatchi executives Hamish Pringle and Marjorie Thompson.[7] In order to identify the emotional end benefits most relevant to consumers, it became of paramount importance to understand who the consumers are, what concerns them most, and what will fulfill their lifestyle aspirations.

Using a variety of methods, from surveys to focus groups to personal interviews, advertisers became experts in psychology and thus learned to understand the motivations behind consumer purchases. From the mid–twentieth century down to the present, marketing techniques have shifted away from mass market thinking and targeting based on demographics—statistical data about consumers—to a niche, and even micro-niche, market mentality based on psychographics.[8]

Psychographics is research that segments consumers based on their personalities, values, and lifestyles rather than their age, income, and gender. These groups are given memorable names that evoke the group psychology. For example, "Bohemian Mix" is a psychographic group defined by PRIZM, a leading marketing segmentation company, as upper-middle-class, ethnically diverse people under the age of fifty-five. More important to marketers is that they tend to like to eat at Au Bon Pain, buy Latin music, read *The Economist,* and drive Audi A4s. "Mayberry-ville" is the name of a rural grouping defined by white people under the age of fifty-five. They tend to shop at True Value, go hunting with a gun, read *Bassmaster* magazine, watch the Daytona 500, and drive GMC Sierras.[9] PRIZM defines sixty-seven different groups, which segment consumers based not only on who they are, but also on what they think and feel, and therefore what they are likely to purchase. Once psychographic groups are segmented in this way, brand companies can determine which of them their products are most likely to appeal to and then target their messages at one or more of them.

"Early adopters" is the best-known psychographic group. An early adopter is the person who has the latest, greatest gadget before anyone else. This feeds the sense of oneself as a "go-to" guy or gal. "Alpha moms" are an example of an early adopter group. According to *USA Today,* these women are "educated, tech-savvy, Type A moms with a common goal: mommy excellence. She is a multitasker. She is kidcentric. She is hands-on. She may or may not work outside the home, but at home, she views motherhood as a job that can be mastered with diligent research."[10] So, an Alpha mom could be a 28-year-old Gen-Y mom/part-time student, a 38-year-old stay-at-home Gen-X mom, or a hard-hitting 48-year-old careerist baby boomer mom: three different consumers with very different demographic profiles. But the psychological motivation to purchase unites these women, and understanding that and creating marketing that feeds that self-perception is how marketers get them to buy. Nintendo did just that when it launched the Wii gaming system, promoting this computer console as a new and innovative tool for exercise, as well as a way to bring the family together. Nintendo recruited Alpha moms for Wii parties, let them try the product, and hoped for positive word of mouth. This promotion was extremely effective. In 2006, when the product launched, Wii sales totaled 1.1 million units and outsold Sony's Playstation—the leader in gaming consoles—by almost 50 percent.[11] By creating a promotion where Alpha moms could be alpha, that is, could know about a new product before any of their friends and thereby look like the trendsetters they see themselves to be, Nintendo successfully used psychographics not only to sell a product but also to support its customers' self-image.

The psychographic label for people who care about the environment and social causes has evolved over the past decade. In the 1990s, this group was first identified as "cultural creatives" in *American Demographics* magazine. The sociologist Paul Ray segmented society into three broad groups—traditionalists (believers in "small towns and strong churches"), modernists (this group values "personal success, consumerism, materialism, and technological rationality"), and cultural creatives. Cultural creatives are well-educated, interested in spirituality as well as social activism, and tend to like to see things from a big-picture perspective—a key reason why they look askance at language-light advertising. In 1997, when this research was done, cultural creatives made up 24 percent of the adult population—a larger group than might have been expected.[12] Let me note that Ray doesn't call this group a psychographic cohort. Rather, he says, the group is based on its members' values. However, these are by definition fundamental to a psychographic group defined by its values, lifestyles, and attitudes, which is why I include this description here. Today, BBMG, a marketing and strategy agency that helps companies integrate sustainability and social innovation, has created a spectrum of cultural caring that it calls "conscious consumers."[13] This spectrum ranks consumers from enlighteneds to aspirationals to practicals to indifferents. This framework in many ways parallels Ray's work in the 1990s. Enlighteneds (10 percent of the population) are the group most engaged in socially responsible behavior, and this is exhibited through their buying habits. Aspiration-als (20 percent of the population) are also socially committed, but they balance that concern against practical issues like time and money. These two cohorts are not identical to Ray's, but they seem to parallel the cultural creatives, and it is notable that this group has increased over the past twenty years. The two remaining segments are less motivated by causes than by traditional product attributes like price and quality. Though fewer, enlighteneds are more powerful in the marketplace than cultural creatives, because they are a particularly vocal group and have access to social media, so-called Web 2.0, unavailable ten years ago. The rule of thumb with word-of-mouth marketing—and social media is its newest incarnation—is that if these passionate consumers like a product, they tell ten people; if they don't, they tell three hundred.

More broadly, a market segment known as LOHAS (lifestyles of health and sustainability) has grown up around products that improve human health, as well as the health of the environment. This category includes well-known companies like Green Mountain Coffee Roasters and little-known ones like Me to We Style, a "social enterprise" that provides sweatshop-free apparel created from environmentally friendly fabrics, with 50 percent of profits going to Free the Children, an orga-nization where children help other children through education, and the winner of the World's Children's Prize for the Rights of the Child (also known as the Children's Nobel Prize). Purchasers of these products and thousands of others like them are called LOHASians.[14] "LOHAS is an idea premised on the assumption that consumers and producers in a capitalist economy are able, through their market labor, to bring about global social change," Monica Emerich, an early LOHASian, explains.[15] Whether we call them cultural creatives, conscious consum-ers, or LOHASians, this belief in the power to sway the market and make it more environmentally and socially conscious is what defines this psychographic group.

Related to socially conscious consumers or not, psychographics is the norm for marketers. The sociologist Michael Schudson posits two important reasons for this. First, women are the primary purchasers of consumer products. Since women may display and embrace certain emotions more readily than men, it is believed that they are more likely to respond to psychological, needs-based sales pitches rather than intel-lectual, reason-based ones. Tied to the need to create emotion-laden sales pitches is the means through which those appeals are communicated, that is, television. Television commercials—and now also Internet advertising—are quite simply much better at eliciting emotion than they are at conveying complex information. This is particularly true when you are trying to convey that message in thirty seconds or less. Second, grabbing consumers' attention trumps providing information, given an overwhelming number of largely undifferentiated commodity-like products. More marketing, louder marketing, cruder marketing became acceptable ways of "breaking through the clutter." The best way for marketers to stand out, however, is to have a thorough understanding of their consumers, so that they will instantaneously connect to the brand message.[16]

Getting people to see your message, never mind connect with it, became more complex as media technologies advanced. That's because people no longer share the same cultural experiences (remember *Friends* on Thursday nights?). Most people now consume media individually. The media environment moved from one dominated by three broadcast networks to one fragmented into hundreds, some would say thousands, of media options. As these choices proliferate, media audiences get sliced into smaller and smaller pieces, so that now instead of being able to reach 30 or 40 or even 50 percent of Americans with one television commercial, marketers are lucky to reach 10 or 15 percent today.

Moreover, while the number of media options has mushroomed, people's time and ability to consume more information are not increasing. People's short-term memory is limited to somewhere between three and nine pieces of information.[17] In television, the rule of thumb has been that viewers are aware of programming on seven channels. Even though the number of programming options has increased to over 150 channels in households with cable, far more if you have satellite TV, and exponentially more if you include YouTube, our brains have not expanded to allow for retaining all of this additional information. Never mind remembering what you have waiting on your DVR, iPod, iPad, or Netflix queue.

Not only do we have limited brain capacity, but also we have limited attention spans, all the more so for being bombarded with new information.[18] You know exactly what I mean if you have more than two tabs open on your web browser. Because of this, marketers are acutely aware that if they want to sell something, they had better stand out in a crowd, and they have to get consumers' attention quickly. To do this, they adorn the landscape with swooshes, yellow arches, and apple logos—what Robert Goldman and Stephen Papson call "sign wars."[19] This is where branding comes in.

BRANDING

What Is Branding?

David Ogilvy said that a brand is "the intangible sum of a product's attributes: its name, packaging, and price, its history, its reputation and the way it is advertised." Thus a brand has little to do with the physical aspects of a product and everything to do with what people think about it.[20]

Take a look around you. From Domino sugar in your pantry to Starbucks coffee, from your Sony TV to the Subaru in your driveway, from your Banana Republic T-shirt to your Target credit card, there's barely a place you can look that you won't see a branded product. In fact, if you have kids, you know just how hard it is to find a backpack or a piece of clothing without a picture of the latest Disney star or Nickelodeon cartoon character.

So why is that? Why turn a simple piece of clothing into a fashion statement, or a car into "the ultimate driving machine"?

Because consumers are more likely to relate to products that have meaning attached to them. Marketers create stories around their products through marketing messages, whether we're talking about advertising or promotion or public relations. These stories, called brand mythologies, are accompanied by a logo and usually a tagline, so that consumers will immediately associate the product with the story when they see the product symbol.[21]

Let's take an example. Basically, an iPod is a piece of media equipment that allows for the transmission of moving pictures and audio entertainment. But is that what you think about when you see an iPod? Of course not. You think of cutting-edge technology and hip, dancing shadows and white ear buds that make you look cool. So, why? Why isn't the iPod simply a piece of machinery that provides entertainment when you want it? Because branding has created a story for you about what that piece of electronics in your hands is. Through numerous commercials, endless promotion and PR (Mac World, stories about Steve Jobs and the secrecy around him and his products, opening new Apple stores, etc.) and ultimately word of mouth, Apple has created a mythology, some would say a mystique, around its products.

In addition to the mythology, there is also the product logo. In this case, the identifying logo could be either the iPod itself or the ubiquitous white earbuds—both of which are distinctive—or the Apple logo. This last has a history that embodies the mythology of being creative (artists and advertising people use Mac computers) and smart and "different," which has been cultivated through years of advertising, from the famous "1984" commercial that introduced the Macintosh during the Super Bowl and launched that game as *the* advertising event of the year to the iconic "Think Different" ads that included creative luminaries in all fields, from Albert Einstein to Amelia Earhart to Jim Henson (with Kermit the Frog).

Most products have traditionally also used a tagline to further embed product information in the minds of consumers ("Just do it" for Nike or "Tastes great, less filling" for Miller Lite). Because of the globalization of markets, however, companies today prefer using simplistic logos that do not require translation across international markets. In the case of the iPod, the Apple logo eliminates the need for words. Another good example where we see this trend is Gatorade: the product is no longer referred to as Gatorade, but simply as "G."

Branding is about communicating an idea through a product. It is about creating meaning—taking a physical object and turning it into more than the sum of its parts. It is about creating a personal connection between consumers and products (or services) through communications that lead to thoughts and feelings that have nothing to do with the product's physical attributes. Branding is about fulfilling a need, providing what marketers call the benefit. So, for example, if we talk about AT&T's historic "Reach out and touch someone" campaign, we are not led to think about how good or bad the technology is, but rather focus on our ability to connect with people we care about. Or take Coca-Cola's more recent "Open Happiness" campaign, which doesn't mention fizzy, syrupy soda, but merely presents us with something everyone wants—happiness. If you are of a certain generation, that idea might also spark up a memory of an older Coke commercial that showed smiling, happy hippies standing on a hillside singing "I'd like to teach the world to sing . . . in perfect harmony." The expectation is that these benefits—connection to loved ones, happiness, and harmony—will become associated with the product. Then the more you as a consumer interact with the product, and the more successfully the product provides you with the hoped-for benefit and/ or fulfills a need, the more likely you are to purchase that brand again and again.

These interactions create connections—marketers would say relationships—between us and the brands we use. This occurs whether we are aware of it or not. We prefer one brand to another, and often we are not conscious of why those preferences exist. For instance, we always buy Morton's salt because that's what Mom always bought, and the girl in the yellow slicker on a blue background reminds us of home. Intellectually, this doesn't make sense, because salt is salt. It's a commodity. But because we have a preexisting relationship with Morton's and Mom, we are willing to pay extra money for that name and its perceived higher quality. Or, women may buy Oil of Olay because they have seen all the research on how it's better than the $700 creams, and they hope by using this brand to eliminate—or at least reduce—the "signs of aging." This is not to suggest that all products are commodities—parity products with no differentiation. Rather, it is to suggest that in the vast majority of categories, it is the brand and not the physical product that we, the consumer, have the relationship with.

But, remember, the brand is simply a story created to sell a product. When Leo Burnett first marketed Marlboro cigarettes, they were sold as a brand for women. The brown filter, in fact, was created to hide unsightly lipstick stains. Today, after decades of the Marlboro Man riding the western plains, it's hard for us to imagine Marlboro as a product with feminine appeal. The reframing of this iconic brand, however, is a great example of how products in and of themselves have no meaning. The brand—the logo, the mythology, the meaning—is the product. The cigarette or the skin cream or the salt is secondary.

These fundamentals of branding remain in effect today. However, the methods of branding are decidedly in flux. Brand managers have less control over the messaging of the brand than they did a decade ago. With Web 2.0, the second wave of the Internet that has fully exploited interactivity, consumers are able to create their own YouTube videos about a product, post comments on Facebook or Twitter, and ultimately spread brand messages to friends, family, and various followers. Because of this, consumers have considerable influence on a brand, especially when it does not live up to its claims or presents its consumers in an unflattering light. In 2008, the "mommy bloggers" took Motrin and its advertising to task when the company suggested in its commercials that putting your child in a sling would lead to back, neck, and shoulder pain. The mommy bloggers considered that to be bashing "baby wearing," and they complained about it—vociferously—throughout the blogosphere. Under pressure from these outspoken consumers, the online ad was summarily pulled. The capacity for direct and immediate feedback means that consumers have more say in the mythologies surrounding the products they use. And, according to the consulting firm Imagination Insight, "as people become increasingly aware of their ability to drive change, they begin to demand more."[22]

Public influence and psychology play into why product companies are connecting their brands with causes—consumers are demanding it, even if they aren't fully aware of why. In the wake of 9/11, when consumers were asked to respond to the statement "I would be likely to switch brands to one associated with a good cause, if price and quality are similar," consumer agreement was 81 percent, up dramatically from 54 percent seven months before.[23] After the tragic events of that day, consumers were encouraged by then president George W. Bush to normalize their lives through shopping. To motivate consumers to get back to the stores, companies responded first by nationalizing their images and then by using charitable appeals.[24] This marketing tactic is so entrenched that today, according to the 2010 *Goodpurpose Study* put out by the PR firm Edelman, a majority of people (52 to 60 percent depending on the product) would actually *pay more for a product* if it was tied to a cause. And consumers expect the charitable connection to be fully embedded in the brand's mythology and the work of the company—it's not good enough just to do a one-shot promotion, the commitment has to be part and parcel of how the company functions. Think here of Ben & Jerry's or The Body Shop or Stonyfield Farms.

Terror management theory (TMT), a psychological theory developed in the mid-1980s, may provide a clue to consumers' positive response to these cause campaigns.[25] TMT hypothesizes that one function of culture is to reduce anxiety around death. Awareness of one's mortality, particularly when put in stark relief after the violence of an event such as 9/11, is likely to lead people to seek out ways to manage their fear. TMT suggests that this will be done either through a cultural worldview that provides value and perhaps promises immortality (for some, this will be religious beliefs), or people will look for ways to bolster their self-esteem. Researchers have begun to apply this theory to consumption practices. Some suggest that one way to buoy esteem and thus reduce one's fear of death is to acquire material possessions; one study noted in particular that those who are concerned about terrorist attacks are more likely to purchase brand-name products and consume compulsively.[26] It stands to reason that cause marketing would enhance the appeal of products connected to charities, because they enhance self-esteem not only through the purchase itself but also through the knowledge of having helped others. Moreover, if these causes are connected to death-related events such as the earthquake in Haiti or the tsunami in Japan, there is all the more reason to justify the purchase to alleviate the fear of one's own mortality in the face of others' tragedy.

New research in social psychology suggests why consumers might even consider paying more for these products. Jennifer Lerner, a professor of public policy and management at Harvard Business School, is a social psychologist who studies how subconscious influences, that is, emotions, affect decision making. Lerner did an experiment to test how sadness impacts financial choices. Sensors measuring skin conductance, sweat response, skin temperature, and so on, were placed on test subjects and baseline physiological measurements taken. Then, among other activities, the test subjects were shown a sad movie, but one that induced only a low level of emotional effect. "The decision-makers in our studies are completely unaware that the sadness is impacting them. And when we ask them, did the film you saw change your responses in any way, they say no," Lerner reports. Once in this state, they are given a number of financial choices to make; the last of which is to say how much they would pay for a water bottle. Those who had watched the sad movie were willing to pay much more than those who had not experienced sadness before evaluating the item—in one case, $10.00 as opposed to $2.50.[27] While studies have not been done that specifically relate this concept to cause marketing, it makes sense that people might be willing to pay more for a product associated with a cause, particularly one that generates sadness, as many of these campaigns do. Whether patriotism or psychology, this trend remains intact today, leading companies to increase their social marketing and integrate these messages into their branding efforts.

This is important information. Most products can't compete on attributes—true physical benefits—because most products are commodities. Shampoo by any name is still shampoo. But if it's a trendy brand like Garnier Fructis and the manufacturer runs a campaign with Locks of Love (www.locksoflove.org), a nonprofit that uses natural hair donations to create hairpieces for financially disadvantaged children who have lost their hair, this may provide consumers with a tipping-point reason to buy it. A cause becomes a product benefit—a means of differentiating one product from another.

This has been dubbed the era of Marketing 3.0. The first era of marketing was the industrial age, discussed above. The second wave was characterized by the widespread use of technology, where consumers have access to numerous products and services targeted to their wants and needs. Marketing 3.0 is characterized as being driven by values:

> Instead of treating people simply as consumers, marketers approach them as whole human beings with minds, hearts, and spirits. Increasingly, consumers are looking for solutions to their anxieties about making the globalized world a better place. In a world full of confusion, they search for companies that address their deepest needs for social, economic, and environmental justice in their mission, vision, and values. . . . Marketing 3.0 complements emotional marketing with human spirit marketing.[28]

Marketers are responding to consumers who want to know what the brand believes in, not simply what it does. This evolution should not surprise us, because it is part of a larger cultural shift. At the same time that marketing is becoming more values-driven, there has been a blending of the sacred and the secular in our culture. The televangelist Joel Osteen sells his *New York Times* bestsellers and DVDs of his sermons during his highly rated weekly TV show, while Oprah Winfrey talks about Jesus and spirituality. Instead of finding faith in traditional religious institutions (only about 25 percent attend services weekly), most Americans—more than 90 percent of whom believe in a higher power—find spirituality through a hodgepodge of secular products such as books, television programming, the Internet, and a myriad of classes on everything from meditation to learning the "law of attraction" promulgated by the best-selling self-help tract *The Secret*.[29] Brands substitute for moral mythologies that used to be found outside of the consumer marketplace.

Baby boomers—a large target segment and one favored by marketers—are aging, and many have found that they have fewer material needs; more broadly, in the current recession, people are having to reevaluate their lives and their values. One result of these social changes has been an increase in the number of people being motivated by personal growth. We've seen this expressed through increased volunteerism, increased interest in socially responsible consumption, and an overall pursuit of doing good, reflected in everything from MBA ethical business oaths to the White House Office of Social Innovation. While we can't reliably explain why this is so, it is likely a combination of an increased awareness of the fragility of life after 9/11, the aging of the population, and the reality that the government has significantly reduced its commitment to social welfare, an issue that will be addressed throughout this book. Whatever the reason, consumers want to express their charitable side—something most Americans no longer do through religious institutions. In the absence of other social and cultural institutions, the consumer marketplace is positioning itself to fill the resulting void.

Brands and Personal Identity Creation

Walk down any street in America and you become acutely aware of how important brands are in creating personal identities. Blackberries. Dunkin' Donuts. UGG® boots. And, yes, yellow bracelets. These are just some of the thousands of brands that we combine to create identities to display to the world.[30]

In marketing circles, this is called "brands as badges." For example, you may think one thing about someone who drinks Budweiser and something else about someone who drinks Samuel Adams. Study after study has shown that under blind taste-test conditions, no one can identify one domestic beer over another. Yet walk around a bar with a can of Budweiser and I'll know everything I need to know about you—or at least I think so. The same idea applies to cars, clothes, cosmetics, and charities.

The demographic age group known as Gen Y (or Millennials or Echo Boomers) has been the one most affected by brand messages. This cohort—born between the mid-1970s and the 2000s and now in their young adulthood—grew up surrounded by media and the brands that support them. They have never lived in a world without MTV, the Gap, and Google. In her book *No Logo: No Space, No Choice, No Jobs,* Naomi Klein criticizes marketers for not only using branding to hide corporate abuses (a topic addressed more thoroughly elsewhere in this book) but also—and more important for the immediate discussion— using branding to overtake public and private spaces. "This loss of space happens inside the individual; it is a colonization not of physical space but of mental space," Klein writes.[31] For Gen Y's offspring—called Gen Z, for now—branded life is likely to be even more intense. American children view as many as 20,000 commercials annually. By the age of three, they are readily able to recognize brand logos and to request products by name.

But it is not just that American kids have been exposed to brands. It is that they look to brands as a means for defining who they are. As Juliet Schor says in her book *Born to Buy,* "more children here [the United States] than anywhere else believe that their clothes and brands describe who they are and define their social status. American kids display more brand affinity than their counterparts anywhere else in the world; indeed, experts describe them as increasingly 'bonded to brands.'"[32]

Millennials and Gen Z are not the only ones affected by this. It's all of us. We can't help but be influenced by the 360-degree "touchpoints" that marketers use. From e-mail to retail, from tweets to commercials, from billboards to bathroom stalls, we are surrounded by marketing. Being immersed in these messages stimulates us to want to buy things— that's their raison d'être—and what we buy affects who we are. "You are what you eat," an old adage says. Today, it's "You are what you buy." This plays into Abraham Maslow's hierarchy of needs, a popular theory among marketers, although discredited in some academic circles, which posits that you move from being concerned with physiological needs to satisfying social needs and esteem-based needs until you reach self-actualization. It is through the acquisition and possession of products that we come to find esteem and social acceptance.[33] Today, we expect those same products to provide us not only with social acceptance but also with self-actualization and transcendence to support higher-order beliefs about ourselves.

Americans suffer from a sense of rootlessness, which fuels our reliance on brands and the stories they embody. We are looking for commonalities that we used to find in our local communities or social institutions that simply no longer exist. Where in the past people might have found connection through a shared understanding of the Bible or a secret handshake, today people have shared experiences with McDonald's or Facebook or Harry Potter. Brands provide not only a shared culture but also consistency. We can count on Kraft, Honda, and Red Bull in a way that we can't be assured about our careers, pensions, and spouses.

There is no better evidence of the use of brands as part of identity creation than the current use of the phrase "I am . . . " in advertising.

I first remember being aware of this in Apple's series of ads that used the lines "I'm a Mac" and "I'm a PC." Two guys on the screen—one buttoned-up and dowdy (the PC), the other cool and laid-back (the Mac, of course). This was the epitome of anthropomorphizing brands. No longer are we users of the product, we are the products themselves.

It didn't stop there, however. Microsoft responded with a series of ads, the most memorable of which was a little Asian girl showing how easy it is to take a picture and e-mail it to her mom and dad (let's not discuss the racial stereotyping attached to using an Asian child to show how easy technology is to use). The commercial ends with the little girl talking into the camera and saying, "I'm a PC and I'm four and a half."

But Microsoft and Apple are not the only ones to use this personification strategy. The current tagline for Jeep is "I live. I ride. I am.

Jeep." On the page, there is a period after "I am," but you hear it in the commercial as "I am Jeep." Nikon, too, recently launched an "I am Nikon" campaign in Europe, which is sure to make it stateside sometime soon.[34]

Brands as building blocks of who we are is not new; what is new is that marketers are so blatant about it. After all, the ads are not saying "I like Jeep" or "I like my PC," but rather "I am a Jeep" or "I am a PC." If we see ourselves as brands—or, more realistically, see brands as parts of who we are—then what those brands represent becomes increasingly important to us.

Ethical Brands

Brands are evolving, then, not only to provide a mythology about a product or service that contributes to our sense of self, but also to communicate values. Such products have been dubbed "ethical brands." An example of an ethical brand is TOMS Shoes, started by Blake Mycoskie. For every pair of shoes bought, a pair goes to a child in need somewhere in the world. As of September 2010, TOMS had distributed over a million pairs of free shoes in a little more than four years. Much like buying a yellow bracelet, purchase of TOMS shoes demonstrates the consumer's commitment to a cause—we're not buying only to get something; we're buying to help save the world. Other examples would include The Body Shop®, which has a long-standing commitment to environmental and women's causes, and Eileen Fisher, which supports women's issues and female entrepreneurship.

The youth marketer Look-Look Inc. takes this one step further by calling these products "conscious brands." It says these brands exist because there is a shift toward postmaterialist values that place an emphasis on expressing oneself and improving the quality of life, and a "shift away from materialist values emphasizing economic and physical security." I think calling consumers "postmaterialist" goes too far, however, even in today's economy. Rather, it is that we are moving away from *luxury* materialism, so-called aspirational or lifestyle brands like Paris Hilton perfumes or Dolce & Gabbana sunglasses.[35] Endless knock-offs and cheap alternatives have devalued upscale products. Consumers, particularly Millennials, are looking for brands with values—not economic values, but social values. They are also searching for happiness, something that is not inherent to purchased goods. The trend, overall, is toward experiences rather than things. The more a product provides an experience (yes, adventure travel, but think, too, of the Apple store, as opposed to the iPod), the more likely it is to appeal to today's consumer.

This search for happiness has led to a search for meaning and community—something traditionally provided by non-market-driven institutions, such as faith communities, the Elks club, or the local bowling league,[36] but of late provided by the consumer culture. People are finding meaning in brand communities.

Brand communities were first noted in 2001 by Albert M. Muniz Jr. and Thomas C. O'Guinn. According to their research, "a brand community is a specialized, non-geographically bound community, based on a structured set of social relations among admirers of a brand." Unlike traditional communities, brand communities do not occupy geographically defined areas, but rather coalesce around branded products. Through marketing communication and interaction between product companies and users, and among users themselves, mostly via the Internet, groups of people create strong bonds, similar to those evident in traditional communities. Specifically, they have a shared consciousness (connection to the brand and one another), they participate in rituals and traditions related to the brand, and they retain a sense of moral responsibility to others who are part of their community.[37]

Nike+ is a wonderful example of a brand community. Runners have always logged their mileage, but in the past this was done with pen and notebook in the privacy of one's home. With the use of a special Nike shoe and an iPod, runners are motivated during their training runs by both their music and a voice that comes through their earphones. Once home, runners sync up their iPods with their computers and their mileage is instantaneously downloaded to the Nike+ web site. While there, runners can check with fellow sprinters, challenge one another, provide training tips, and so on, as one might do in a gym or locker room. While I could not find information on how many runners use the site, we do know that this community had run more than 435 million miles as of September 2011. That's more than 17,500 laps around the globe.

This is not simply traditional brand loyalty. It goes beyond that. Communities demonstrate membership legitimacy (you have to know "the secret handshake") and oppositional brand loyalty (my brand is better than yours). For example, Saab owners honk at one another, and Mac users consider working on a PC downright blasphemous. In brand communities, rituals, tradition, and storytelling are based on product experiences, which can be either personal interactions with a brand or events created by the manufacturer. These rituals and traditions perpetuate meaning and cohesion for the group. Moral responsibility is a bit different in brand communities than in traditional faith communities. For example: here, it has to do with integrating members into the group and helping them properly use the brand.

These brand communities clearly remind us of how fractured our physical communities have become. As this has occurred, marketing companies have stepped in to fill the void. Initially through online communities, but now through a combination of online and offline events, such as annual meetings or barbeques, organizations work to maintain their brand communities. These events serve to foster relationships among community members, further cementing connections to one another and the brand. Shared experiences, rituals, and myths make these communities as real as traditional ones, even if the source of connection is a marketed product.

Within cause marketing, there are no better examples of this type of community than the ones created around fund-raising events such as the Avon Walk for Breast Cancer (a two-day event) or the AIDS/Lifecycle, a seven-day ride from San Francisco to Los Angeles. These multi-day events are really multi-month, and for some multi-year, commitments. In the case of the Avon Walk, for example, the company provides walkers with newsletters about how to train for the walk eight months in advance. Included in these newsletters are information about how to train with others (thus creating community) and fund-raising tips. Community-building is furthered through connections made on the walk and communications after the event ends, which encourage participants to make it an annual ritual. Thus, Avon and the Breast Cancer Walk become an integral part of participants' lives, and all the personal relationships around that event—steeped in intimacy, caring, and perhaps even happiness—become connected to the Avon brand.[38]

Let's stop to note here that I did not include Avon in the list of ethical brands above. Nor would I include it on a list of brands producing real social change, even though it is raising significant amounts of money for research. There's a very good reason for this. According to Samantha King, author of *Pink Ribbons, Inc.: Breast Cancer and the Politics of Philanthropy,* "Fund-raising experts claim that thons [like the Avon Walk] have become popular not so much because of their money-making potential (often funds raised through thons make up only a small percentage of any organization's annual income . . .), but because of the publicity they generate for the foundations that

sponsor them."[39] Many would argue that this type of event is important because of its ability to generate awareness of breast cancer, AIDS,
or some other cause. This argument is valid to a point. It is also likely
true that the (mostly) women who spend months and months physically preparing for these events and hours and hours creating viral
promotions to attract donors are unaware that their effort is more
about marketing a brand than about alleviating suffering. Would all
of these women still be so vested in the event if they were conscious
of this deception?

Avon invests heavily in its Breast Cancer Walk and raises significant amounts of money for the cause, but the fact is we know very
little about whether Avon products themselves might potentially cause
cancer. I tried to find out for myself by contacting Avon's vice president
for sustainability and corporate responsibility, Tod Arbogast. While he
initially intimated that he would be willing to chat, after I e-mailed
him my questions about where Avon stood in making sure that its
products were noncarcinogenic, and if it was working toward reducing
packaging waste—a significant environmental issue for the cosmetics industry—he never got back to me. I could only assume that he
did not have anything positive to say. Investigating further, I went to
goodguide.com, a web site founded by Dara O'Rourke, a professor
of environmental and labor policy.[40] Goodguide's goal is to provide
unbiased health, environmental, and social performance information
so that consumers can purchase products that reflect their values. As
the site says, "We believe that better information can transform the
marketplace: as more consumers buy better products, retailers and
manufacturers face compelling incentives to make products that are
safe, environmentally sustainable and produced using ethical sourcing
of raw materials and labor." According to this site, Avon produces
several products—not all—that contain ingredients considered to be
carcinogenic. Products containing ingredients that are considered toxic
for everything from kidneys to skin to the cardiovascular system were
mostly cosmetics—products that would be used by women. The company's social ranking also rates very low, which is surprising given
its philanthropic work. Avon is better than average, however, when
it comes it environmental impacts, something the company does not
highlight.

Avon demonstrates the standard operating procedures of most consumer packaged goods (CPG) companies—promote first; align your
corporate values later (if at all). From a marketing perspective, it makes

perfect sense that the company would support a women's issue like breast cancer research. However, it is also true that if Avon really cared about women's health, it would start by producing products that don't make women sick in the first place.

BUYER BE AWARE

As mentioned, after 9/11, consumers began to show a propensity to purchase products associated with social causes, a trend that has continued. At the same time, people were becoming more civic-minded, particularly Millennials—those born between 1979 and 2001—a population segment whose attention marketers covet. According to the National Conference on Citizenship study *America's Civic Health Index 2009: Civic Health in Hard Times,* this demographic group is the leader when it comes to volunteering: 43 percent of Millennials volunteer, as compared to 35 percent of baby boomers. In addition, members of this group use social networking sites to "promote civic causes, express their opinions on issues, and gather information related to civics."[41] This altruistic nature has been given a decided push by the ongoing recession. Americans have had to reevaluate not only their consumer habits but also fundamental choices in their lives, such as what they do for a living. As corporate jobs disappeared, more jobs were expected in the public sector, and while people waited for those jobs to materialize, volunteerism skyrocketed. In addition, "applications to the Peace Corps and Teach for America meanwhile, are up, as are those to some divinity schools and public policy programs."[42] In sum, there is an overwhelming trend toward focusing on things that matter. Marketers are acutely aware of this trend and are finding ways to take advantage of it.

Advertising agencies have always wanted to know what matters to consumers, but today consulting firms and conferences have sprung up around finding ways to tap into what matters most to consumers from a social-engagement perspective. These companies are responding to a trend that the Amsterdam-based research company trendwatching.com calls "Generation G," with the G standing for generosity, not greed, as might have been the case in the 1980s. Trendwatching.com describes the generosity trend in the following way:

GENERATION G | "Captures the growing importance of 'generosity' as a leading societal and business mindset. As consumers are disgusted with greed and its current dire consequences for the economy—and while that same upheaval has them longing more than ever for institutions that care—the need for more generosity beautifully coincides with the ongoing (and pre-recession) emergence of an online-fueled culture of individuals who share, give, engage, create and collaborate in large numbers.

In fact, for many, sharing a passion and receiving recognition have replaced 'taking' as the new status symbol. Businesses should follow this societal/behavioral shift, however much it may oppose their decades-old devotion to me, myself and I."[43]

As this suggests, companies are being urged to combine making the world a better place with selling us more stuff. Some are doing this legitimately (TOMS, discussed earlier, being a good example), but many more are deceptive in their marketing practices.

Let me give you an example from my own experience. Dawn dishwashing liquid ran a promotion where for every bottle of Dawn purchased a dollar would go to save wildlife—or so I thought. I needed dishwashing liquid anyway, and I'd seen the ad so I thought, "Okay, I'll buy Dawn. Why not?" On the bottle was a picture of an adorable white seal with enormous imploring eyes that seemed to say, "Save me, save me!" Next to that photo in BIG WHITE TYPE was "1 Bottle = $1." I purchased the bottle and, of course, thought a dollar would be contributed automatically to the Marine Mammal Center and the International Bird Rescue Research Center, as I'd seen in the commercial. I was wrong. It wasn't until I rinsed out the bottle to recycle it that I saw the asterisk. In teeny-tiny little mouse type, it stated that I had to go to a web site (dawnsaveslife.com) and register my purchase in order for the donation to be activated. Later, P&G continued this campaign during the Gulf Oil disaster. If consumers were smart enough to go to the site, they were met with the following:

> Dawn has reached its goal! Thanks to thousands and thousands of Everyday Wildlife Champions like you, Dawn has successfully reached its $500,000 donation goal to the MMC and IBRRC wildlife conservation organizations— and far ahead of schedule.[44]

It turns out that there was a "glitch" on the part of Procter & Gamble, which subsequently took down the notice, increased its commitment to $1 million, and extended the promotion until 2011. That's fine on the face of it. However, the web address has changed, making it more difficult to find, and the company is no longer promoting this campaign and has gone back to a traditional marketing campaign promoting the product's benefits.

Procter & Gamble does do good work, some of which is discussed in subsequent chapters. What this example demonstrates, however, is the issue at the very crux of problems related to cause marketing: corporations can do good, but only when marketing is secondary to the cause and the corporation's long-term, concerted commitment to it. (I want to add that this opened my eyes to the fact that Dawn, like many dishwashing liquids, contains petroleum by-products—thus, the "solution" was an underlying contributor to the problem.)

Another example is Americans' good-hearted response to the 2010 earthquake in Haiti. The Red Cross used texting as a means to get money to Haiti faster, or so at least thousands of people thought. The impression given (and this ties into the personalized economy discussed above) was that as soon as someone texted "Haiti," their $10 would be whisked away as quickly as buttons were pressed. In reality, the money got there thirty to ninety days later, depending on when the donor's cell-phone bill was paid.[45] This, of course, was much later than people expected, and well after the crucial first couple of days.

The predicament in all this is that so many companies have wrapped themselves in the blanket of philanthropy today without having any significant effect on solving social problems. This has not gone unnoticed. A majority of consumers (61 percent) are increasingly looking for details about cause campaigns, and even more (75 percent) want to be sure that their actions will have results in the form of either a positive effect on the social issue in question or funds raised.[46] Some (unfortunately, only very few so far) are starting to realize that being responsible entails working to solve social problems, not simply using a band-aid approach. At the 2010 Sustainable Brands Conference, Jason Saul, CEO of Mission Measurement, a social-impact consulting firm, noted that the new driving forces of social innovation entail creating an intentional core business strategy in which philanthropy is woven into the business, rather than being pieced together from leftover time and money. Saul gave as an example Walmart's $4 prescription drug program, which saved consumers billions of dollars and provided medication to thousands who could not otherwise afford it, not only solving a social problem (rather than simply helping to improve a situation or making it less bad) but also generating a profit. This is very different from the majority of past campaigns, including walkathons and what I call the "spend to send" approach, which has been the most publicized.

MTV's response to 2005's Hurricane Katrina shows the difference between looking as though you're solving a problem and actually solving it. Like many other organizations at the time, MTV created a mechanism for raising money to aid hurricane victims. If viewers downloaded certain songs, money from the sale would go to the American Red Cross. MTV didn't stop there, however. According to a former CSR executive at MTV whom I interviewed, the company fielded research that found that simply clicking a button left young donors feeling helpless and unfulfilled. Were they really doing something? Couldn't they do more? The answer was yes. Out of this disaster came the inspiration for Alternative Spring Break, a program developed by MTV and United Way, in which two students were selected from each of the fifty states to travel to Louisiana for a week. There, they built houses with Habitat for Humanity, instead of perhaps tanning themselves and partying on the beaches of Puerto Vallarta. The response to the initial call was overwhelming—thousands of young people submitted essays about why they should be selected for this venture. The prevailing response by those chosen was that it was the most important experience of their lives. Moreover, Alternative Spring Break continues as an organization on hundreds of college campuses throughout the country. Not an easy fix, for sure, but one that has continuing, verifiable benefits.

Here we have examined the pull for responsibility from the consumer side. Over the next two chapters, we'll look at the way the cause–product landscape is responding to our need for brands with values, while also providing corporations with the best means to sell their products. Unfortunately, this is often to the detriment of charities, and, more importantly, to the people and the planet those charities are meant to serve. We'll begin by examining the corporate takeover of caring. Subsequent chapters will spell out the price we pay as individuals and as a society for ceding charitable works to the marketplace.

2

How Corporations Co-opt Caring

Strategic Philanthropy, Cause-Related
Marketing, and Corporate Social Responsibility

Beyoncé appears on the TV screen in a beautifully shot black-and-white
commercial, reminiscent of 1980s Bruce Weber/Calvin Klein advertising. First, we see a pair of five-inch black stilettos as she walks into
frame. Then, the camera pans up her body as she kneels on an empty
sound stage with a stark white backdrop. Dressed in a plain white
T-shirt and jeans, her hair blown-dry straight, she speaks directly and
earnestly into the camera.

Beyoncé is not announcing her latest concert or her newest album.
She is there to demonstrate her commitment to feeding the hungry—not
through her own Survivor Foundation but by teaming up with General
Mills's Hamburger Helper. Yes, that package of noodles and flavoring
mothers started using in the early 1970s to extend their families' food
budgets.

This commercial launched "Show Your Helping Hand" (SYHH), a
campaign that in conjunction with the country's leading hunger relief
organization—Feeding America—proposed to deliver 3.5 million meals
to food banks. The spot ends when Beyoncé asks viewers to go to the
campaign's web site, www.showyourhelpinghand.com—the hand being
both the consumer's helping hand and Hamburger Helper's dancing,
giggling anthropomorphized hand logo—for more information about
how they, too, can help feed America's homeless.[1] From the web site,
we learn that General Mills will donate the small cost of a single food-
bank meal, up to a specified maximum, for each code found on a box

of Hamburger Helper that is entered online. In addition, consumers are encouraged to donate directly to Feeding America and to bring non-perishable food to Beyoncé's concerts, conveniently listed on the web site. Running tallies show how many meals have been paid for, how much money raised, and how many pounds of food donated.

On the face of it, this seems like a great idea. Hamburger Helper—a recognizable household name—ties in with A-level talent to draw attention to the issue of hunger at a time when more and more Americans are going hungry due to increasing unemployment and the continuing recession. In addition, the campaign is implemented in conjunction with Feeding America, the leading distributor of food through local food banks. Food banks get food; Feeding America gets funding; hungry people get fed. So what's the problem?

Beyond trying to imagine that Beyoncé would scramble up some Hamburger Helper never mind eat it, the explosion of cause-marketing campaigns and other pro-social corporate activities like this have shifted attention away from causes and onto corporate interests. Just as Livestrong bracelets moved the focus from cancer to consumers, this sponsorship moves the focus from hunger to Hamburger Helper (or, more likely, Beyoncé).

In so doing, the promotion does far more for the corporation and the celebrity than it does for the homeless and hungry. In this case, it falls out in the following way: Hamburger Helper is a product whose sales have been in serious decline because of competition from ready-made and microwavable food options. By tying in with Beyoncé, General Mills not only brings attention to its faltering brand through endless publicity, but may also hope to increase its significance for a younger, hipper audience. By requiring consumers to input special codes to generate a donation to Feeding America, the brand company also captures personal data about consumers. This is important because with the decreasing effectiveness of television commercials and other more conventional forms of advertising, the need for database development has increased. After all, when was the last time you watched a television commercial? From a more strictly public relations standpoint, General Mills's tie-in with Beyoncé was responsible for generating significant tabloid exposure for Hamburger Helper, and extensive "free" publicity is one of the obvious reasons for linking a product (and a cause) with a celebrity. Finally, the connection to Feeding America brings with it the patina of a company with a heart—"We're not just a food company interested in profits; we're a food company that cares about feeding hungry people." The choice of Feeding America as a partner bears high-lighting: Feeding America has become one of the largest cause tie-in partners in the country, and General Mills is one of its top ten donors through campaigns with a number of its food products. A large charity partner and the multiple connections between the two organizations generate incremental publicity and added goodwill for the corporate partner.[2]

Just as General Mills attains an aura of goodwill, so does Ms. Knowles. But this is not *just* about charity for Beyoncé. General Mills was one of two main sponsors of Beyoncé's "I Am . . . " tour. The other was L'Oréal Paris, which makes far more sense, because she is a spokesperson for its line of makeup. In today's market, sponsorship of this tour probably set General Mills back several million dollars, which bought it (some) increased sales, a database of committed consumers, and the glowing image of a caring, (almost) hip company; Beyoncé got increased exposure (and funding) for her concert tour and the per-ception (which may be genuine) that she is a compassionate celebrity. Win-win on the corporate side.

Did Feeding America benefit from this campaign? Of course. More than 2.8 million meals were delivered by mid-2010. But—and you have to read the fine print to find this out—money to deliver those meals *was not generated by the promotion.* Rather, most of that funding is attributable to a $500,000 donation from Beyoncé and General Mills.[3] Fewer than 50,000 meals were donated based on consumer participa-tion, a number that suggests that the campaign was not successful in generating the level of participation the company expected, even while it provided other corporate benefits.[4] Just a quick aside about this lack of success: consumers—that is, you and me—aren't stupid. If the product isn't any good, or the promotion doesn't make sense or is disingenuous, it doesn't matter how many bells and whistles you put on it, we're not going to buy it. General Mills seems to have understood this. "Show Your Helping Hand" remains Hamburger Helper's cause initiative, but Beyoncé has been replaced by the country music star Tim McGraw, who seems to be a more appropriate fit for the brand.

"Show Your Helping Hand" is just one example of how hundreds of consumer companies have gone about aligning their products with social causes in an effort to sell more of them or to improve sagging corporate reputations. In some cases, this has meant fund-raising through product purchases; in others, the social cause is related to how the company does business: American Apparel not using sweatshop labor or Scotties tissues planting three trees for each one it cuts down. While this corporate-cause promotional practice was just a trickle only a decade ago, today, more and more products, services, and corporate entities are touting their positive social initiatives in their advertising.[5] According to the 2010 *PRWeek/Barkley PR Cause Survey*, 75 percent of brands now utilize cause marketing, which is a significant jump from the 58 percent it was in 2009, and most marketing executives (97 percent) "believe it is a valid business strategy."[6] We've seen environmental messages on everything from cars to lightbulbs to Walmart, of course, but now marrying product sales to charity exists for causes from child abuse to hunger to AIDS to cancer research. Cause marketing is being used to sell everything from McDonald's to tampons to text messaging.

So why do this? Why the social connection? As we saw in chapter 1, much of it has to do with a push from consumers—you and me—and the ability that we have to influence the market through Twitter, blogging, and Facebook. But that's not the only reason. Patrice Tanaka, CEO of CRT/Tanaka, told me that tying a consumer product to a cause has become "the price of admission."[7] She should know. As a leading public relations practitioner and one of the groundbreakers of cause marketing when she created the Liz Claiborne campaign against domestic violence, Tanaka has been instrumental in promoting the connection between brands and causes. But while it has become necessary in the minds of marketers to find appropriate cause-brand connections, they rarely effect real change. Rather, the appearance of responsibility and self-congratulatory cause-marketing campaigns—both of which serve to further corporate interests—are the rule rather than the exception.

This marriage of corporation and cause goes by many names—cause-related marketing (CRM), corporate social responsibility (CSR), social entrepreneurship, and most recently social innovation. CSR was introduced in the 1960s, and CRM in the 1980s, but it was not until the past decade with the growth of the Internet and more specifically the past few years, with the expansion of Web 2.0 and the broad distribution of social media, that we have seen this business strategy take hold in the consumer marketplace.

Our first step in understanding how and why companies believe in the effectiveness of this corporate strategy—and how and why they are using it to get us to buy more stuff—involves looking at the history of CSR and its cousin CRM.

THE CHANGING FACE OF CORPORATE PHILANTHROPY OVER THE PAST FIFTY YEARS

You may have never heard the terms "corporate social responsibility" and "cause-related marketing." However, you have more than likely been party to a campaign that falls under one of these umbrellas. Most often, as consumers, we think of these initiatives as products tying in with a social cause—McDonald's and the Ronald McDonald House, Tide's "Loads of Hope," or a pink ribbon on just about anything. We might also relate this to companies creating "green" products, like Toyota's hybrid Prius or Sun Chips's introduction of a biodegradable bag that disintegrates in the sun.

While it is these things, social responsibility entails far more. It also relates to complying with government regulations and donating money and even implementing employee volunteer programs. According to Harvard's John F. Kennedy School of Government web site, "Corporate social responsibility encompasses not only what companies do with their profits, but also how they make them. It goes beyond philanthropy and compliance and addresses how companies manage their economic, social, and environmental impacts, as well as their relationships in all key spheres of influence: the workplace, the marketplace, the supply chain, the community, and the public policy realm." By this definition, promotional campaigns like "Show Your Helping Hand" are only a very small part of this strategy, even though it is the type of initiative that most corporations tout as CSR.

The essence of responsibility remains the same—and admirable. However, the definition of CSR has been ever-changing since its inception over fifty years ago. In the beginning (the 1960s), CSR was a strategy much as defined above, whereby businesses would fully integrate philanthropy, ethics, and regulatory compliance, as well as labor and environmental issues, into their day-to-day operations. In short, CSR was about being a good corporate citizen, with an emphasis on highlighting corporate ethics.

This philosophy made perfect sense given the era. It was a time of revolution and societal change. There was a cultural acceptance of social justice and a broadly held belief that society was obliged to help those less fortunate. It was the time of Robert Kennedy and Martin Luther King Jr. It was the era of the civil rights and environmental movements, and citizens, corporations, and the government were all expected to be part of "the solution."

Even against this backdrop, though, CSR had an inauspicious beginning. Proponents of CSR were hardcore promoters of "doing good," with little care or concern about corporate profits. This attitude stemmed in large part from the fact that early CSRers did not come from corporate backgrounds. "They spoke in the off-putting accent of moral superiority, and they betrayed ignorance of business realities, making demands that threatened to weaken the competitive positions of companies" Daniel Yankelovich observes.[8] Because of this offensive attitude, most companies not only did not embrace this new business strategy but rejected it outright. The prevailing response to CSR was to fall back on the Milton Friedman school of economics, which held that a corporation's only responsibility was to make money for its shareholders.[9] Providing jobs was in and of itself a service to the community, these CSR rejecters said. The few companies that did accept CSR usually did little more than write a check.

CSR lay all but dormant—with a few notable exceptions, like Ben & Jerry's and The Body Shop—until the 1990s. CSR's rise in popularity at that time was not because of a sudden burst of altruism on the part of corporations and their leadership, but because of regulatory and economic changes. In the 1980s, during a period of massive deregulation, Ronald Reagan significantly cut corporate taxes—something that corporate America heartily endorsed. However, in cutting the tax rolls by more than $130 billion between 1982 and 1984, the president simultaneously gutted the welfare system. Social programs were slashed—economic development by "$2.4 billion, food stamps by $10.8 billion, and job training by $15.9 billion."[10] Corporations found themselves bombarded by requests for funding, and throughout the 1980s, they responded by increasing their philanthropic giving.[11] Corporate contributions swelled to $4 billion in 1984, up from $2.5 billion in 1982, and increased further to $5.9 billion by 1993.[12] However, this was nowhere near the $29 billion cut in government social spending.

It wasn't simply this increase in corporate giving that led to a change of heart about CSR. Rather, it was an economic change that occurred a decade later. When corporations increased their largesse in the 1980s, they did not align corporate giving with product promotion (à la Hamburger Helper). At that time, using philanthropy to promote your brand was considered self-serving, if not uncouth. Corporate perspectives on philanthropy changed in the 1990s, however, when increasing calls for efficiencies arose throughout the corporate sector. The philanthropic increases of the 1980s needed to become strategic advantages in the

1990s. Much as television networks in the 1980s looked for ways to make TV news rooms profitable—something that would have been unthinkable in the time of Walter Cronkite or the Huntley-Brinkley Report—in the 1990s, corporations looked for their philanthropic works to contribute to the bottom line. This reincarnation of CSR became known as strategic philanthropy.

The Eastman Kodak Company is a good example. When Kodak restructured and downsized in the 1990s, it changed its mission to focus on a global perspective and reorganized to create a combined community relations and contributions—that is, philanthropy—program. While the budget was reduced for contributions, community relations (what today would be the corporate responsibility department) was tasked with additional duties. In conjunction with other departments of the company, community relations revised its strategic objectives to include investing in urban markets, developing business-to-business partnerships with nonprofits in addition to for-profit ventures, leveraging donations to improve sales prospects, and strategically making grants that help to open global markets.[13] Establishing this new approach aligned fully integrated philanthropy with the goal of generating increased sales. This was very different from the more traditional contributions approach, which required simply writing a check. It was this sort of thinking that ultimately led to the widely held belief in corporate America that charity and volunteerism should provide a return on investment (ROI), another new twist on CSR.[14]

Two other events at this time contributed to the expansion of corporate responsibility. In a 1994 *Harvard Business Review* article titled "The New Corporate Philanthropy," Craig Smith suggested that the *Exxon Valdez* disaster was instrumental in connecting business to charity. In order to clean up the oil spill, Exxon needed the expertise of environmental groups, but it had no such relationship (prior to this time a relationship like that would have looked self-serving on the part of Exxon and seemed like selling out on the part of the environmental group). At a loss to respond effectively to this environmental disaster, Exxon executives vowed that in the future they would not be found wanting in this way, and the company made a concerted effort to court planet-conscious groups.

In a second example, Nike was taken to task for abhorrent labor practices in factories that produced its sneakers and sweats during the early 1990s.[15] Made aware of the problem by human rights groups and then pressured by the public more broadly, the company responded by instituting a monitoring program to oversee working conditions. It also helped create the Fair Labor Association, an organization made up of companies, colleges, and social organizations that acts to improve working conditions in factories worldwide. These changes significantly improved—but did not erase—Nike's negative image. Today, Nike continues to pursue corporate responsibility with initiatives that include "Step It Up," which promotes dance competition and athletic participation to fight childhood obesity in urban markets, and "Reuse-A-Shoe," which recycles old sneakers into running tracks and other athletic surfaces. Unlike other companies, however, Nike is very low key about its corporate responsibility efforts.[16]

At the same time that strategic philanthropy and public scrutiny were reigniting interest in CSR, corporations became aware of a new promotional tool: cause-related marketing (CRM). CRM "is when companies partner with charitable organizations to help non-profits better achieve their goals. Cause-related marketing is attached to a media campaign, with money generated for the cause through the sale of products," according to the marketing research firm Mintel. A long-running example you might be aware of is the relationship between Procter & Gamble (P&G) and the Special Olympics. Consumers buy P&G products during designated annual time periods, and a percentage of the sale goes to the nonprofit.

CRM began in 1983 when American Express (Amex) created a promotion around the rebuilding of the Statue of Liberty (which, aside from its patriotic aspect, did not tie into American Express per se). Amex agreed to contribute one penny for every card transaction and one dollar for every card issued during the final quarter of 1983. The campaign was incredibly successful by any measure. Not only did Amex collect $1.7 million for the restoration project, but use of its credit cards increased 28 percent, and the company received enviable press coverage. Thus, just as strategic philanthropy married charity with business, CRM campaigns tied corporations to causes that improved their public reputations, while also promoting brands and increasing sales.

Campaigns could either be internally produced (like the Amex example) or corporations could attach themselves to existing umbrella campaigns, like breast cancer research—synonymous with the now ubiquitous pink ribbons of the Susan B. Komen Foundation—a trend that has continued to expand into the 2000s, and one extensively examined in chapter 3. Either way, businesses jumped on the CRM bandwagon. By the mid-1990s, corporate sponsorships—initially, mostly sports-related and then more targeted to social causes that appealed to their audiences—were the fastest-growing segment of corporate marketing budgets, increasing to nearly $2 billion in 1994, up from a mere $200 million just ten years before. By 2009, American corporations more than doubled their spending on CRM campaigns alone to $1.51 billion, according to the IEG Sponsorship Report, up from $733 million in 2001.[17]

After the turn of the millennium, these campaigns were also fueled by concerns that investors and consumers—understandably—no longer trusted corporate institutions. After the Enron, Martha Stewart, Bernie Madoff, and Tyco cases, to name a few, company after company looked for ways to improve its sagging corporate reputation. Investors—particularly baby boomers—began using their money to express their opinions in the market. Instead of marching in the streets as they did in their youth, they now capitalize companies and portfolios that reflect their social sensibilities. A whole industry has sprung up to help investors find and rate socially responsible companies. Socially responsible investing (SRI) is still small, but it continues to be a growing investment segment, even in these hard times, and corporations want to be evaluated in a good light by these groups.

Finally, the expansion of social media such as Facebook and Twitter, as well as the Internet more generally, fueled the spread of cause campaigns. As noted earlier, the effectiveness of traditional advertising tools, particularly television commercials, has decreased. Media fragmentation—hundreds of TV channels instead of a handful of broadcasters—created an environment where commercials do not reach the mass audience they once did. In addition, with the creation of the TV remote, and later the VCR and DVR, people learned to avoid ads either by zapping to another channel or zipping past them. As the Internet became more widely available, marketers followed.

The Internet does several things that television does not. First, it allows for information gathering and customization. When you buy something online—say a book from Amazon.com—the web site collects purchase data, on the basis of which it may suggest other purchases. Marketers also create campaigns that help generate a consumer database. In cause campaigns, consumers are asked to input personal information when they submit product codes activating corporate donations. The company thus acquires their e-mail addresses and details of their product preferences, facilitating further sales pitches. This use of technology to interact with consumers is called customer relationship management (confusingly, also known by the acronym CRM). Having more and continuously updated information about consumers enables companies to customize products and services.[18]

Furthermore, social media enhance interactivity between you and the product producer, you and your friends, and, ultimately, your friends and the product producer. Word-of-mouth marketing is the holy grail of any consumer campaign. Social media expedite this process. Consumers become product "evangelists"—asking their friends to join in and help a cause, which simultaneously touts the benefits of buying the product. Companies love this, because person-to-person selling has high credibility; people trust their friends more than a corporation. Whereas in the age of television, people might have mentioned a campaign in passing, online campaigns are created to encourage pass-along through social media. Corporations become the beneficiaries of person-to-person selling that helps drive traffic to additional promotion through Facebook, Twitter, and YouTube, sites that are virtual treasure troves of marketing research.

Multipronged interaction is increasingly being implemented in conjunction with cause-related marketing campaigns with the expectation that helping with a cause will motivate consumers to participate. These are some combination of a product purchase that requires going to a web site and putting in a code, and then "liking" a Facebook page and inviting your friends to sign on too. Some campaigns may also entail asking consumers to blog or tweet about the product or the campaign. Examples of these appear throughout this book, including "Glad to Give," "Pepsi Refresh," and Weight Watchers' "Lose for Good." Even before the advent of social media, these campaigns were considered to be highly cost-effective.[19] The added layer of consumers doing much of the promotional work makes them even more appealing to marketers.

Cause marketing works. Through the mid-2000s, a majority of consumers (79 percent) said that, all else being equal, they would switch to a brand associated with a cause.[20] Today, however, consumers are willing to *pay a premium* if there is a charitable connection. Moreover, research published in 2009 found that tying a product to a cause not only increases profits but also has a "spillover effect," leading to increased sales for the *entire line of products connected to the brand*. These sales increases bring in earnings well above the cost of the company's charitable donations.[21] It is also true that spillover effects occur when charity products are used as loss leaders at the retail level, that is, the charitable product is used to lure consumers into a store, where they will probably pick up additional merchandise. One example is Gap's relationship with (RED), where research suggests that Gap likely increased the prices of both (RED) and non-(RED) products.[22] In another example, Bath & Body Works put a candle lighter designed by Harry Slatkin, a maker of upscale candles, on sale during the Christmas holidays, with 100 percent of the proceeds going to the charity Autism Speaks. The item sold out almost immediately, and surely numerous candles with it. It should also be noted that the following year, the Slatkin & Co. Zippo Lighter was on sale at Bath & Body Works again, but with no cause attached.[23]

Most responsibility initiatives remain at the level of cause marketing. However, CSR is growing at an astonishing rate. *Corporate Responsibility Magazine,* a leading trade publication, which puts out a "100 Best Corporate Citizens" list, conducted a Corporate Responsibility Best Practices survey to which more than 650 companies from around the world and across dozens of industries responded. Its findings demonstrate the increasing importance of responsibility to American business: in 2006, only 1 percent of U.S. companies had a designated corporate responsibility officer. Today, that number is 35 percent (still significantly lower than in Canada and Western Europe, with 47 percent and 65 percent respectively). Almost half (42 percent) report to the company's CEO, which means these are positions with authority and not merely window dressing. And, most telling for our discussion, "two-thirds of companies report that at least one of their product or service offerings rely on a marketing message wherein corporate responsibility is the key value-driver for the brand."[24]

Much of this growth in corporate responsibility is driven by what is now called "sustainability." Like CSR, this has numerous definitions—300 by one estimate. There seems to be agreement, however, that it covers both sustaining the planet through improved environmental initiatives and sustaining the company with supportive labor practices and increased profitability. It includes not only what the company does, but how its partners and suppliers—members of the value or supply chain—affect the wider environment. It requires paying for externalities—accounting for the true cost of a product, such as eliminating e-waste or recycling products after consumers no longer need them. In her book *Plentitude: The New Economics of True Wealth,* the economist Juliet Schor explains how accounting for externalities can change an industry's reported bottom line:

> One study of the U.S. electric power industry quantified "off the books" (i.e., currently unaccounted for) liabilities associated with three types of emissions

(carbon dioxide, sulfur oxides, and nitrogen oxides). When these are added to official net operating after-tax profits for 2004, the industry total of $22.2 billion in earnings is converted into a net loss of $28.2 billion. Only four of the thirty-three companies included in the study remained profitable after accounting for pollutants they were releasing.[25]

Unlike cause marketing, then, espousing sustainability necessitates a fundamental shift in how a corporation does business. Accounting for those costs falls under what is known as the triple bottom line (TBL or 3BL), which requires that companies account for and audit their impact on "people, planet and profits."[26] Thus *stakeholders*—people (labor and local communities) and the planet (environmental concerns)—are as important as *shareholders* (those traditionally concerned with profit). Becoming sustainable requires a 360° analysis of one's business to find ways to source, manufacture, and recycle products that reduce, or better still eliminate, the company's carbon footprint (a concept known as "cradle to cradle," a term coined by William McDonough and Michael Braungart).[27] Most companies that have taken this initiative have found that they not only reduce pollutants and waste but also save material and fuel costs, thus increasing their profits.

Corporate ethics, strategic philanthropy, and sustainability all fall under the umbrella term corporate social responsibility (CSR). While it has many names and a vast majority of companies write about their CSR initiatives, the reality is that few have implemented the full spectrum of what it was meant to be and do. A review of the top-selling books about this issue shows (glaringly so) that stories about the same companies are told over and over again—Interface Carpets, Starbucks, Stonyfield Farms, Ben & Jerry's, and a half dozen or so others. Presumably, this is because the authors could not find more shining examples. I have found some additional bright points, but admittedly not many. Most companies continue to create consumer-driven, cause-related marketing campaigns and call them CSR.

LEVELS OF RESPONSIBILITY

Companies can demonstrate responsibility and their commitment to pro-social programs through a number of actions. In 2001, Minette Drumwright and Patrick Murphy published an exhaustive list of ten marketing activities related to doing good: traditional philanthropy, strategic philanthropy, cause-related marketing, licensing agreements,

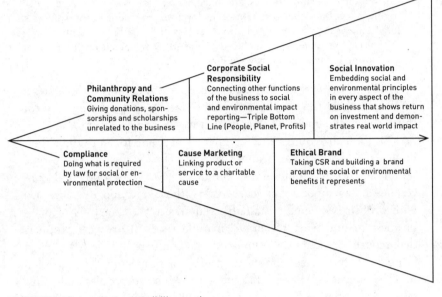

FIGURE 1. Corporate responsibility continuum.

. social alliances, corporate volunteerism, strategic corporate volunteerism, enterprises, sponsorships, and company advertising with a social dimension.[28] While all these pursuits are part of responsibility, that lineup is a bit too fine-grained for our purposes. The framework I use here was created by Chad Boettcher, former SVP of social innovation at Weber Shandwick, an international public relations company.[29] Boettcher has a long career in the field of social responsibility, including stints at Nike and MTV. He developed Goodzuma.com, a collaborative platform where people come together to "crowdsource" ideas for a better world (more on crowdsourcing below), has won several Emmy Awards for his work, and is a much-sought-after speaker at industry and academic conferences. He has worked with numerous corporate clients including Pepsi, Polo Ralph Lauren, and Samsung. Figure 1 depicts the spectrum of corporate social responsibility impacts, based on his experience. Boettcher called this an "embed impact cone." With his permission, I have renamed it the Corporate Responsibility Continuum.

As a company moves from left to right across the corporate responsibility continuum in figure 1, an increasing commitment of resources is required, which in turn generates an increasing ability to influence the social landscape. Responsibility can be demonstrated in six ways, or steps: compliance, philanthropy and community relations, cause marketing, CSR, ethical brands, and social innovation.

There are a couple of things to note about this continuum. First, these steps are not mutually exclusive; nor is this list meant to suggest that one progressively leads to another. For example, a producer of an ethical brand—say, TOMS shoes—is naturally involved in cause marketing, because every time it promotes its shoes, it promotes its cause. Second, all of the steps listed are already familiar, except the newest form of responsibility, dubbed social innovation, which takes CSR to its most fully executed level, requiring that companies completely integrate, or embed, accountability into every aspect of what they do. Finally, sustainability—a problematic concept because of its strong association with the environment, without encompassing other social issues—is not shown in figure 1, because it is an aspect of social innovation (and, one might argue, of some of the other steps as well).

Let's go through the responsibility continuum step by step, with some examples to illustrate exactly what each of these processes means.

Compliance: Doing Only What the Law Requires

This is the most basic level of corporate responsibility. For most companies, compliance means observing regulations that relate to environmental and employment issues. It may include additional regulation, particularly for food and drug companies. At the very least, every company can, or should, be fulfilling these obligations.

Unfortunately, not all do.

In April 2010, there was an explosion on the Deepwater Horizon offshore drilling rig in the Gulf of Mexico. Over the next 87 days, millions of barrels of oil poured into the waters south of Louisiana, Alabama, and Georgia and began pushing toward the beaches of Florida. Called "the BP oil spill"—a disturbing misnomer, inasmuch as it brings to mind images of spilled milk, say, as opposed to gushing crude—it became arguably the worst environmental disaster in American history.

Two years earlier, BP had been included in a book called *Green Biz: 50 Green, Profitable Companies Reveal Their Strategies & Successes* put out by CERES (pronounced "series"), a highly respected coalition of investors, environmental groups, and public interest organizations that works with companies to create sustainability initiatives and provides information on socially responsible investing. BP was included in a group of companies—Alcoa, Bristol-Myers Squibb, Goldman Sachs, and Pacific Gas and Electric—that were being recommended based on their commitment to biodiversity and land conservation. The authors of this book note that supporting these issues is as much about "enlightened self-interest" as it is about philanthropy, which is certainly the case for the former British Petroleum.

In the late 1990s, under the leadership of CEO Lord Browne, the company had made what appeared to be a serious commitment to the environment. With all the fanfare associated with social responsibility announcements, Browne admitted in a speech at the Stanford Graduate School of Business that global warming and climate change were serious global concerns—the first oil company executive to make such an acknowledgment. This was no small deal. Stanford is a business school with a long-standing commitment to responsibility, including publishing a leading academic journal, the *Stanford Social Innovation Review*. This announcement thus did not go unnoticed or un-acted-upon. Between 1997 and 2007, BP reduced operational emissions, developed alternative energy sources, and was funding biofuel research. According to company estimates (a source we are unlikely to trust these days), BP reduced greenhouse gas (GHG) emissions by 2.4 million tons. BP Alternative Energy was launched in 2005, with a commitment to invest $8 billion over ten years in renewable energy sources like solar and wind power (and natural gas—a questionable inclusion in this list). A biofuels division was launched in 2006, including a $500 million commitment over ten years to the Energy Biosciences Institute at the University of California, Berkeley. While these investments seem like a substantial amount of money, one needs to take into account that BP earned $20 *billion in profits in 2005 alone.*

Over the same period of time, BP was becoming one of the largest oil companies in the world, growing from a $50 billion company to a $265 billion company in part through swallowing the likes of Amoco and the Atlantic Richfield Company (ARCO). It was also during this time that the company launched its Helios logo—a sunflower image embedded in green, suggesting happiness and friendliness to the environment. In addition, it changed its name from British Petroleum to BP, which in advertising was promoted as "Beyond Petroleum" and on the company web site was presented as standing for the newly combined company's aspirations: "better people, better products, big picture, beyond petroleum."

Despite its shiny, happy logo, BP has been a company fraught with problems for years. It was accused of price-fixing in 2004. The following year, fifteen workers were killed and almost 200 more were injured in a Texas City, Texas, refinery explosion. This was followed by the discovery of burst and corroded BP pipes spilling more than 200,000 gallons of crude oil in Alaska, which came to light through the process of governmental oversight, not as a result of internal corporate initiative. Ironically, these environmental hazards led to escalating oil prices—resulting in record profits for BP.[30] BP "took full responsibility for its disastrous miscues," something we heard again a few years later from Tony Hayward, the successor to Lord Browne and the man of many malapropisms.

In the summer of 2010—*after* the oil spill disaster—BP was hit with the largest fine ever imposed by the Occupational Safety and Health Administration (OSHA), in connection with its Texas City refinery. Initially, BP was fined $21 million for safety violations that led to the Texas City blast. Additional fines of $50.6 million have since been imposed on the company for 270 safety violations. After millions of dollars in fines, the deaths of fifteen workers, injuries to scores more, plus billions of dollars paid to the families of victims, another billion spent since 2005 to fix the plant, $500 million committed to bring it up to code, and as party to one of the worst environmental disasters in American history, BP still was not in compliance.[31]

I include this cautionary tale as a reminder that while compliance is basic, it is not simple, and that it is not in our best interest to rely solely on the market to alleviate society's ills—corporations won't do it alone, and we shouldn't expect them to. Compliance is not something that companies can promote. After all, what are they going to say? "We're fabulous! We obey the law!" Rather, compliance tends only to become visible when it is *not* adhered to.

Philanthropy and Community Relations: Donations Unrelated to Business

Moving across the responsibility continuum, organizations can begin to provide support for community groups in the form of donations or employee volunteering. This step may also include sponsorships or scholarships unrelated to the business. Most companies are already involved in this type of activity; some may have relationships with organizations like United Way, or they may have their own foundations. For example, AT&T and Philip Morris (now Altria) have long histories of supporting the arts, notably museums and ballet companies. While not directly related to their businesses, these relationships help elevate corporate reputations by aligning the business with social causes that attract upscale, influential audiences.[32]

Time Warner

The entertainment conglomerate Time Warner uses a semi-traditional approach to philanthropy. It supports the arts, but seeks to address underserved audiences and artists, rather than to influence its target consumers. Time Warner's corporate grants are thus community-focused and only tangentially related to its businesses.

Time Warner's corporate philanthropy has two goals: to develop diverse talent and to provide broad access to the arts. Some might see this as strategic philanthropy, because Time Warner is cultivating artists and audiences, and certainly a case could be made for that. Moreover, these initiatives have a long-term communal goal rather than a short-term revenue one. Based on my conversation with Dan Osheyack, Time Warner's vice president for philanthropic initiatives, the company doesn't see what it does as strategy philanthropy, at least not in the traditional sense.[33] In part, this is because Time Warner does not brand itself as a product-manufacturing company, or even the way some entertainment companies do (think Disney). After all, when was the last time you said, "I must go see the latest Time Warner film"? Rather, funding creates opportunities for artists who would not otherwise have a voice in the market and audiences who cannot afford to participate in it.

As it relates to artist development, the company has an initiative called "Diverse Voices in the Arts," through which it helps to provide opportunities for emerging playwrights from diverse backgrounds and ethnic groups to work with theater companies in New York. It has also worked with the Sundance Institute to help develop stories for stage and film. This involved not only funding but input from HBO and Warner Bros. executives. Furthermore, Time Warner funds programs to nurture talent in New York City public schools. Through its Youth Media and Creative Arts Initiative, the company has created after-school programs in the arts—an area hard-hit by budget cuts—for underserved youth.

While the company has a number of initiatives that aim to develop audiences, the one that Dan Osheyack seemed most passionate about (and the one that seems most inclusive) is the ticket initiative at the Signature Theatre Company. In 2005, Time Warner funded the entire season, so that every seat in the theater cost only $15—just slightly more than a movie ticket and far less than Broadway's $150-plus prices. The initiative continues today (with the slightly increased price of $20 per ticket) and has led to 180,000 people being able to see plays by August Wilson, Tony Kushner, and the Negro Ensemble Company, among others. Audiences were diverse (26.6 percent identified themselves as people of color) and included many usually unable to attend such events (24.3 percent earned less than $50,000 annually).[34]

TAXI and the Homeless

This instance is a bit atypical, but it is a wonderful example of innovative thinking. After celebrating its fifteenth anniversary in business, the Canadian ad agency TAXI wanted to find a way to give back to the community. Spurred by the problem of homelessness in Canada's extremely cold weather, the company's executive creative director, Steve Mykolyn, came up with "The 15 Below Project," which distributes a specially designed jacket that is breathable, waterproof, and lightweight. Most important, the lining consists of pockets throughout the jacket, which can be stuffed with newspaper as needed to provide adjustable insulation. Paul Lavoie, co-founder, chairman, and chief creative officer of TAXI, explained: "It's a lifeline for people without homes. They're a pretty low-cost, immediate way to address a huge issue. . . . This won't eliminate homelessness, but it can make a lot of people more comfortable."[35] Money to fund this initiative was generated by auctioning 15 Below Jackets on eBay that were signed by socially conscious celebrities including R.E.M., Nicholas Negroponte, the cast of *The Daily Show* with Jon Stewart, and Sir Elton John. These celebrities also donated signed books, albums, television scripts, backstage passes, and other items to help generate funds. In 2009, 3,000 jackets were distributed through the Salvation Army. TAXI is looking for a corporate sponsor to take the program national.

Some companies are thus doing good works, whether with or without an immediate impact on their bottom lines. But there are, of course, philanthropic campaigns that have ulterior motives, such as funding pet projects of politicians that have the ability to help bolster a company's bottom line. Philip Morris is one.

Philip Morris

In a 2008 article titled "Ethical Conduct in Public and Private Arenas," Laura Tesler and Ruth Malone show "how Philip Morris's corporate philanthropy serves as a link between corporate image and legislative objectives to influence public health."[36] In systematically reviewing internal documents—many of which were made available through the Legacy Tobacco Document Library (a database of internal tobacco company documents related to how cigarettes are researched, manufactured, and promoted)—they were able to show that Philip Morris used philanthropy, not only to improve the company's reputation vis-à-vis its tobacco business, but also to garner favor with politicians who could affect legislation negative to the corporation.

In 1997, the company initiated "Philip Morris in the 21st century" (PM21), a campaign to improve its reputation and "to respond to and shape a political, regulatory and attitudinal environment that permits the Company to achieve its business objectives."[37] This was also in response to the public's intense scrutiny of the tobacco industry after the CEOs of the major tobacco companies had each stood in front of Congress in 1994 saying, "I believe that tobacco is not addictive." The hope was to separate consumers' views on tobacco from the company that sold the cigarettes.

Strategic philanthropy was an important aspect of this campaign, because it was shown to have a positive effect on the company's public image. It supported causes like hunger relief (which made sense because the food producer Kraft was Philip Morris's parent company), domestic violence abatement, and humanitarian aid. The company aligned itself with reputable nonprofits like Second Harvest and even had ghost writers fashion op-ed pieces that were pitched to local papers by the company's public relations firm. These news pieces contained sections that described Philip Morris as an exemplary corporate citizen.

In addition, Philip Morris made a concerted effort to influence politicians who affected tobacco legislation. As early as 1990, the company amassed a database of the favorite social causes of members of Congress. Through promoting charities of interest to legislators and inviting them to attend company-sponsored philanthropic events, Philip Morris helped to "thwart state and local cigarette, beer, and food excise taxes and tobacco marketing restrictions." In all, the researchers found that the company was able to achieve legislative objectives in nineteen out of twenty states where some type of philanthropic investing was done. Lobbying also no doubt helped, but promoting the company as caring is what bolstered the bottom line in multiple ways.

Since philanthropy is integral to a company's reputation, public relations departments have traditionally handled cause marketing. As we are beginning to see, however, philanthropy is increasingly moving out of PR and into the marketing department, because it has become key to product sales.

Cause Marketing

Cause marketing links branded products and services to charitable causes. Brands can be connected with causes through an internal foundation, an outside organization or a combination of the two. Chapter 3 addresses at length what I call "hypercharities," with their pink ribbons, red dresses, and so on. Here I focus on individual corporate campaigns. In providing these examples, my hope is to help people distinguish the good from the not so good.

There are so many of these campaigns, it's almost hard to know where to start. Some are fairly innocuous, in that they are typical cause-related marketing campaigns, providing what one expert I spoke with called "symptom relief." An example is Milk-Bone's "It's Good to Give" program, where a portion of each purchase goes to Canine Assistants, which provides service dogs to disabled people. This should not be confused, however, with Glad Products "Glad to Give"—a campaign that virtually mimics Hamburger Helper's: consumers are meant to buy Glad products and input codes online ($1 per purchase goes to charity), "share recipes for giving" (tips for instilling service-mindedness in kids), and/or host a bake sale, with all proceeds going to Cookies for Kids' Cancer. My problem with this campaign is twofold: first, the obvious attention being directed to the brand ("*Glad* to Give"), and second the gimmicks used to play on mothers' heartstrings. For this last, they hit all the notes—horribly sick children, teaching charity to your own children, and associating caring with food (and decidedly unhealthy food at that). Never mind that this deflects us from thinking about the environmental and possible health issues associated with the many plastic products that Glad manufactures.

Let's look at a few examples in a bit more depth so that you can see the many layers of issues associated with such campaigns.

Weight Watchers: "Lose for Good"

Weight Watchers International, Inc. (WWI), is a leader in weight loss both in the United States and around the world. Operating through company-owned and franchised stores, WWI provides education and information to its members, who attend weekly meetings and/or follow its program online. There are today an estimated 1.4 million Weight Watchers members.

In September—a popular time of year to promote weight loss because of back to school (a new beginning), and in anticipation of the holidays—Weight Watchers runs "Lose for Good," a promotion combining weight loss with fighting hunger. The program name can be understood in two ways: the WWI plan helps you lose weight "for good" (meaning forever), and by losing weight you do good by helping donate to charity (the amount of money given to charity is tied to the amount of weight lost by members). The program launched in 2008.

For every one million pounds lost during the six-week promotion, WWI would donate $250,000, with the total capped at one million dollars. Both online and in-store weight were tracked and included in the total. Of the "earnings," 70 percent went to Share our Strength (www.strength.org), a domestic organization that works to eradicate childhood hunger, and the remaining 30 percent to Action Against Hunger (www.actionagainsthunger.org). Share our Strength is most known for promoting local events, including the Great American Bake Sale, a campaign that encourages communities to hold bake sales to raise money, and the Great American Dine Out, where one week each fall, restaurants donate a portion of their earnings to help fight hunger. Action Against Hunger is a global organization that sponsors multiple initiatives to eliminate the underlying causes of hunger around the globe.

In addition to the monetary donation by Weight Watchers, there was a "grassroots" overlay whereby each store could choose to collect food for local food banks. In 2009, more than 3,300 drives were organized. One final component added the same year was a social media element called "Lose-A-Palooza." This was a one-day event when Weight Watchers would donate money for each blog post, tweet, or other social media mention of "Lose for Good." The amount for each individual posting was not disclosed and the total incremental donation was capped at $25,000—in 2009, the donation totaled $23,530.

The actress and sometime Playboy Playmate of the Year Jenny McCarthy was the spokesperson for "Lose for Good" in 2009. Two years early, McCarthy had lost sixty pounds after her pregnancy while on the WWI program and was asked to grace the cover of *Weight Watchers Magazine*. This was the first time a celebrity had appeared on the magazine's cover, and newsstand sales jumped 10 percent. In light of this, the company sought to expand its relationship with McCarthy, hence her spokesperson status. She also made sense for this position, because she would appeal to a younger client base.

Issues. On the positive side, Weight Watchers' "Lose for Good" campaign is not a hit-and-run operation. It has taken place for several years running and has been a success for WWI and helpful to the charities. On the other hand, the promotion is convoluted and confusing. What I have outlined here is buried deep in the company's fine print. Moreover, Weight Watchers hyped the success of the campaign's local food donations, but when one of my students asked at several local WWI offices, no one there could explain exactly how they worked. As for "Lose-A-Palooza," you'd be hard-pressed to find a campaign that is more self-serving. Ditto goes for the choice of Jenny McCarthy as spokesperson.

"Give a Day, Get a Disney Day"

The Walt Disney Company's "Give a Day, Get a Disney Day" campaign was conceived to promote volunteerism in America. The concept was simple: one million people would receive free admission to a Disney theme park when they volunteered a day at an approved volunteer organization. The promotion was slated to run throughout 2010, and the free ticket had to be redeemed by December 15, 2010.

Broadly, this promotion was a smart one, because it tied into the growing zeitgeist of volunteerism, which was on the rise during the ongoing recession. From the company's point of view, it would help to spur sales, because fewer people were traveling during the recession (it was the time of "staycations"). In giving people tickets for one day, the assumption was that they would stay (and pay) for additional days, as well as for additional family members.

Because this was Disney—a company that rarely does anything in a small way—the campaign was promoted to the hilt. This included commercials starring the Muppets (owned by Disney), a special episode of *Extreme Makeover Home Edition* on ABC (owned by Disney), and multi-page spreads in leading women's magazines like O, *The Oprah*

Magazine (not owned by Disney, though her show aired primarily on ABC stations). The campaign was such a "success" that Disney had to shut it down by mid-March. It had done such a good job of promoting "Give a Day, Get a Disney Day" that it reached the allotted limit of one million volunteers ten weeks into the event. By mid-March, there were no longer any opportunities for promoting volunteerism or to continue helping organizations, other than a line on the campaign web site that said, "And even though the program has come to an end and you can no longer earn a free Disney Theme Park ticket, we encourage you to volunteer in your community by searching for opportunities through the HandsOn Network, its affiliates and partners. You can search year-round for volunteer opportunities at: www.Handsonnet work.org."

Issues. Disney was able to generate substantial interest in volunteering and bring people to organizations that desperately needed the support. Many were so flooded with volunteers that they had to turn them away or start waiting lists. The campaign provided people with an incentive to donate their time—something many had never done before but were glad to try, given the enticement. However, beyond techno-logical issues—of which there were many—this campaign demonstrates the fundamental problem when it comes to promoting the corporation over the cause. The extensive promotion around this campaign was mostly in some way related to Disney properties—not to the causes being helped. For example, a time-lapse video created in conjunction with the campaign (which the company undoubtedly expected to go viral) showed people constructing the largest canned food "sculpture" ever built. Made up of 115,000 cans, it reads "Celebrate Volunteers!" and includes several Disney characters with tools in their hands, like a shovel and a paintbrush.[38] This sculpture was all about getting publicity around setting a Guinness world record, rather than that the food was going to food banks after the structure was disassembled.

Instead of keeping the focus on the corporation, efforts should have been made to turn the cameras on those in need, or at very least the volunteers. Moreover, a Disney promotion celebrating guests' birthdays the year before had capped the campaign at 1.2 million free tickets. Certainly, Disney could have done at least the same for those freely giving their time for a good cause through "Give a Day, Get a Disney Day."

Dove's "Campaign for Real Beauty"

In 2002, Unilever was facing slowing growth in its Dove product line. Like many manufacturers of "personal care" products today, the company stopped talking about product attributes and began looking for something else to promote. Research revealed that more than 50 percent of women were disgusted with their bodies. Women's self-esteem thus became the benefit Unilever sought to associate with the use of Dove products.

In 2004, the company launched the "Dove Campaign for Real Beauty." Television commercials, magazine ads, and billboards suddenly featured real women, not models, of all ages, shapes, sizes and colors dressed only in bras and underpants. The success of this promotion was crowned with the ultimate in middle-aged female consumer acceptance—an appearance on *Oprah*.

By 2006, the campaign moved beyond its initial promotional elements to include a social campaign. Unilever created the Dove Self-Esteem Fund, which aims to change Western perceptions of beauty by targeting programs that help build girls' self-esteem. Money from the sale of Dove products goes to support one of three charities: Girl Scouts of the USA, Boys & Girls Clubs of America, and Girls, Inc.

Issues. This is a highly celebrated campaign, and for good reason. First, it is a long-term initiative. Dove continues to use this campaign almost a decade after it first started. Second, the campaign works on multiple levels: there is information to help mothers and mentors talk to girls about self-esteem, as well as a "girls only" section of the web site, and there are videos and workshops to provide additional ways to disseminate information. Also, while the site (and the advertising) claims that money goes to one of the three charity partners listed above, and it would be great if that were true, there is no information that explains how much of your purchase goes to charity.

Broad public criticism of the campaign didn't arise from the advertising. Rather, it was a viral video on YouTube called "Evolution" that led to the backlash from the press, bloggers, and interest groups. The video was a scathing attack on the beauty industry, calling on parents to talk to their daughters about esteem issues before the advertising industry does. The campaign, including this video, seems forward thinking, until you realize that Dove is owned by Unilever, an international conglomerate that is the maker of Slimfast, and Tresemmé hair-care products, among other things. Several Unilever products—most notably the Axe line, whose commercials show women shamelessly throwing themselves at men—are flagrant perpetuators of the beauty myth that Dove claims to be attempting to dispel. As an *Advertising Age* article said in 2007: "That doesn't mean the company should give up the Dove work. What it does mean is that Unilever and other large companies must realize that the days of the populace never making the connections between brands with conflicting messages are gone."[39]

A few campaigns show a glimmer of hope that companies can be innovative around cause marketing without making it all about the brand.

British Airways: "Change for Good"

In the mid-1990s, British Airways instituted a campaign called "Change for Good," which both provided a service to its customers and raised funds for UNICEF, the United Nations Children's Fund. The concept was simple and clever. When traveling internationally, passengers often have leftover foreign currency in their pockets, and the amount is typically too small to be worth converting. British Airways collected this spare change in envelopes during flights and passed it on to UNICEF.

The advertising firm Saatchi & Saatchi calls this campaign cause marketing because British Airways promotes it. What makes "Change for Good" different from other marketing initiatives we've looked at, however, is that it provides a service without requiring a purchase.[40]

Triscuit and Home Farming

Building on a trend that is part of the DIY and health movements, Nabisco, a subsidiary of Kraft Foods, began a campaign in 2010 to promote home farming via the company's Triscuit crackers. Farming in urban areas is growing around the country. To support this, Nabisco included seeds in boxes of Triscuits and created a web site (www.homefarming .com) giving advice to help both beginners and seasoned pros grow their own food. Working with the nonprofit organization Urban Farming, the company created fifty community farms in twenty cities. It also aligned with Paul James, host of HGTV's *Gardening by the Yard,* who visited some of the local farms and provides tips on the web site.

There's even a map so visitors can find other gardeners in their area. Finally, the campaign got a push when the founder of Urban Farming appeared on the *Ellen DeGeneres Show,* a down-to-earth version of *Oprah.*

Certainly, you could criticize the fact that an international conglomerate that manufactures overprocessed food is the purveyor of this information, and a number of bloggers did. However, and this is an idea to bear in mind, if for no other reason than to keep from getting too cynical: isn't it better that people get interested, informed, and maybe even excited about home farming, no matter where it comes from? After all, it's not as though the vegetables are going to come out of the ground with a Triscuit logo.

Corporate Social Responsibility: Aligning Business with Social and Environmental Impacts and Reporting on It

Unlike cause marketing, corporate social responsibility (CSR) does not simply involve slapping a logo on a marketing campaign. Rather, it requires an increased level of commitment, and the cause is integral to the work of the corporation. CSR will work differently for different companies, depending on the category they compete in. For example, for a food company, alleviating hunger is an obvious social issue. Automobile manufacturers will likely demonstrate how they are creating more fuel-efficient cars. An important element is that this step includes reporting on how a CSR strategy is being implemented.

The issue with CSR (as opposed to social innovation, discussed below) is that the focus is on (1) the corporation, and (2) the communications. It is a responsive model, not a proactive one, and it tends to be about creating a campaign or an initiative or a product so that you can talk it up to the investment community. Companies have responded in droves. According to the consulting company KPMG, 80 percent of 250 global companies produce a CSR report, either as part of their annual report or more commonly as a separate document that appears on the corporate web site. KPMG expects this to become standard operating procedure.[41] (Others will have broader definitions of CSR, but I use this more limited definition here to clearly delineate it from social innovation, which ultimately is what CSR sets out to be, but in most cases is not.)

Here I provide an example of good marketing packaged as good works.

Clorox: Burt's Bees and Green Works

Clorox bleach has been a household product since before most of us can remember. It was first sold in 1913 and remains the Clorox Company's most lucrative brand, accounting for $1.5 billion, or 28 percent of sales, in 2008.[42] Bleach, Clorox or generic, is one of the most environmentally unfriendly products on the planet. Given this and the growing environmental trend, Clorox set out to "green" its image.[43]

In addition to household cleaning products, the Clorox Company produces a long line of well-known brands from Glad wrap and containers (see above) to Hidden Valley salad dressing to Fresh Step cat litter. Its green line of products includes Brita filtration systems, Burt's Bees, and a new line of household cleaning products called Green Works, launched in January 2008. Here we'll focus on the last two.

Burt's Bees, perhaps best known for its beeswax lip balm, has a long history of success in the natural food–health care marketplace. The packaging used to have a picture of the curmudgeonly Burt, but has since been redesigned to display a beehive, suggesting a natural, environmental image.

Burt's Bees remained a small producer until 2004, when the company was sold to a private investor group. With the influx of funding, distribution of the products moved into mass-market outlets like supermarkets, chain drugstores, and mass merchandisers, in addition to smaller outlets like bookstores. The company's growth attracted Clorox, which bought it in November 2007 and was able to further expand the brand's distribution and improve performance by discontinuing underselling products.

This acquisition demonstrates the trade-offs when a small company is bought by a larger conglomerate, a continuing trend as sales of sustainable and ethical products increase. Numerous manufacturers of such products have been purchased by multinationals, including Ben & Jerry's (Unilever), Stonyfield Farms (Groupe Danone, makers of Dannon yogurt), and Honest Tea (40 percent owned by Coca-Cola). Owners of the original companies argue that "scalability"—the ability to reach millions of people less expensively who wouldn't otherwise use the product—outweighs the benefits of keeping the company small and privately owned. That may be true. However, it also allows the conglomerate to use the brand to claim responsibility—which is the case with the bees and the bleach.

In its sustainability report, Burt's Bees claims, "Organic sources simply don't exist for all the ingredients we need. . . . For now, we'd rather be 100% truly natural than only partially organic." The "natural" designation has no real merit. While "organic" is regulated, and specific benchmarks must be met in order for a product to use that designation, the same is not true of "natural." Thus, organic is real; "natural" is marketing. Additionally, the company's web site says it "commits to the highest standards of fair trade and working conditions in the sourcing of our products." However, the products are not labeled as fair trade, because here too the company would have to prove it. More positively, the company is switching to post-consumer-recycled (PCR) materials and eliminating shrink wrap; its factory in North Carolina was made 100 percent carbon neutral, and it established The Burt's Bees Greater Good Foundation in 2007, which donates at minimum 10 percent of sales from its web site sales to charity.

While Burt's Bees increases the Clorox Company's credibility in the health care category, the creation of Green Works has propelled the company's environmental image in the household cleaning segment. Green Works sells a variety of products, including an all-purpose cleaner, a toilet bowl cleaner, a bathroom cleaner, a glass and surface cleaner, and a hand-dishwashing liquid. These products bear the Clorox logo—a key indicator that the company is looking to reframe the image of its main brand. Like BP's, Green Works' packaging and marketing colors are white, yellow, and green.

Within two years, Green Works was the leading natural household products brand, with $200 million in sales and 42 percent of the market. It more than doubled the size of the eco-friendly cleaners category. A key reason for its success is its ability to undercut the prices of its competitors. Green Works products cost 10–20 percent more than conventional products, while smaller producers have to charge 60 percent more (the scalability issue).

From a consumer perspective, Clorox was able to tap into the environmental market with consumers who might not lean toward green products. Love or hate the bleach, Clorox is a trusted name and helped bring new people to the category.

As for the products themselves, they are "99% natural," which we know means very little. The company does list the ingredients on the bottle, something that is not done for most household products. Even so, as noted by Treehugger.com, a respected blog on environmental issues:

> Clorox is right: each of those ingredients, aside from the two specifically mentioned [preservative (Kathon) and colorant (Milliken Liquitint Blue HP dye and Bright Yellow dye X)], can be "naturally-derived." They say their

alkyl polyglucoside comes from coconut oil and their ethanol and glycerine from corn oil; while that's better than using petroleum-derived alternatives, there are still major issues with rainforest habitat destruction relating to harvesting coconut oil and all sorts of issues with corn-based ethanol. So, like many things we mention on TreeHugger, Green Works is better than a conventional alternative, but not perfect.

Clorox attempted to ward off critics from the start. One way it did this was with the FAQs on its web site, which include the following:

"Is Clorox merely jumping on the green bandwagon?"

Answer: "We've been working on natural products for the past 5 years. We set ourselves a difficult task—to set the standard for natural cleaning and create products that clean with the power you expect from Clorox. In fact, we delayed Green Works products from hitting the shelves by 6 months to further perfect the formula. We are fully committed to continuing to develop natural products that continue to set the standard for natural."

The other far more controversial method was to get the endorsement of the Sierra Club, whose logo appears on all Green Works packaging. In exchange, Green Works helps to support Sierra Club's conservation efforts. In 2008, Clorox donated close to half a million dollars to the Sierra Club. The "alliance" between these two organizations is problematic. Nonprofit organizations are not allowed by law to endorse consumer products. So if you look closely you will see that while the products bear the logo (the only thing that consumers are likely to see and read), small print states: "Sierra Club logo is used with permission, which does not constitute sponsorship or endorsement of any company or product." So the next question has to be: what is it there for?

Some would say that we should support Clorox in doing this work and taking the time and the research and development money to create better products. I might have included myself in that number, except for the fact that one of my interviewees told me that Bill Morrissey, the leading sustainability officer at Clorox, attends the trail of sustainability conferences promoting "what a great environmental steward Clorox is and how 'not bad' bleach is—that's their message—bleach isn't as bad as you've been told." Clorox never would have made that bold move without having first created the image of being a more environmentally correct manufacturer.

For additional context, let's compare Clorox with another manufacturer, 3M—a company with a long-standing reputation for innovation, as well as a commitment to the environment.[44] As far back as 1970, 3M has looked to design, or in many cases redesign, products to be eco-friendly. In one example, the engineers redesigned sandpaper, a product harmful to the environment because of the solvents used in its production. After fifteen years and $2 billion spent—a serious commitment on the part of 3M—it developed a sandpaper without the use of solvents. Period. Yes, 3M did it for the environment, but it was also for the company. Through the redesign, 3M saves 30 percent on its material costs.[45] In the end, then, both companies undertook these initiatives out of self-interest. However, one did it to help both the environment and the company; the other did it to make money and talk about its environmental stewardship.

Ethical Brands: Building a Brand around a Social Cause

Moving beyond CSR, this step entails creating a product or service with a social and/or environmental benefit intricately woven into the brand. Specifically, ethical products are those labeled "local," "fair trade," "eco-friendly," "sustainable," "cage-free," or "organic"—this last designation being the most important, because it is the only one that is regulated. They may also be connected to charity without the product itself being in some way healthy or ethical; Ben & Jerry's, for example, is often berated for contributing to obesity.

Unlike the other steps in the corporate responsibility continuum, this one is a consumer product segment, and it is growing like wildfire. According to Datamonitor, a corporate research firm, "5,129 new ethical products were launched globally in 2008, marking a world's record," and 2009 introductions were expected to surpass that.[46] Most of these products (73 percent) were food or beverages; the remainder includes health and beauty products, household products like cleaners, and even light bulbs. Moreover, the United States is the leading producer of ethical brands, having launched 8,463 products of this type between 2005 and July 2009. This is nearly four times that of the United Kingdom (number two in ethical products), which introduced 2,318 over the same time period. Because of these new products, retail sales in this category were estimated to be $38 billion in 2009 and could reach as high as $62 billion within five years. Driving the sales of these products are stores like Whole Foods Markets and Trader Joe's, but increasingly they are also finding their way into Costco, Sam's Clubs, and Walmart.

Not surprisingly, this kind of growth has attracted large consumer brand companies. In fact, many of your favorite ethical brands are owned by big multinationals. For example, Kashi is owned by Kraft Foods, Naked Juice by Pepsico, and Tom's of Maine by Colgate-Palmolive. What is also not surprising is that companies are using kids to attract parents to these products. Concerns about appropriate nutrition are driving sales of organic products for every young demographic from infants to teens. Anyone who ever bought YoBaby from Stonyfield Farms or Annie's Mac & Cheese with the rabbit on the box knows what I mean.

While it is true these are ethical brands, some of the spirit of being an ethical brand gets lost when the company is merged with a larger conglomerate. An organization called B Corp that is trying to mitigate that is discussed later in the book. Here I want to provide examples of two smaller companies that fully embody the spirit of an ethical brand.

Madécasse

I met Tim McCollum when he came to talk to my class on social innovation at New York University. He's young—in his mid-thirties—smart, self-deprecating, and has a good sense of humor—qualities I found in most people who work in sustainability and social justice. Tim and his partner, Brett Beach, came up with the idea of Madécasse—a company that produces fine chocolate—after having spent two years in Madagascar with the Peace Corps.[47]

What I didn't know was that 85 percent of the world's cocoa comes from Africa. However, not even 1 percent of it is processed on the continent, and it is in the final production from bean to bar that the value is created. So, while Africa grows the crop, multinational companies like Nestlé, headquartered in Switzerland, for example, reap the lion's share of the profit.

Tim and Brett had the crazy idea of producing chocolate in Africa—crazy because, as Tim joked in class, "it's hot in Africa." However, if they could make it work, they would have a financial impact that far exceeds what could be done simply through fair trade. They could help to significantly raise the standard of living in Madagascar, one of the poorest countries on the planet.

True ethical products exist to make the world a better place not only because of the product—who doesn't like chocolate?—but through the act of producing it—in this case, raising the standard of living for exceedingly poor people. As it says on the company's web site: "It's a unique partnership, where we travel by oxcart to work with the [farming cooperative called Ezaka], share their table for meals, and together produce a unique style of cocoa. Through this relationship, and your purchases of our chocolate, we provide Ezaka with training, equipment and a stable market. And Ezaka provides us with cocoa, and a constant reminder of why we started this business." Now that's making a difference.

"Life is good"

You've seen the T-shirts. They have a very smiley stick-figure character (his name is Jake) riding a skateboard or rowing a boat above the saying, "Life is good." That line is not just a saying, it's the name of a company started by two brothers, Bert and John Jacobs. In fifteen years they have grown to be a $100 million business.[48]

The company is built on the philosophy of optimism and the belief that they could build a brand with meaning. "Optimism focuses on what's right with the world, rather than on what's wrong," says Bert. "It's tremendously empowering." As for the brand, he notes, "There's a reason why the phrase 'Life is good' works. Note that we don't say 'Life is great!' We say life is good, period. Three simple words. People connect with it instantly."

Integral to the brand is the ability to spread that optimism. This is done through the Life is Good Kids Foundation. Its primary beneficiary is Project Joy, an organization that "fosters the development of at-risk children through the art of play." Money for the foundation is raised through the purchase of designated products and through an annual Life is Good Festival, where all the profits from the festival support Project Joy. (This year the company also created shirts saying "optimism has no borders" to raise money for relief efforts targeting children in Haiti.) This has led to more than $4 million going to children's causes.

What these examples demonstrate is that companies can pick an issue that they want to have an impact on. While these are more local in their effect, they are in many ways more powerful because of that.

Social Innovation: Embedding Responsibility and Return on Investment

The newest incarnation of CSR is called social innovation, and it represents a philosophical shift in corporate do-gooding. It is an integrated web of corporate responsibility, sustainability, strategic philanthropy, cause marketing, and advocacy that is underscored by a holistic approach that embeds "doing good" into a corporation's DNA. While we usually think of the word in terms of embedding reporters in, say, Iraq, in truth embedding is to incorporate or contain as an essential part or characteristic. The idea is that this will allow corporations to think more broadly and act more creatively, while still serving the needs of stakeholders and the bottom line. Done correctly, social innovation improves corporate perception, reduces operational costs, *and* produces incremental revenues. Companies become more vested in committing to this practice because it shows a return on investment (ROI) and demonstrates real world impact. More important, because it helps the company—and now there are methods to demonstrate that it will help the company—it is more likely to do it and stick with it.

The key difference between CSR and social innovation is the element of publicity and the true level of corporate commitment: CSR is about telling everyone what you are doing (even when some companies don't deliver on their press releases), whereas social innovation is going about the business of making a difference and then "getting caught doing something good," according to John Rooks, president of the socially conscious marketing company SOAP Group.[49]

ACTS: Authenticity, Customization, Transparency, Sustainability

Fundamental to social innovation is the concept of ACTS—authenticity, customization, transparency, and sustainability. Authenticity means that the company supports a cause that is integral to the product it produces. Customization allows for the consumer to affect how "good works" are done. Transparency—one of the most important elements of being ethical—means that the company is open and honest about the work it does. Sustainability relates to both the environment and the company's bottom line, that is, it must be an initiative that can be sustained over a long period of time. These elements work in conjunction with one another and are what make a company truly helpful, as opposed to simply marketing-minded.

Authenticity is the most self-explanatory of these aspects of social innovation. It means that the company creates programs that are natural extensions of the brand and develops campaigns that solve social problems that are in its purview. We have already seen some of this with the examples above like 3M and Madécasse.

Because consumers expect products to be customized to their needs and because consumers have become more vocal when they are unhappy about corporate actions, integrating consumers into the decision process—customization—is an important element in creating social innovation campaigns. This is done through what is called "crowdsourcing."

Crowdsourcing is using the power of technology and communication to tap into the wealth of ideas available through multiple sources. You might have seen a Best Buy commercial where a girl is standing in a stadium asking for advice about her cell phone. The arena is packed with sales assistants from Best Buy—all of whom are ready to answer her question, but not all of whom can answer every issue. That's a visual demonstration of crowdsourcing.

The brand-innovation firm BBMG has created a permanent community for crowdsourcing called The Collective. The Collective is a social network (think Facebook) where 2,000 conscious consumers can voice their opinions to shape the policies and products of consumer companies. BBMG feeds a survey or invites participation in an online forum on an ongoing basis. Consumers' input is then used in developing new programs and brands that have a socially innovative overlay. However, participants in The Collective can interact and voice their opinions at any time. This is a systematized way to get group feedback and input. Most companies are not yet at this stage.

Integral with open communication is the idea of transparency. This is a word that has been thrown around a lot lately in terms of corporations and government as well. For many companies simply writing a CSR report becomes a stand-in for transparency. Others attempt transparency but fall short, like General Mills with Hamburger Helper. Truly innovative companies take transparency very much to heart, and the web sites of the best ones demonstrate it. 3M, again, is a very good example here, as is Chipotle, discussed below.

Finally, sustainability is about developing initiatives that sustain both the planet and corporate profits. This is the key difference between social innovation and cause marketing or corporate social responsibility—it puts the focus equally on the business *and* the cause.

Social innovation is a long-term process that may take ten to fifteen years, and it has to start at the top. Everyone in the company nonetheless needs to feel a sense of ownership in the process. Employees must advocate for innovation, and know that if an idea is approved, they will be given the resources to implement it. The most successfully responsible companies are those that have a C-level executive whose job it is to foster responsibility within the organization. Someone within the organization has to be thinking about this consistently, have the tools to make a difference, and have clear, performance-based objectives. Finally, social innovation seems to me to be what CSR at one time hoped to be. It is about how a company does business as much as how it makes profits. It is about knowing where supplies are sourced and how products are recycled, and it's about knowing that the people who make the product are fairly treated and earn a fair wage both here and around the world.

Chipotle Mexican Grill

Chipotle Mexican Grill is a semi-fast-food restaurant chain that fully embeds social innovation into its business practices. Chipotle sells made-to-order burritos and tacos from almost exclusively organic and locally grown produce, as well as naturally raised, antibiotic-free beef, chicken, and pork. Founded in 1993 in Denver, the company has expanded to over a thousand stores around the country. Sales for fiscal year 2010 were more than $1.8 billion, and Chipotle was #60 on *Fortune*'s list of the 100 fastest-growing companies.[50]

Chipotle built its business on providing a great product and a unique customer experience—an idea that is driven by the company's founder, Steve Ells. Steve (that's what they call him on the web site, demonstrating the company's accessibility) attended the Culinary Institute of America. He's a foodie's foodie, and providing the best-tasting product is what drives the business. This has meant from the beginning that Chipotle committed to using food from local, and preferably organic, farms. Steve may have been aware of the mushrooming local food and organic trends, but he also knew that this food quite simply tastes better.

The guiding principle for Chipotle is "Food with Integrity." As it says on the company's web site: "[This] isn't a marketing slogan. It's not a product line of natural and organic foods. And it's not a corporate initiative that will ever be finished or set aside to make room for other priorities. It's a philosophy that we can always do better in terms of the food we buy." Food with Integrity has all of the hallmarks of good social innovation. It drives the company to look continually for new and better means to improve products for its customers, while doing it in an increasingly beneficial way—for the company, the customer, and the community.

A recent initiative demonstrates this continuing commitment. In the summer of 2007, Chipotle began using Polyface Farm as its pork supplier in Charlottesville, Virginia. Polyface is a local organic farm made famous by the author Michael Pollan. The switch to Polyface began slowly—no public announcement and only a sign in the store on the days the product was available. But even this slow rollout required significant logistical changes. New cooking equipment was necessary. New recipes were developed. Special temperature-monitoring technology was needed for the farm's delivery van. And the company had to work in tandem with the farm to get it up to speed to produce the quantity needed by the restaurant. This took seventeen months. And while initially the company is paying a higher price for this product, the expectation is that through economies of scale, the organic farmers will decrease their costs at the same time as industrial farm costs will be increasing due to the rising prices of fuel and animal feed, ultimately reducing or eliminating the cost differential.

Chipotle is a different kind of company, not only for how it produces its product, but how it promotes its business. Unlike most fast food chains, or even sit-down restaurants like Appleby's, Chipotle built its brand through public relations efforts and not advertising—marketing that is considerably less expensive as well as more accepted by consumers. Through a combination of online engagement, local events and promotions, and select sponsorships, the company was able to increase its visibility as it expanded into additional markets. Of course, the selection of promotions and sponsorships had to marry up with the company's philosophy as well as its promotional needs. For that reason, the company sponsors a cycling team, which makes good sense as a tie-in with Chipotle's commitment to health, as did the company's promotion of a PBS cooking show. All of this led to successful word-of-mouth promotion, most notably a web site created by customers called chipotlefan.com, an enterprise that has nothing to do with the company itself.

Chipotle takes transparency to heart. On its web site, you can find where Chipotle serves naturally raised animal products (100 percent for pork and chicken, but only 50 percent for beef; so, if you want to avoid eating beef that is not naturally raised, you know not to order it from certain locations). The company opened its first green restaurant in 2002 in Texas. More recently, the company opened green restaurants in Minnetonka, Minnesota, and Gurnee, Illinois, the latter certified as platinum based on the Leadership in Energy and Environmental Design (LEED) rating system.

Social innovation has made Chipotle one of the most successful fast food companies on the planet. While what has driven the company is its owners' own sense of how they want to run their business, these practices have also turned out to be very good business, period. We've already discussed how consumers are changing the landscape. However, there are other environmental business factors that are forcing companies to make changes. In the case of the food industry, in addition to consumers driving the market for organic and seasonal food, the restaurant industry overall is being forced to contend with concerns about food safety and fluctuating fuel costs—concerns and costs that can be eliminated or significantly reduced through "doing good." Using organic produce and naturally raised animals reduces many of the safety issues inherent in large corporate farms. Sourcing local produce by definition cuts fuel costs. Here, too, we see that social innovation embeds what the company does with what makes the most sense in a changing business environment.

In sum, Chipotle represents social innovation at its best. It uses the best ingredients—organic and locally grown—to produce a superior product. It lets its customers know what it is doing. It gives back to the community through causes that match the corporate philosophy. It cares about its workers and works to build long-term relationships with its suppliers. This is the definition of ecology, where one part of the system affects the other.

WhiteWave Foods

Another company that demonstrates the vision of social innovation is WhiteWave Foods, a wholly owned subsidiary of Dean Foods.[51] While you might not know the name WhiteWave, you likely know its brands— Silk soy milk, Horizon organic milk, and International Delight coffee creamer.

I first learned about WhiteWave's sustainability and social justice initiatives in June 2010. Ellen Feeney, vice president of responsible livelihood, gave a presentation that stopped me in my tracks. The first thing that hit me was her job title. Feeney is not the VP of CSR; she is the VP of responsible livelihood. Framing the position in this way sets up her duties to be holistic and people-focused, which I found out to be true when she later explained that her job entails environmental initiatives, community involvement, employee volunteerism—VIA (which will be explained more fully in a minute), philanthropy and nonprofit partnerships, and event sponsorships. Projects, therefore, not only improve sustainability but reduce company costs through reduced resource use (greenhouse gas, waste, water), responsible sourcing, and improved packaging. Still, the comment that made the biggest impression—and something I hadn't heard from anyone else—was this: "I have to empower employees to think about sustainability when I'm not in the room."

Feeney expanded upon this idea when I spoke with her a few months later. "No matter how much you embed it in the culture and no matter how vibrant it is, not everybody can be at every meeting. I can't be at every meeting from a sustainability point of view. So what I need to do is to make sure that all of the people in that meeting are thinking through this sustainability screen. Does it work all the time? No." But the company has put structures in place that enable this kind of thinking to occur more often than not.

It starts with the company code of ethics, which states in part: "We expect you to help us build a sustainable business for the future and encourage you to look for opportunities to improve our environmental performance." WhiteWave helps employees do this through a program it calls Values in Action, or VIA. VIA exists as a tactic to use employee engagement and employee education as a foundation for embedding sustainability, Feeney explained. "The theory being that we needed to invest in educating each and every employee about what sustainability is, what responsible sourcing is, why it matters, who cares, what are some of the other tenets of corporate social responsibility, what's fair trade, all of that, what is it, why does it matter? And then the challenge was: How do you educate employees when they're already really busy with their jobs?"

So with the full support of leadership, the company set about creating a program that would reward employees for everything that they did in their lives that was making the world a better place. This was set up so that employees could use their own judgment—thus generating ownership—as to what fulfilled that mission. They could volunteer at their kids' school or donate money to a nonprofit; they could replace their light bulbs at home or donate their hair to Locks of Love. Each action earns the employee a point when he or she logs it into VIA. To help achieve full compliance, random gifts are given. Employees who enter only once can win a prize. So the system is not set up for employees to prove how responsible they are, but rather to enable everyone to be part of something bigger. "When the economy was better, we did

some pretty amazing prizes. The first year we started off with iPods in
'06 and then we did a really nice bicycle, because riding your bike to
work, or taking alternative transportation was one of the other ways
you could earn points, and we have a really vibrant bicycling group
. . . and one year we even did an energy-efficient high-def television.
We really got people's attention, and it wasn't about who logged the
most points—that's what we wanted to be clear about—it's whatever
you do, no matter how small, whatever, logging a point one time will
get your name in the hat for this. As you can imagine, we have 100
percent participation."

VIA is not just about rewards, however. It's about education. At
the heart of VIA is an Internet site that includes tutorials and definitions where employees can learn all about sustainability and renewable
energy and other company initiatives. Recently, it has added online
modules, mini-lessons in a PowerPoint format. These modules—Sustainability 101 and Recycling 101 and 102, so far—take about half an
hour, and there are questions at the end. The company tracks how many
employees have finished the module and what they scored, making it
possible to judge how effective the program is. Finally, employee ori-
entations are used as an opportunity to teach newcomers about what
responsible livelihood is at WhiteWave, including how they can get
involved, or Feeney and her team will set up a booth in the lobby and
answer questions as people enter and leave the cafeteria.

Incrementally educating middle- and upper-level thought leaders is an
important strategy in making WhiteWave a more sustainable company.
In conjunction with providing knowledge, the company worked with
managers to embed responsible livelihood or greenhouse gas reduction into their personal goals and objectives, that is, management was
bonused based on achieving livelihood goals. "We started really small.
We started with the top ten and then we built the top fifty list and then
it built out to the top 100 list. . . . The person would have the chance
to write their own goal, or we would craft it for them and they could
fine-tune it. The theory being we'll save you the time and you have final
edit, or you can write it and come to us and we'll help tweak it. That's
been amazingly successful, because what that does is . . . create buy-in
at the highest level from the senior leadership team—they get it, they
want it—and then we have all this grassroots support that continues
to generate all these good ideas—from the bicycling clubs saying we
need lockers for our bikes to all these real passionate causes that the
employees would take on."

Deciding what gets implemented is determined in a couple of ways. The model is set up to empower employees to make their passions reality. One example given was of an employee who was interested in Alzheimer's disease, something affecting many people in regard to their parents. The livelihood group helped him put on a brown bag lunch and bring in an outside speaker. He now organizes a run for everyone in the company to participate in as a fund-raiser—and in addition to helping others in the company learn about Alzheimer's, this becomes a means to generate VIA points. The other consideration for implementation is whether the initiative fits within the company's three pillars of philanthropy and sustainability: food security, renewable energy, and sustainable agriculture. "Those three pillars have served us really well, because they can be stretched a little bit here and there—the food security one can be stretched to include a nutrition program for kids in the Denver area, the sustainable ag one can be stretched a little bit to include a sustainability initiative happening at the Denver Zoo that we want to support. . . . If somebody's interested in something beyond those we'll consider it, and we may load information on the VIA web site, we may help them organize an event; it doesn't mean the organization's going to get money from us, but we will still give them product donation or employee time."

What makes WhiteWave and VIA exceptional is that they can put numbers to their initiatives. In 2009, they achieved the following results:

volunteer hours: 5,893

bus rides: 799

carpool days: 5,350

bicycle commuting miles: 16,897

hair donations: 95 inches

changes to CFL bulbs: 1,946

It is only when a company makes this kind of commitment and embeds the program into its work that real change can begin to happen. "Instead of having an employee program out here and 'isn't that nice' and a sustainability program that you're trying to get some teeth into, it integrates it, which I think is critical," Ellen Feeney told me. "Not only does it integrate it but it actually quantifies it so you can measure it. It's not just this soft little blah, blah, blah. It's something real, which I think is key."[52]

Is this solving all the problems of sustainability and social justice? No, of course not. However, it is a powerful first step in changing how people think, which is the seed to true, sustainable innovation. And what makes this appealing to companies—a number of whom have contacted WhiteWave because of its success with this program—is the ability to quantify the effect in terms of both actions taken by employees and dollars saved by the company.

CAN CORPORATIONS REALLY EFFECT SOCIAL CHANGE?

Paul Ray presciently predicted the path that marketers would take when he said: "The appearance of the Cultural Creatives in America is a very hopeful thing for our society, for it offers a chance to create a more positive new culture. Business can play a major role in that cultural development, and serve the leading edge of many consumer markets by catering to the new values."[53]

They can, but the question is "are they?" Some companies are, or at least they are trying.

There are many instances of companies having a positive impact around the world, David Vogel points out: Mattel has improved working conditions in China, and Nike has done the same in Vietnam; Ikea is helping to educate children in India, and Home Depot has changed its procurement policies to help save old-growth forests.[54] Given the number of organizations that have been created around sustainability and social innovation, I don't believe initiatives like these are a fad. More telling, however, is that doing good works creates wealth for corporations, and that is what is going to keep companies motivated to implement socially conscious initiatives. The bottom line for any product that aligns itself with a social cause has to be whether the initiative is transparent, that is, whether the company fully discloses information about how money is raised and used, *and* demonstrates a tangible effort on the part of the corporation leading to a positive effect. These are the key elements not only for providing real, long-term results but also for creating valuation for a company, according to Pamela Cohen, founder of CCW, a consulting firm that creates financial models demonstrating the impact of social responsibility efforts on the bottom line.[55]

Corporations will use social innovation (or some elements of it) because of its ability to impact their brands positively. Brands communicate value and values to consumers. They also create value for corporations. Coca-Cola, valued at $70.4 billion; IBM, at $64.7 billion; Google, at $43.5 billion; and Disney, at $28.7 billion were some of the leading brands in 2010.[56] More and more, those brands will contain a mythology of innovation in order to stay competitive.

I want to be clear that my critique exists so as to find real solutions to difficult problems; it is not about corporate bashing. While the Beyoncé Hamburger Helper campaign is misguided, overall General Mills is one of the good guys. It donates a lot of money and product, which does help to reduce hunger in the short term. So, too, Beyoncé donates her time and money, and she does not have to do that. (However, given her status as an icon and a role model for young girls of all ethnicities, but most certainly for those of color—the group most affected by childhood obesity—it would have been far better for Beyoncé to have promoted a healthy eating campaign than a product with nominal nutritional value.) Truly, delivering close to three million meals is nothing to sneeze at. The company even changed the size of the noodles in Hamburger Helper in order to make the box smaller and thereby reduce environmental waste—also a good thing.

However, with this initiative—and others like it—we need to stop looking at the marketing (which is after all illusion) and start looking at the cause (which is very much reality). Most of these campaigns deal with the symptoms instead of the root problem, because the root problem is not something that they can address. Hunger isn't about not having enough food; it's about not having a job and enough money to pay for food. Also, most of these initiatives are measured by the dollars donated or the number of volunteer hours; these are useless criteria. The real bottom line is results—the elimination of a carbon footprint, the number of people pulled out of poverty, or the number of jobs created. The goal is to move more companies toward social innovation and away from cause-related marketing campaigns—eliminate them completely if we can.

The next time you are deciding if you are going to buy a product attached to a cause, try asking yourself the following questions:

- Does the product serve the social good? If not, can the company make one that does, or does another company make it better?
- Can it be produced more sustainably?
- Has the company been transparent about the promotion?

- Do you know exactly how much of the purchase price you are paying is actually going to the cause you want to support?

- Does the company have a long-term commitment to the cause or is this a one-shot, "make me look good" marketing campaign?

Or, you could just ask yourself: is XYZ company creating the problem just so that it can create the solution? A good question, and an even better marketing trick.

Critics say more could be done if government regulated things that are now voluntary, such as reducing emissions or adhering to humane labor practices. David Vogel's response is: "While this may well be true, it should not be allowed to obscure the significance of the improvements that *have* taken place."[57]

I say let's do both—regulate *and* voluntarily improve!

3

The Birth of the Hypercharity and the Rise of "Charitainment"

As you sipped your grande latte in Starbucks, did you notice an ad with red parentheses surrounding a trio of drinks? If you did, there's a good chance you have no idea that the ubiquitous coffee beanery is part of a coordinated, multicorporation branding effort whose goal is to upsell you to a more expensive beverage so that a few pennies from the sale will go to charity. The marketing effort signified by those parentheses is (RED), a branding campaign that marries upscale consumer products—everything from Starbucks coffee to iPods to American Express cards—with a charitable organization, the Global Fund. When you purchase any product parenthesized in red, a portion of the proceeds go to funding AIDS medication in Africa.

This sophisticated marketing has been a boon for product sales, but the disappointing news is that it has been a bust for you, the consumer, and nowhere near the boon one would expect for the people supposedly being served by the Global Fund. You have, unfortunately, been coaxed into thinking that the money you give to support this campaign actually goes to paying for sorely needed aid. Truth is, far more money was spent to advertise this venture than will ever make it to the shores of Africa.

(RED) is a perfect example of the corporatization of charity gone terribly awry. Its launch shows exactly where the emphasis lies when commerce becomes the conduit for compassion.

Let's start with *The Oprah Winfrey Show* on October 13, 2006. There's Bono, lead singer of U2 and world-renowned philanthropist, sitting on Oprah's couch and explaining how he and Bobby Shriver have come up with the idea for (RED). Bono connects with the audience by sharing his understanding of how most of us don't have the time or inclination to be activists. We do, however, have time to go shopping, he tells us, and who can deny that? Bono's big idea, then, is to combine the promotional power of shopping malls and big business with the act of raising money to save lives in Africa. He enlists an eager assortment of consumer product companies to create (RED) products, and in no time at all, T-shirts at the Gap read "INSPI(RED)" and a pair of jeans or an MP3 player becomes a means to, in Bono's words, "change the world."

Oprah is all over this one. A short clip about dying children in Africa is shown, but this doesn't make for good television, and, more important, because (RED) is about shopping, the stars do not stay seated in the studio for long. Before the first commercial break, Oprah is leading Bono by the hand down Chicago's Magnificent Mile, a section of Michigan Avenue known to be one of the ritziest shopping districts in the world. Wading through throngs of screaming fans, these two mega-celebrities stop by a Gap store, where they survey a display of (RED) products. At this point, Oprah's cameras are panning the store, providing Gap with millions of dollars in free air time, all the more priceless when celebrities Christy Turlington and Penelope Cruz pop in and "surprise" Oprah and Bono to talk about their support for (RED).[1] Oprah hugs and thanks them, and then proceeds to do her bit to save lives in Africa by buying dozens of (RED) items, which she and Bono happily tote out of the store in Gap shopping bags.

Next, they're in an Apple store to pick up (RED) iPods. But before they can begin to shop, they are met by Lisa, a salesperson, who says, "Let me show you the new nano." Winfrey gushes, "Oh, my gosh," as does Bono, "Wow!" Oprah orders ten of the iPods, which have already been conveniently packaged, so that the dedicated shoppers can head off to their next stop to do more good.

As Bono and Oprah walk out of the Apple store, a disembodied voice—none other than hip-hop superstar Kanye West—beckons them to come to the Motorola store. There they meet Kanye in person, who extols the virtues of the (RED) campaign, while admiring the new Motorola phone he purchased in Paris the week before. We learn that the phone is "ultra thin" and "ultra light," it costs $79.95 with a two-year contract, and $17 of that cost will go to the Global Fund. Oprah is so sold on the cell phone that she buys ten of them on the spot.

The last stop for our shopping buddies is the Armani store, where Oprah buys ten pairs of sunglasses that are similar to Bono's trademark sunglasses (presumably for her ten best friends) as well as a single oversized watch (for her significant other Stedman Graham, perhaps?).

THE RISE OF THE "HYPERCHARITY": MORE BRANDS AND MORE BRANDING

(RED) is just one example of a growing phenomenon that I call the "hypercharity."[2] A hypercharity is an organization that is structured and promoted to appeal to large corporations looking to tie in with a charity partner for maximum marketing exposure. These organizations have adopted sophisticated marketing techniques and harnessed the resources of consumer product companies to raise more money for their causes, often with one or more celebrities attached. What makes these philanthropic organizations different from those of the past is not only their size but also the fact that *they* have become branded entities. Campaigns like (RED) or the Susan G. Komen Foundation, which gets companies to produce pink products in October and places pink ribbon logos on everything from blenders to credit cards, are marketed as "values brands" specifically to appeal to consumer goods manufacturers and their customers. Note that I speak of a charity partner, not a nonprofit partner. That is because not all of them—notably (RED)—are nonprofit organizations. More on that in a minute.

Just as other cultural and political institutions, such as religion, education, and the arts, have turned grudgingly to branding, so too the charitable marketplace finds itself forced to become expert in the tools of the marketing trade. Of course, putting names and logos on charities is not new. The American Cancer Society, United Way, and the MDA Labor Day Telethon to benefit the Muscular Dystrophy Association, to name a few, have had well-established identities for years. What is new is creating a well-known brand that will be used as a tool to perpetuate the sale of consumer products. A yellow bracelet (cancer) or a red dress (women's heart disease) becomes a way of branding charitable works and selling merchandise from athletic gear to clothes to Coca-Cola.

What is new in terms of the hypercharity is that these behemoths have reached the tipping point, so that brand companies see being part of these organizations as something they *must* do. "When clients come to see me, they ask for a (RED) campaign," Alison DaSilva, executive vice president of Cone, one of the leading strategy and communications agencies in this sector, told the Harvard Social Entrepreneurship Conference in 2010.

While these campaigns do some good, their underlying raison d'être is marketing. Not only marketing, but marketing made easy. By marrying up with a hypercharity, large corporations get a marketing-friendly environment attached to a charity that appeals overwhelmingly to women with children (moms are one of the most profitable consumer segments, representing $3.3 trillion in spending) and an off-the-shelf promotion, all while having a limited commitment—certainly more limited than if they had to execute it themselves. These charities exist to help brand companies extend their marketing message—and remember, the message has to be values based in the new world of conscious brands—while also extending the marketing message of the charity. Oh, and yes, further the charity's fund-raising ability.

As a group, these organizations have been accused—rightfully so—of focusing more on the brand than the charity, lack of transparency, and squeezing out smaller and more local causes by virtue of their size. There are also individual concerns about them, examined below. An important element in the selling of a charity—whether a hypercharity or not—is to have celebrities attached to it, a situation so rampant it has acquired its own moniker: "charitainment"—turning charitable works into mass entertainment. Contrary to popular marketing lore, purchasing products for good is not as simple as "buy, be good, be done."

Pink Ribbons: Is It Susan G. Komen? Breast Cancer Research Foundation? Does It Matter?

I was flying from New York to Boston when a flight attendant came on the loudspeaker to announce that in addition to the usual soft drinks and juices, they would also be serving Minute Maid Pink Lemonade for $2, and 100 percent of the proceeds would be going to the Breast Cancer Research Foundation (BRCF). I realized, then, that it must be October—National Breast Cancer Awareness month.

To learn more about the promotion, I pulled out my Delta *Sky* magazine. It was awash in pink—I mean *really pink*. Melissa Etheridge, singer, songwriter, and famous cancer survivor, graced the cover under the headline, "Pink Rocks: How **Breast Cancer** Became the Mother of Cause Marketing" (boldface in the original). Etheridge is connected to this cause not only through her own bout with cancer, but also through having written an anthem for it, "I Run for Life," which the Ford Motor Company approached her to write (proceeds from the song go to two cancer foundations, and the song is used in conjunction with Ford's Warriors in Pink campaign).

Perusing this magazine—and I swear you can't make this up—there were pink promotions for hotels, a $295 pink "puffer vest" (what you would likely call a down vest and buy at Eddie Bauer for about $80), and a 135-piece all pink tool kit, including power drill and hammer. More specifically, there was the Hard Rock's "Get into Bed for a Cure" promotion, where your hotel room would be "decked in pink" and 25 percent of the room rate would go to the cause (the 1980s all-girl rock group The Bangles were the talent attached to this).[3] Or you could purchase in-flight wireless on Delta's *pink plane* and the wireless company Gogo would donate 100 percent of the session to the Breast Cancer Research Foundation. (How many pink Delta planes are there you might ask? Just one.) And, for a more down-to-earth example, there was the lemonade promotion; I learned that the drinks had been donated by the Coca-Cola Company (Minute Maid's parent), and that this campaign had been running for the past four years.

When I got home, it seemed as though every magazine and newspaper editor on the planet had drunk the pink Kool-Aid. Of course, being a mother in my forties, I was a prime target for these campaigns and thus more likely to see them. Even so, you too might have seen some of these examples:

- Target's weekly circular had a page called "do more in pink," offering a series of athletic products from bicycles to golf clubs to yoga mats, while Best Buy offered pink Sony laptops ($110,00 going to BCRF) and pink flash drives (50 cents of each purchase going to Susan G. Komen, up to $100,000).

- A "Give Pink Get More" Bloomingdale's ad offered Big Pink Umbrellas ($6 of the $12 purchase price went to BCRF) and Little Pink Cards (store gift cards). Customers were asked to charge a $15 fee to their Bloomingdale's credit card (all of which went to BCRF). In turn, when they charged purchases on the store's card, they would get a gift card, depending on how much money they spent (example: $25 gift card for spending $250).

- SmartSource, the weekly insert of coupons in your Sunday paper, was chock-full of pink opportunities—Playtex tampons (already conveniently in a pink box), Bake for the Cure from the makers of Karo syrup and baking powder, and the Dial family of products, including soap, Soft Scrub cleanser, and Purex laundry detergent, among many others.

My favorite, though, was an ad in the *New York Times* for Saks Fifth Avenue with the headline "Key to the Cure" (a concept that is never explained in the ad, but is a promotion that Saks has done for the past ten years). The main visual in the ad was of Heidi Klum wearing a pink and white shirt by Michael Kors. How do we know that it is by Michael Kors? First, because it says so in the ad, but also because there are two oversized MKs—the Michael Kors logo—designed into the top of the shirt. Now anyone who has watched *Project Runway* knows that Kors, a regular judge on the show, is a "top American designer" (as Klum so gushingly calls him). Anyone looking quickly through the paper would automatically assume that the ad was for the show and not a cause. This, of course, is the problem. Sure, there was the requisite pink ribbon on the bottom of the ad, but what is the reader's net takeaway? Based on everything we know about how advertising works, that ad did far more for *Project Runway*—and Heidi Klum and Michael Kors—than it ever did for Saks Fifth Avenue or breast cancer.

So who's behind this pinking of the autumnal landscape? Our first hypercharity: the Susan G. Komen Breast Cancer Foundation. Susan G. Komen for the Cure, as it is now called, was founded in 1982 by Nancy G. Brinker. She created the organization to help find a cure for breast cancer after her sister, for whom the organization is named, died of the disease at the age of thirty-six. Over a twenty-year history, Komen has generated *more than 1.5 billion dollars* from a combination of race events, contributions, and sponsorships. Through all of this, it has "become the largest source of nonprofit funds dedicated to the fight against breast cancer in the world,"[4] primarily through a systematic, concerted effort to attract and retain significant corporate sponsorships.

But why breast cancer? Why does this disease appeal to corporate marketers, while so many others do not? Samantha King, author of *Pink Ribbons Inc.*, delineates several reasons why this malady is so marketable: (1) it is a "blameless" disease, because its risk factors are tied to genetics and age, (2) women are its victims, just as they are the target audience for most marketing companies, (3) the breast is the "very symbol of femininity," and (4) the pink ribbon is sweet and reminds us of our girlhood innocence.[5] Combined, these elements make breast cancer causes, and Komen in particular, a valuable tie-in for a wide swath of consumer product companies.

Corporate partnerships are Komen's lifeblood, and these relationships have been assiduously nurtured over time, creating benefits for both parties. Komen does this by working with brand companies to create unique campaigns that get consumers engaged over the long term. Here are two campaigns with which you might be familiar:

- Yoplait's "Save Lids to Save Lives" campaign (www. yourlidmatters.com) urges consumers to send in the pink lids from their yogurt containers during September and October. Yoplait donates ten cents for each lid mailed in, with a guaranteed donation of up to $1.5 million. This campaign has been running for more than a decade.

- Ford has been a sponsor of Komen for sixteen years and has raised $105 million for the organization. Its participation works on multiple fronts: encouraging employee involvement in "Race for the Cure," exposure through media, and Ford's "Warriors in Pink" campaign (www.fordcares.com), which encourages participants to upload videos about their breast cancer experience.[6]

Carol Cone, founder of Cone Inc. (she is now with the PR firm Edelman), known as the "mother of cause marketing," says that these integrated, multiyear campaigns are what made Komen successful: "it's [about] creating community both internally with your colleagues and externally with your stakeholders."[7] By stakeholders, she means investors and consumers.

Hundreds of companies, including the manufacturers of female-friendly (though not health- and environment-friendly) products like Lean Cuisine, Clorox bleach, and Pepperidge Farm baked goods, are among Komen's sponsors. Not all of the corporate participants have extensive, integrated campaigns like those of Yoplait and Ford. They all, however, use the logo: the pink ribbon.

Komen was not the first to use the pink ribbon; Avon and Estée Lauder did that in 1993, and all three organizations use it still. That more than one organization uses the logo surprised me. Before researching this topic, I thought all the ribbons on all the products were related to Komen. While most of them are, a large number are connected to the Breast Cancer Research Foundation (an organization started by Evelyn

H. Lauder of Estée Lauder, whose ad you've more than likely seen—a nude woman with her back to the camera, a red satin cloth draped over her shoulder and across her buttocks). Still other ribbons are for the Avon Foundation, the organization behind the multiday breast cancer walk each October. But even these are not the end of it. Some companies, like Lee Jeans, create their own pink ribbon events and raise money for a designated charity. In this case, the company established Lee National Denim Day, when $5 of the price of every item sold that day is donated to the Entertainment Industry Foundation (EIF), a Hollywood organization founded by Samuel Goldwyn of MGM fame.[8]

Whether charitable foundation or individual company, if you look at the ribbon logos closely, you will notice they are not the same. Some have dots, some look as though they are dancing, some appear frayed at the edges; that's because they are from different organizations. These variations can occur because the use of the logo is unregulated. The reason why is important: the ribbon is not associated with raising money for any one organization and sometimes *doesn't raise money at all*. The success of the pink ribbon as a branding tool is so accepted that some companies simply stick the logo on their packaging and say they are raising awareness. Most consumers never second-guess the pink ribbon (or the idea that money from their purchase is going to breast cancer research), because it has become such a recognizable—and trusted—logo.

Because Komen is the leader of the breast cancer fund-raisers, it has the biggest stake in making sure the pink ribbon is not misused. It is imperative that Komen retain access to corporate funds, and it needs to ensure that those partners maintain an appearance of philanthropy rather than greed. If not, Komen's reputation could be sunk. To this end, Komen, unlike many others, requires that its partners clearly state how the product sale will benefit Komen, as well as delineate if there is a limit to the amount of the donation. Komen also heavily monitors the use of the logo. A story in the *Wall Street Journal* in 2010 highlighted the organization's increasingly litigious nature around the use of its tagline "for the cure," as well as the use of the logo.[9] Managing the logo is not just for the corporate sponsors but for the cause itself. The full extent of this was explained to me by someone who had attended the Cause Marketing Forum in Chicago in 2010, where an executive from the Komen Foundation spoke. "She was talking like a capitalist . . . a hardcore business person . . . she presented the case that they were concerned because other breast cancer groups were getting credit for what they are doing. She was literally talking about [market] share. So if anyone's doing something around breast cancer that's our market. We need to brand it. We need to make sure we keep control of it." What this story demonstrates is what happens when the charity itself becomes more important than the cause that it serves; when it becomes about the pink instead of about the people.

Pink has reached a point where it may be too much of a good thing. In October 2009, the *Boston Globe* published an article called "Sick of Pink"—a sentiment evidently felt by many but expressed by few.[10] The article reviews issues associated with breast cancer promotion, chief among them the exploitation of cancer survivors, many of whom believe their disease is being used by corporations to claim philanthropy when what these companies are most concerned about is profits. This fear is justified. "The response I've heard from corporations when I challenge them about [commodifying cancer] is 'Who cares, as long as the money is going to a good cause?'" Samantha King says. The ultimate hypocrisy was Komen's decision to tie in with KFC (formerly Kentucky Fried Chicken). In April and May 2010, pink buckets of chicken selling for five dollars led to 50 cent donations to Komen—and a lot of headaches. This alliance ignited the wrath of the media as well as numerous watchdog groups, including Breast Cancer Action, the organization behind Think Before You Pink (thinkbeforeyoupink.org), which questions the use of pink ribbons and calls for transparency between corporate sponsors and consumers. When someone somewhere does not take a minute to evaluate the duplicity in this type of partnership—connecting women's health to a product that leads to obesity, which is a contributing factor to breast cancer—we know we have reached the pinnacle of commercialism and consumption taking precedence over caring and a cure.

From Pink Ribbons to Red Dresses

Following on the success of pink ribbons, the National Heart, Lung, and Blood Institute (NHLBI, a division of the U.S. Department of Health and Human Services) created *The Heart Truth®* (www.nhlbi.nih.gov/educational/hearttruth) in 2002. This campaign targets primarily women between the ages of forty and sixty, with an emphasis on women of color, who are disproportionately affected by the disease.

The campaign's "aim was to develop and promote a *women's heart disease brand* [italics added] that would create a strong emotional connection with women," according to *Social Marketing Quarterly*.[11] That brand is The Red Dress®, which has as its logo a simple red spaghetti-strapped silhouette, with a white heart over the left breast.[12] Attaching meaning to this brand entailed connecting the logo to the message: "heart disease is the #1 killer of women." To do that, the organization created a marketing campaign that uses stories of real women—mothers, women of various ethnic groups in their twenties and over (use of younger women demonstrates that it can happen at any time)—and what they have had to do to overcome the disease. Through these emotional stories, the campaign hoped to elicit empathy among its target audience that would in turn lead to motivating these women to change their unhealthy lifestyles.

The heart of this campaign is the National Wear Red Day, which takes place on the first Friday in February (a smart marketing choice, because it is a time when people are thinking about red hearts and Valentine's Day). On that day, women and men are invited to wear red to show their support for the cause. In addition, *The Heart Truth* established a partnership with the fashion industry through the Red Dress Fashion Show. Each year since 2003, big name designers like Vera Wang and Donna Karan have participated in creating a frock for the Red Dress Collection during Fashion Week in New York City. These dresses are then worn by celebrities like Felicity Huffman, Angela Bassett, and the pop star Fergie.[13] In 2009, this got an additional promotional push when a competition to create a dress for the Red Dress Fashion Show took up an entire episode of *Project Runway* (this show was also tied to breast cancer, though not so directly), likely due, in no small part, to Heidi Klum's being the "Diet Coke heart health ambassador" and to Diet Coke's being the title sponsor of *The Heart Truth*.

To disseminate the heart health message, the organization used a three-pronged strategy of media relations, institutional partnerships, and community involvement. Media partnerships were essential, because they not only provided stories about the campaign (important because readers are more likely to trust editorial content over corporately paid-for advertising) but also provided introductions to their advertisers, many of whom in turn became corporate sponsors. Those media partners include female-targeted outlets such as *Women's Day*, *Glamour*, and Lifetime Television for Women. By the beginning of 2008, more than 2.1 billion people had been exposed to messages about *The Heart Truth*, much of this is being attributed to celebrity attention surrounding the campaign, including support from then first lady Laura Bush.

NHLBI established partnerships early on with a group of founding organizations. These were the Office of Women's Heath (also a division of HHS and a critical source of funding), WomenHeart: the National Coalition for Women with Heart Disease (an organization committed to women's heart health, focusing on advocacy, education, and support), and the American Heart Association (AHA). The relationship among these groups is fuzzy, particularly in the case of the American Heart Association. The NHLBI and the AHA claim that their connection is simply to co-brand National Wear Red Day, an event that includes most other campaign partners. However, the AHA has appropriated the campaign by creating its own initiative around women's heart health called "Go Red for Women." AHA also has its own red dress logo (its logo is a bit jauntier—it looks like the dress is blowing in a breeze—and does not include a heart), and it promotes the first Friday in February as "Go Red for Women" Day.

It is unclear whether this has led to confusion among consumers, but it has certainly caused confusion—and consternation—among the medical community. First, in February 2010, the Center for Science in the Public Interest (CSPI) protested to the NHLBI about the appearance of the red dress logo on cans of soda, saying: "overweight and obesity are prime risk factors for heart disease, and the agency shouldn't be bolstering the dismal reputation of the Coca-Cola Company, the world's biggest manufacturer of obesigenic soft drinks. . . . Though Diet Coke is the ostensible sponsor, it is the entire Coca-Cola product line that is basking in the credibility conferred by a government heart-health agency."[14] The director of NHLBI defended its actions, saying in part, "We can be effective only if we are able to reach wide and diverse audiences through nationwide health campaigns that find people where they are." Coca-Cola also offered a defense, saying that it had helped provide free health screenings to thousands of people through its sponsorship.[15] Subsequently, at the American College of Cardiology (ACC) meeting in March 2010, the AHA was called to task for allowing its logo to appear on cans of Diet Coke. The AHA responded to the ACC that it was not its logo, but the logo of the NHLBI. A spokesperson from *The Heart Truth* agreed that it was its symbol and defended its actions saying that the use of the logo was about "getting out a public health message," a riff on that ever-popular refrain of needing to increase awareness. Whether with respect to *The Heart Truth* or Go Red for Women, however, this discussion highlights the underlying issue—the red dress logo on the packaging implies endorsement of a Coca-Cola product, either by the U.S. government or the American Heart Association. This is yet another way in which causes—in this case, women's health—are being subordinated to the consumer market.

Aside from Diet Coke, there is no shortage of corporate sponsors for *The Heart Truth*. McNeil (makers of Tylenol and St. Joseph aspirin), the jewelry designer Swarovski (makers of the Red Dress pin), and Bobbi Brown cosmetics are just a few of the more than one hundred corporate sponsors.[16] Separately, Go Red for Women (AHA's initiative) has its own list of sponsors including Macy's, Campbell's Soup, Merck, RiteAid and many others (see www.goredforwomen.org for a full list of national and local sponsors). These sponsorships are necessary in order to get out the message, but they also fund the third element of the strategy—community events. NHLBI provides a traveling exhibit of red dresses and educational information about heart health that is sent to targeted cities around the country. This is in addition to other local events such as health fairs, fashion shows, and statehouse rallies.

The need to create this campaign demonstrates the power of the pink ribbon. Prior to the creation of *The Heart Truth,* only 34 percent of women knew that heart disease was the leading cause of death among women. "Most thought that breast cancer was their greatest health threat," and in focus groups leading up to the campaign several women "expressed anger that they had never 'been told that before.'"[17] We can conclude that these assumptions were in no small part due to the ubiquitous pink ribbons. In 2007, heart disease killed 306,000 American women, in comparison to 82,000 killed by strokes, 70,000 by lung cancer, and 41,000 by breast cancer.[18] The reality is that heart disease far outranks other female health concerns—it is more deadly *than all forms of cancer combined.* (Breast cancer *is* the biggest killer of women between the ages of 35 and 54; for women overall, however, heart disease may be a bigger issue. I say "may be" because those numbers should be considered skewed because "cardiac failure" is the ultimate cause of death for all of us, and this is often noted as the cause of death, even if there is another underlying factor.)

There is no doubt that *The Heart Truth* has been successful in achieving its goal of increasing women's awareness of heart disease. In 2010, 62 percent of women surveyed knew that heart disease was the leading cause of death for women, almost doubling pre-campaign awareness. With this increased understanding came increased action to improve the health of women, as well as of their families. This campaign also highlights the importance of committing to a long-term strategy. It was only by its fifth year that it began to generate awareness of heart disease, and ultimately action to reduce health risks. Even with these gains, however, women still fear breast cancer more than they do any other malady.[19]

The Heart Truth is a social marketing campaign and differs from most of the others we've looked at in a very essential way. Its mission is to improve women's health habits through information and health screenings, rather than through raising money for research or medical assistance. According to Philip Kotler and Nancy Lee, social marketing is when "a corporation supports the development and/or implementation of a behavior change campaign intended to improve health, safety, the environment, or community well-being."[20] This explains why *The Heart Truth* needs to raise significantly less money ($65 million versus the billions for pink ribbons), while focusing on media relationships to get out the message. However, while *The Heart Truth* has done well in disseminating its message, it may unwittingly be undermining this work through corporate sponsorship.

The (RED) Campaign

On the face of it, (RED) seems much like the other hypercharities we've been looking at.[21] It is a recognizable brand with a ubiquitous presence on consumer products supported by celebrity spokespeople. That, however, is where the similarities end. Where the road diverges is why charities that promote themselves for the purpose of corporate profits have taken a turn for the worse.

As noted in the beginning of the chapter, (RED) was founded by Bono and Bobby Shriver with money raised going to a single entity—the Global Fund. Unlike the other charities discussed, (RED) aligns itself almost exclusively with high-end consumer products with hardcore marketing muscle behind them—Apple, Starbucks, GAP, and American Express, among many others. (RED) recently signed up Nike, which surprisingly did not jump on board in the early stages. Nor did Nike create an exclusive shoe—something it does at the drop of a hat—for (RED). It merely produced red laces for the 2010 World Cup. True, Nike Corporation was involved slightly earlier with a sneaker, but that was with its secondary brand, Converse. Thus, we have to wonder: does Nike know something most of us don't know?

The most serious concern about (RED) is its lack of transparency. This occurs on multiple fronts. First, how much money from the sale of each item actually goes to the cause? Of course, opacity is an issue for all the hypercharities (though some have attempted to remedy this—remember that Komen requires partners to specify their donations). However, it comes up as glaringly more nefarious for (RED) when the products being purchased are $200 cell phones, $149 iPods, and $1,029 Bugaboo baby strollers. Confusion continues when you go to www.joinred.com where it states "up to 50% of the profits go directly to those who need it"—a comment that is decidedly vague. Admittedly, some of the companies involved are straightforward about their donation structure: Apple gives $10 for each (RED) iPod, Amex gives 1 percent of sales generated on its (RED) credit cards,[22] and if you scroll past the supermodel on the Bugaboo web site, you'll see that it donates 1 percent of revenue across its entire product line.[23]

With some other corporate partners, however, things are a bit murkier. A Gap T-shirt, for example, has provided endless consternation, appearing in multiple articles that criticize (RED). Sarah Dadush, a law fellow at New York University, did successfully calculate how much was donated from a $28 GAP shirt. Using the "impact calculator" that converted product purchases into the number of days of medication provided—a tool that no longer appears on (RED)'s web site—she found the donation to be approximately $3.60 per shirt, or about 12 percent of the purchase price. Whether a Gap T-shirt or a cup of Starbucks (from which 5 cents goes to the fund), consumers don't pause to consider the effect—or the effectiveness—of their purchases. As Sarah Dadush astutely puts it, "Empirical research is needed to determine whether these dollar amounts meet consumer expectations of a charitable return on their investment. It is at least conceivable that at a certain ratio of profit to charitable contribution, consumers would opt to buy a cheaper item (at H&M rather than the Gap, for instance) and simply donate the difference (or more) to charity."[24]

Moreover, it is very easy for consumers to get sucked into the idea of doing something good when it also allows them to give into their consumerist impulses. The following is anecdotal, but it is not hard to imagine scenes similar to this playing out on a regular basis across the country. One of my students, Danny, works in an Apple store in New York City. One day, a woman came into the store and was strolling listlessly past the iPods. She started walking away, so he asked if he could help her. She replied, "I was going to buy an iPod but I don't really need it." Danny suggested, "Why don't you get the red nano? Money from your purchase goes to help provide medicine to people dying of AIDS in Africa." The customer responded, "Oh, okay, I'll take two." When

I asked Danny if he knew how much money went to (RED), he said he had no idea, and the company didn't tell him (though it provides extensive training on everything else). He also noted that the customer never asked. Thus, the transaction becomes not about the cause but about giving the customer a "reason why" to buy. Research bears this out as a trend, particularly when it relates to "frivolous" purchases. Just as in this story, the cause becomes the means to rationalize unnecessary purchases.[25]

Lack of transparency extends beyond the level of funding. It starts with the organization itself. (RED) is a brand—a logo with an accompanying mythology. That is it. Period. The brand is owned by The Persuaders LLC, a limited liability company incorporated in Delaware, which you might be aware is the corporation capital of the nation because of its liberal tax code.[26] The Persuaders sells the license to use (RED) to its corporate partners (Apple, Starbucks, and so on) to create (RED) products. Money from the sale of those products is then donated to the Global Fund. What makes this scenario particularly interesting is that The Persuaders does not donate the money to the Global Fund, the corporate partners do. This structure enables The Persuaders to circumvent laws regulating charities. Moreover, part of the agreement between The Persuaders and the Global Fund is that money generated by this campaign be listed as an aggregate number in the organization's financial disclosures, something that is not standard practice for this NGO. Thus, because The Persuaders is a privately held company, there is no way to learn how its money is being used, and because the money sent to the fund is reported as an aggregate, there is no way to determine if this structure is successful as a money-generating tool for charities. Is the Gap T-shirt raising all the money? The Amex credit card? The Motorola phone? There's just no way to know.[27]

This corporate structure is what makes (RED) fundamentally distinct from the other hypercharities—it's not a charity. It's a for-profit corporation that makes money from its corporate partners by selling them licenses to use the brand. The licensing agreement entails a five-year commitment reportedly costing between $3 million and $5 million. Associated with that agreement is the requirement that the licensee create and promote a (RED)-branded product.

By now, you should have a good idea as to why Nike did not jump into this arrangement at first. In addition to the money spent on the licensing agreement, product development, and production, Nike would have been using *its* marketing prowess and *its* advertising dollars to sell what was then an unknown brand. (RED) contributes nothing to companies in terms of marketing funding; only the use of the logo and the expectation that all partners will significantly promote the brand. (There is, perhaps, incremental financial benefit for the brand company in addition to the hoped-for sales. While there is a limit on how much money a company can claim as a corporate tax write-off in terms of donations, this is not true of advertising, which is a legitimate business expense. If charitable donations get slotted into the advertising line, they become tax deductible.)

While perhaps not the best arrangement for marketers, this structure is very advantageous for the Global Fund. The Persuaders negotiates relationships with corporate sponsors. Big-name marketers—and bigger-name celebrities—sell the (RED) brand, increasing awareness of the need to provide medicine for AIDS sufferers in Africa through extensive advertising campaigns and by raising money for the cause through product sales. The Global Fund receives additional promotion through (RED)'s other initiatives. Recently, this included a documentary called *The Lazarus Effect,* produced in conjunction with HBO, that shows what antiretroviral medicine can achieve in Africa. According to the (RED) web site, more than $150 million was raised—the largest corporate contribution the Global Fund has received to date (approximately one-third of this group's funding, a total of $5.87 billion since 2002, comes from the U.S. government).[28] In addition, as opposed to one-time donations as with other cause marketing campaigns, this structure allows for contributions to be continuously generated over the five-year period of the marketing agreement—which is why the founders call this model sustainable, an interesting choice of buzzword.

But is it sustainable? The jury is still out on that. Five-year contracts are coming to an end, and companies are going to have to reassess the value of being associated with the brand. Given how little companies now promote (RED)—much in evidence when you have to dig very far into a company's web site to find (RED) products—I suspect there will be a number of dropped sponsorships. At a minimum, it is likely that few will re-up at the high licensing fee initially required. What we do know is that almost a third of the money raised thus far was generated from a one-time art auction. On Valentine's Day 2008, in conjunction with Sotheby's and the Gagosian Gallery, (RED) raised $42 million from the sale of donated artworks.[29] Since then, (RED) has also added a music site and produced concerts to raise money for the Global Fund. But this funding cannot be deduced from the aggregate number, so there is no way to know how successful this is. What we do know is that it can be continuous, since it is run by the organization itself.

Defenders of (RED), and cause-related marketing generally, have two main responses to those who criticize them for lack of transparency and other transgressions. First, these campaigns weren't designed to eliminate social ills, just improve an unfair and unjust system. No one expects that selling high-end consumer products will eradicate AIDS or solve the hunger crisis; these are tasks that can only be solved at the governmental level. True enough, and the funds raised might not have come through other means; that is, those who bought a (RED) T-shirt probably wouldn't have sat down and written a check. The second argument, which doesn't have the same credibility, is that the campaigns are designed to increase awareness. (This is happening, of course, while increasing profits and making consumers feel good about possibly unnecessary purchases.) Increasing awareness is a good thing, but is that what is really happening? Aren't people already aware of the AIDS crisis in Africa in the age of 24-hour news cycles and broadband internet access? Or that people go hungry, or that millions of women die of breast cancer?

(RED) has, understandably, had more than its fair share of criticism. The first brouhaha associated with the campaign was an article in *Advertising Age,* a leading trade magazine, which claimed that in the first year, the campaign partners spent $100 million on advertising, while generating only $18 million. Bobby Shriver responded that these numbers were incorrect, but *Advertising Age* stood by its story.[30] In March 2007, *The Independent* (London) looked into the charges against (RED) and found that:

- (RED) raised $25 million within six months of its launch in 2006—five times the amount given by the private sector to the Global Fund (the recipient of donations) in the period since 2002.

- (RED) has not spent $100 million on its advertising campaign. The organization states that the Gap has spent the most money to market its (RED) products ($7.8 million), and total expenditures are less than $30 million.

- (RED) has given Americans "who are too idle or too self-centered to actually get up and do anything" a chance to fight AIDS simply by purchasing (RED) products—thus capitalizing on an untapped portion of the general population.[31]

To be fair, no matter what is true about (RED) as it relates to fund-raising, it is not alone in "spending dollars to raise pennies." This charge has been leveled at numerous CRM campaigns, which seem to be motivated by tax write-offs and product promotion as much as by fund-raising.[32]

The high profile of (RED)'s founders, however, contributes to the ferocity of the criticism. Face it, the tie-in with Bono is a two-edged sword—he generates awareness, and corporations sign on because they get a face-to-face with one of the world's leading pop stars. However, he also creates a very large target if things do not go well, which may be an issue as contracts lapse. Bono is so integral to the promotion that "participating companies can pull out of the scheme if Bono is not involved in the future. If the Fund's projections are correct, then this would mean that in the future almost 10% of the Fund's work would depend on the interest and health of one rock star."[33]

Admittedly, the U2 front man has done significant work in helping to alleviate poverty and raise awareness of AIDS in Africa, and his commitment is genuine, as evidenced by his more than twenty years of work in the field. Before (RED), Bono's work was focused on ONE. According to its web site (www.one.org), "ONE is a grass-roots campaign and advocacy organization backed by more than 2 million people who are committed to the fight against extreme poverty and preventable disease, particularly in Africa. Cofounded by Bono and other campaigners, ONE is nonpartisan and works closely with African policy makers and activists." ONE is also closely aligned with the evangelical movement in the United States, in part because Bono used the "evangelical circuit" to spread the word about ONE. The extent of this connection is considerable. In 2006, Michael Gerson of *Newsweek* "asked young evangelicals on campuses from Wheaton to Harvard who they view as their model of Christian activism. Their answer is nearly unanimous: Bono."[34] But this organization, too, has run into controversy of late. In September 2010, it was reported that the ONE campaign sent pricey gift boxes (four each, not just one) to New York reporters in hopes of getting news coverage in conjunction with the UN "Summit on the Millennium Development Goals" and to push President Obama for African AIDS funding. The same report noted that based on 2008 IRS filings, the latest available, ONE took in almost $15 million in donations, while paying out $8 million in salaries. Only $184,732 was distributed to three charities.[35] ONE has countered these allegations, saying that it is not a charity but an advocacy organization—the goal is awareness and lobbying, not providing direct funding.

ONE encourages lobbying Congress; (RED) does not. ONE advocates engaging local media; (RED) does not. ONE promotes recruiting and organizing on college campuses and through churches; (RED) does not. (RED), rather, promotes buying more (RED). Period. In other words, (RED) is not like ONE, although young consumers probably don't see much difference.

Critics, however, do. Buylesscrap.org, a web site created by the marketer Ben Davis, admonishes us: "Shopping is not a solution. Buy (less). Give more." Along with fake ads that redesign the Gap logo as "Crap" and are headlined (Red)icu(less), Point(less), and Meaning(less), there is a long list of charities, with links to their web sites. Buylesscrap.org promotes direct donation to these causes and asks that we reject "the ti(red) notion that shopping is a reasonable response to human suffering." Put that way, it's hard to argue.

Feeding America

Feeding America—the country's leading distributor of donated food to food banks around the country and "the nation's largest charitable hunger-relief organization"—is the newest of the hypercharities.

In May 2010, *Advertising Age* ran an article entitled "How Feeding America Became the Go-to Cause for Marketers" that begins as follows: "IS IT POSSIBLE TO PLAN a cause-marketing campaign without Feeding America? It sure doesn't seem like it—which is why the nation's largest food bank is closing in on the 'it status for marketer tie-ins.'"[36]

Barely a blip on the marketing radar just three years ago, Feeding America is now one of the top charities to tie in with, much as Komen has been and continues to be. It counts Walmart, General Mills, Kraft Foods, United Airlines, and PepsiCo among its many corporate partners.

In 2006, Feeding America wasn't Feeding America; it was Second Harvest. Under that moniker, there were few corporations banging down the door. In order to increase the organization's profile, it hired a corporate CEO (Vicki Escarra from Delta Airlines) and a new head of marketing (Wendy MacGregor, who had significant experience at advertising agencies Leo Burnett in Chicago and Starcom, one of the world's largest media-buying companies).

Bringing in strategic heavy hitters like the Boston Consulting Group and Interbrand, the organization executed marketing studies including segmentation and consumer-engagement research, as well as brand identity studies. A key finding of this research was the lack of recognition for the name Second Harvest versus the newly coined Feeding America. The new name tested higher among consumers, which MacGregor attributed to it being more descriptive of what the organization does.

Important for this discussion, the name change has also been significant in terms of its ability to bring in corporate partners. According to the director of cause marketing, Laura Traut-Coyle, the name change "has helped cinch major deals such as the Pound for Pound Challenge," a tie-in with General Mills and the TV reality series *The Biggest Loser,* discussed below. What also helps is that the organization is a client of Cone Communications, one of the leading cause branding and responsibility agencies marrying corporations with charitable partners. "They certainly have had a lot more interest from corporate partners. . . . For them it's really about making sure they're creating really powerful partnerships, and how they turn the interest into longer, deeper partnerships," according to Erica Vogelei, an account director at Cone.

Contributing to this organization's appeal for sponsors is its connection to Hollywood heavyweights. Feeding America created an Entertainment Council, which includes approximately forty volunteer celebrities, including actors like Jennifer Aniston and Ben Affleck, musicians such as Sheryl Crow and Josh Groban, and the celebrity chefs Rocco DiSpirito and Mario Batali. One example of a campaign that took advantage of this arrangement is "Stamp Out Hunger." In conjunction with promotional partners, the U.S. Postal Service and Campbell's Soup, and spokespeople (and Entertainment Council members) Courteney Cox and her then-husband, David Arquette, Feeding America implemented the country's largest one-day food drive. For this campaign, people were asked to put nonperishable food in bags by their mailboxes. Letter carriers would pick up the bags and donate the food to local food banks.

A visit to the Feeding America web site shows the full extent of its connection with corporate America. Overall, there are financial, product, and media partnerships, as well as corporate promotions. Financial partners participate at four different levels—leadership, mission, support, and partner. Each of these levels is associated with an increasingly large amount of support, with leadership partners donating $10 million or more in cash and kind, while ordinary partners donate between $50,000 and $100,000. Not surprisingly, leadership companies include many of the largest food producers (ConAgra, Kellogg, Kraft) and retailers (Walmart, SuperValu, Kroger).[37] Product sponsorships are broken down into product companies, retailers, transportation partners, and trade associations. The only media partner listed is CMT, though it has connections to numerous individual television shows through its corporate sponsors.

Here are two of the more complex campaigns for Feeding America:

- Oscar Mayer's Good Mood Mission
  The Good Mood Mission started with Kraft Foods, Oscar Mayer's corporate parent, donating a million pounds of food, with the ultimate goal of donating three millions pounds. To generate the incremental two million pounds of food, consumers needed to go to www.GoodMoodMission.com and give examples of things that make them happy. Each "good mood" translates into one pound of food donated. If someone shared their good mood with five other people via social media, five pounds were donated. And if someone became an Oscar Mayer fan on Facebook, ten pounds of food were donated.

- General Mills's Millsberry.com
  General Mills's "kid-friendly" web site Millsberry.com encourages children to interact with the company online while doing good. "Citizens of Millsberry are urged to start their own pizza farm, learn how to maintain crops, watch them grow, and harvest them—all while helping others. General Mills will make a donation to Feeding America based on the number and type of pizzas grown, up to $50,000." Notably, this may raise money for a good cause, but it is also advergaming, the process of exposing young children to brand messages while playing video games.

These are sophisticated marketing campaigns. They do not merely ask consumers to buy a product. They require the consumer to interact significantly with the product company—visit its web site, sign up for Facebook, and so on. This is the reality of marketing in an age when television is no longer the most effective means of delivering a product message. However, it also makes the cause seem ever more like a come-on for the products it is associated with.

These changes have led to the biggest growth period in Feeding America's history. In 2009, it fed 37 million Americans, up from 25 million before the new management came on board. This growth was, in part, due to more efficient food distribution, but the majority can be attributed to corporate sponsorships and retail programs. Funds raised increased by 34 percent to $75 million, and food salvaged or donated increased 22 percent to 2.6 billion pounds. Some of this increase may have been serendipitous: the organization rebranded itself at a time when homelessness and hunger were increasingly on the minds of most Americans. It was also a time when marketers were increasingly looking for causes to partner with.

On the other hand, the issues remain: (1) the focus is increasingly about attracting corporate sponsors, and (2) the sponsors become more important than the cause. While Feeding America has achieved success—and it is success—it will need to ramp up the volume to continue growing. There is every indication that it plans to do that. Feeding America has developed metrics to demonstrate return on investment to its partners and it uses a company (Harris) to track its brand. While this may be a "virtuous cycle" that "helps the company from an image standpoint, but also [in terms of] brand awareness and brand attributes," as suggested by Wendy MacGregor, it overshadows the cause of feeding those in need.

Environmental Charities

Consumers claim that environmental concerns are worthy of cause marketing initiatives. The planet—at 57 percent—comes in fourth on the list of most deserving causes according to one report.[38] Given that, it's surprising that there aren't any environmental hypercharities.

This is not to say that there aren't planet-conscious organizations with numerous corporate sponsors. There most certainly are. Groups like the Nature Conservancy and the World Wildlife Fund (WWF) come to mind in this regard.[39] However, none has become as ubiquitous as the charities examined thus far. Even newer group 1% for the Planet—an organization made up of businesses that donate 1 percent of their sales to environmental groups—doesn't fall into this category, because it isn't promotionally oriented, not necessarily a bad thing.[40]

What also makes this curious is the increasing interest in global warming, which has been significantly and consistently fueled by the media for more than a decade. FAIR (Fairness and Accuracy in Reporting) tracked reporting on the topic and found more than 3,500 articles in top-flight media outlets like the *New York Times,* the *Wall Street Journal,* and the *Washington Post* just between 1988 and 2002. Television news outlets have also given environmental concerns significant coverage since even before the 2010 BP Deepwater Horizon oil disaster. Al Gore's *An Inconvenient Truth* hit movie theaters in 2006 and went on to win an Academy Award for Best Documentary as well as a Pulitzer Prize for Gore. Every April, in honor of Earth Day, publications from *Real Simple* to *Vanity Fair* devote entire issues to this concern.

Several reasons may account for environmental organizations not "breaking through the clutter." First, green is now mainstream. Consumers have come to expect that the products they are purchasing (or can choose to purchase) are environmentally correct. According to the Boston Consulting Group's "Global Green Consumer Survey," a majority of consumers (66 percent) believe that it is "important or very important for companies to offer green products," and an even higher percentage (73 percent) want companies to have "a good environmental track record." This belief is not just intentional; it has translated into increased purchases of green products, from 32 percent to 34 percent.[41] Green is so mainstream that there are Green MBA programs around the country at such prestigious institutions as Stanford, University of Michigan, and Carnegie Mellon. Second, there is nothing personal about the environment. You can't say "my mom is dying of the environment" or "my sister is an environmental survivor." Without that ability to connect on a deeply personal level, environmental issues are at a distinct disadvantage in a market-driven world. Finally, environmental organizations don't all work to solve the same problems—some are concerned with global warming, others with saving animals. It's not as simple as the rallying cries around breast cancer or hunger. While I'm not advocating that any of these organizations become a hypercharity, there may be learning here in terms of needing to find out what about the environment specifically will lead people to want to make a difference.

ENTERTAINMENT, CHARITY, AND PRODUCT SALES

With Melissa Etheridge, Bono, and Courteney Cox, we have already seen how celebrities play an important role in the marketing of charities tied to product sales. Celebrity spokespeople—the more, the better—bolster the appeal of one charity over another. This creates a bandwagon effect for product marketers, attracting more and more corporations to the same social issue, because they see it as an opportunity for extensive free publicity. We saw this in the (RED) campaign, as well as a growing number of hunger and health initiatives.

Celebrity philanthropy—or, more broadly, "charitainment," that is entertainment for charitable purposes—has taken on a more expansive dimension since the 1990s. This is attributed to several factors, such as the ubiquity of the media and with it the growth of celebrity culture, as well as the increasingly competitive nature of the nonprofit sector, which has driven the use of celebrities to increase attention—much the way branding is used more generally. Celebrities help bring attention to humanitarian issues that might not be on the popular radar. And, because we tend to believe celebrities we like (and often those celebrities are ones we see every week in a television series and therefore have a parasocial relationship with), we are more likely to trust what they have to say. Finally, celebrities move products: when Oprah endorsed Amazon's Kindle e-reader in October 2008 (when it was selling for $359), search traffic for the item increased 479 percent, and visits to Amazon were up by 6 percent.[42]

Celebrity philanthropy is not a recent idea. Audrey Hepburn and the United Nations is an example that comes readily to mind. Others you might think of are Michael J. Fox and Parkinson's disease or the Betty Ford Center and substance abuse.

Let me be very clear: I am not talking about these or other celebrities who volunteer their time or create their own foundations that are in no way tied to product sales. For example, Sean Penn created the Jenkins-Penn Haitian Relief Organization in the wake of the hurricane in Haiti. He has given time and money and energy to bring attention and much-needed aid to that part of the world. George Clooney, who needs no additional press attention, has trained a spotlight on the atrocities in Darfur and rallied musicians and actors to raise money for Haiti. Celebrity when used in the name of easing a social ill is to be lauded and supported. It is when the cause is connected to a product (and sometimes the product is the celebrity) that the messaging gets pretty muddied. Are celebrities selling the need to assuage hunger or are they shills for Campbell's V8?

A most egregious version of this sort of celebrity self-promotion occurred in the fall of 2010. At that time, Cincinnati Bengals' wide receiver, VH1 reality celebrity, and endless Twitterer, Chad Ochocinco, took the next obvious step in his path to media overexposure: he created a limited edition cereal (named for, you guessed it, Ochocinco himself), with a portion of the proceeds going to Feed the Children. There was only one problem—the box included a phone number where cereal eaters could make a donation to the cause over and above the donation generated by the purchase. Instead of reaching the charity, however, they got a breathless woman asking for a credit card and requiring callers be over the age of eighteen "if they wanted to join the party."

While Ochocinco is not responsible for this mistake (Feed the Children took the blame for submitting the wrong number), he is responsible for the product's promotion. In an effort to push sales, the athlete tweeted that fans should order the cereal online and "Start your day with a lil suga!!!"—a questionable pronouncement if this product is targeting children, and even more questionable given the erroneous sex line phone number. More telling, in response to the publicity around the mistake, Ochocinco said: "In a positive light, it's bringing more attention not just to Feed the Children and the cereal but also myself. I hope people do understand it's something good."[43] Good for the kids, or good for him?

It is so expected for celebrities to be associated with charities that *Good Housekeeping* magazine has a monthly section that features different celebrities and their charities, called "Why I Give." It is not alone; other women's magazines like *Woman's Day* and *InStyle* also provide celebs with opportunities to promote their good works. *InStyle*'s version makes the most sense, however, if charity is the goal. It provides readers with a highlighted box called "How You Can Help." This "call out" presents an array of options for becoming involved with celebrity charities by donating money, purchasing a T-shirt, or posting your picture on Twitter or Facebook to show your support for the cause. Admittedly some of these seem more genuine than others. For example, Charlize Theron's foundation to build soccer fields in her native South Africa is part of an ongoing commitment to help her home country; on the other hand, Kristin Davis's support of pachyderms because of her many trips to Africa doesn't provide the same sense of generosity.

Whether heartfelt, put on, or put together to improve a sagging reputation, PR firms work diligently to align celebrities with talent. Perhaps the best-known (at least in celebrity circles) is Trevor Neilson of Global Philanthropy Group. According to a *New York Times* article titled "Charity Fixer to the Stars," Neilson and his company have advised the likes of Bono, Demi Moore, Ashton Kutcher, and Angelina Jolie (who is no longer a client), among many others, on philanthropy. It is also reported that the company currently has a roster of twenty clients, some of whom pay upward of $200,000 annually for their services. That's fine. Neilson is entitled to be paid for the services he provides. What makes me crazy is the idea that he has to research "which cause a celebrity should champion" extensively and then teach the celebrity the talking points around the cause.[44] I don't know which is worse, that the celebrities don't have enough passion on their own to determine what is important to them, that someone has to teach them what the issues are, or that these put-on packages of celebrity causes are supposed to be educating us, the public, on what we should care about. And, for many celebrities, one cause is just not enough. On the web site, looktothestars.org, you can find a database of celebrity-charity connections ("1575 charities, 2240 celebrities and counting . . . "). A search of Beyoncé Knowles, for example, brought up fourteen charitable connections; Angelina Jolie, twenty-three; and Bono, thirty-one.[45]

Where we see the nexus of entertainment *and* charity *and* consumerism most taking root today is on an increasing number of reality and game shows. This includes one of America's highest-rated TV programs, *American Idol,* which has for several seasons generated tremendous returns from advertising (a thirty-second commercial at one time went for $700,000) and money charged to viewers voting for their favorite contestant. In light of this embarrassment of riches, the show created *American Idol Gives Back*. Through what is quite simply a highly produced, celebrity-doused telethon, money is distributed to five beneficiaries—notable among them is the Global Fund, also supported by (RED). Charity concerts have their roots in musical celebrities coming together for causes, significantly the Concert for Bangladesh in 1971 and later Live Aid in 1985. These older campaigns, however, were not pushing sneakers or cell phones, they were simply raising money.

The success of charity as entertainment cannot be underestimated and where we see it most often is in our own living rooms. Reality programming, which we've seen proliferate over the past decade, is the perfect format for combining caring with pop culture. Television networks like these programs, because they do well in the ratings, are inexpensive to produce, and provide ample opportunities for product placement, while simultaneously acting as entertainment CSR.

TV Charity: Reality, Reality, Reality

Time magazine called 2005 "The Year of Charitainment." It was a year that saw multiple telethons for the Asian tsunami and Hurricane Katrina. It was also the year of Live 8, a series of concerts to raise money for the "Make Poverty History" campaign in the United Kingdom. These were produced by Bono and Bob Geldof, founder of the Live Aid concert televised twenty years earlier to raise money for famine relief in Ethiopia. In terms of recurring television programming, we had *Extreme Makeover: Home Edition,* Oprah building communities in areas hit by Hurricane Katrina, and *Three Wishes,* a show starring the Christian rocker Amy Grant, wherein she acted like the proverbial genie.[46]

Once "civic potentialities" were the purview of public television, most notably through providing educational programming, the media scholar Laurie Oullette explains. However, with deregulation, changes in technologies, and increased competition, "doing good" has moved to the realm of reality television. These shows are a microcosm of market forces, where celebrities, viewers, television networks, non-profits and sponsors present and play out a framework of public-private partnerships. "Reality entertainment . . . intervenes directly in social life, enacting 'can do' solutions to largely personalized problems within emotional and often suspenseful formats."[47] Celebrities, entertainment, and product sponsorship become the conduits for showing viewers how to make the world a better place through individualized solutions.

Extreme Makeover is a good example of the misdirection of such programs. It is also an important example because of its use of product placement, the act of inserting product promotion within a television program. Product placement (now often called branded entertainment) has increased in popularity because of the proliferation of reality television shows, the increased use of DVRs, which allow viewers to skip commercials, and the ability to watch an increasing number of shows online. Sears, Ford, and Pella Windows are just a few of the brands that have been highlighted on *Extreme Makeover.*[48]

While we see the upside of *Extreme Makeover*—building homes for large families with a disabled child, or one for a family whose father died in the World Trade Center Towers on 9/11—we often don't see or think about the downside. In one famous case, a family that had had a new home bestowed on them had to file for bankruptcy. More generally, these homes are typically built in middle-class neighborhoods. The final homes are anything but middle class, which carries with it the issues of taxes and resale. In terms of celebrity, beyond the ubiquitous host Ty Pennington, in the 2009–10 season, *Extreme Makeover* increasingly brought in celebrity guests to help build a new home. I suspect this was to help boost the show's ratings—a tactic often used in television. What is not quite as kosher is bringing in celebrities to help them improve their image. The example that comes to mind is David Duchovny. Shortly after having gotten out of rehab for sex addiction, Duchovny appeared on *Extreme Makeover* as both a humanitarian—he took time out of his "busy schedule" to help build a house for a family with a sick child—and an environmentalist—he helped set up an organic garden and talked about his own environmentally friendly lifestyle. Extreme makeover, indeed.

The premise of *Extreme Makeover* entails a social cause element—redesigning homes for people who most need them. NBC's *The Biggest Loser,* a reality program in which morbidly obese people compete to see who can lose the most weight (and the show that is the most prolific user of product placement), is an example that demonstrates when a campaign is overlaid onto a program.

When the show began in 2004, it was a program like most other reality series. Several seasons ago, it launched a campaign to get viewers to lose weight along with the contestants. In January 2009, it added the "Pound for Pound Challenge." This campaign asks viewers to pledge to lose weight (though there's no verifying that they actually do). For every pound "lost," money/food will go to Feeding America. This promotion is a partnership among the TV show, the charity, and numerous corporate sponsors, including General Mills, Subway, and 24 Hour Fitness. I focus here on General Mills because it is the campaign's leading corporate sponsor.

General Mills gets the benefit of reaching fitness-conscious consumers (who presumably want to eat General Mills's cereal or other products), while tying in with health-minded companies like 24 Hour Fitness health club, and Jenny-O Turkey as well as the show's celebrities—Bob Harper, Allison Sweeney, and weekly guest stars. Viewers do not only pledge to lose weight; they participate by purchasing General Mills food products. The Challenge asks consumers to send in specially marked General Mills products that carry the Pound for Pound seal. For every Pound for Pound Seal received, General Mills donated 10¢ to Feeding America, with a cap of $275,000.[49] (This is similar to Yoplait's campaign, and in each case one has to wonder why consumers wouldn't simply donate the cost of the stamp to the charity rather than send a seal in for a 10¢ donation.)

The Biggest Loser obscures the cause issue and turns it into entertainment more than other campaigns we have looked at. First, the show gives time to the Pound for Pound Challenge. These segments include showing celebrities, like the teen rock star Nick Jonas and the Olympic skater Scott Hamilton, donating time at local food banks. Another aspect of this struck me when the campaign was launched. To promote the delivery of food to the homeless, they showed clean, happy people picking up bags of food from the set of *The Biggest Loser.* This can only be interpreted as an effort to make viewers feel comfortable in their giving. Finally, the web site allows viewers to submit videos showing their weight loss. This is done all in the hope of being included on the TV show—the ultimate in turning the focus away from the needy and toward the giver.

In an unsurprising twist, *The Biggest Loser* has moved on from hunger to . . . wait for it . . . breast cancer. Announced with print ads highlighting the show's stars and the headline "100% COMMITTED," the program promoted its special episode devoted to Ford's Warriors in Pink. The blurring of celebrity and sponsor and charity was seamless. This episode was the series' traditional makeover show, and each contestant was dressed in some sort of pink attire for their walk down the runway. Contestants vied for a chance to win a Ford SUV, and the celebrity spokespeople were attired in Ford Warriors in Pink clothing throughout the show. Committed, perhaps. But to what and for how long, we don't know.

Finally, let's look at *Celebrity Apprentice,* a spin-off of the successful show *The Apprentice.* Each week, contestants work in groups to create projects around branded products—one week it's Levi's; the next week it's Universal Studios theme parks (owned, not coincidentally by NBC, the network on which the show appears). The group that wins gets to stay to compete another week. The losing team appears in front of Donald Trump, who will tell one of the team members, "You're fired."

In 2008, the show was revamped for the teams to be made up of B-, C-, and D-level celebrities, who were playing to raise money for charity instead of for a chance to apprentice with "The Donald." Other than this, the format remained the same, so that celebrities were interacting with products and promoting their causes at the same time—the ultimate in charitainment integration.

The exchange below demonstrates that this program is not all about the causes, but indeed about commerce. Curtis Stone, a celebrity chef, is one of the semifinal contestants. In order to make it to the final round, he must interview with Bill Rancic, the winner of the first season of *The*

Apprentice. They are sitting across from each other for this important final reality test:

B: *I guess my question is why are you here?*
C: Bill, I've worked with Feeding America and have done so for quite a while. I'm super passionate about the charity. They have food banks, they have shelters.

B: *That's a canned answer. Why should you be here?*
C: I should be here because I'm a natural leader. I've done it all my life. When you run busy kitchens, you're dealing with chefs from all walks of life, front of house stuff and different nationalities, you really got to know how to harness people's energy.

B: *You've only stepped up as project manager once, and to me I have to say that raises a red flag. It's a little weak.*
C: Yeah. I understand that. Look, everything I've done we've won. And then this last one . . .

B: *But you've only done one.*
C: Yeah, that's right.

B: *That's going to come up.*
C: Of course my goal of being here is to raise money for Feeding America.

B: *But it doesn't hurt to sell some pots and pans and cookware . . .*
C: Of course. One of the major reasons that everyone comes onto this show is to carry on building their profile so that they can increase their business potential . . .[50]

When I saw this, I have to admit I was surprised that they were quite so blatantly honest. It suggests that combining celebrity and entertainment and product sales has become second nature, an accepted fact of the way the world is.

The problem with popularizing social issues through celebrity is that they become secondary props in trumped-up morality stories. White knights—millionaires who are sometimes well-known celebrities—are the primary focus of the show, while the poor are cleaned up for display and their problems are solved in an hour. This masks the systemic social dysfunction that creates issues like poverty and disease and obesity. Unfortunately, CSR as entertainment is likely to become more popular as our country sinks further into hard times and as our president prods us toward service—both providing ready-made opportunities for TV-style reality.

Let me provide one example of a better way to mix charity and celebrity. In June 2009, Stephen Colbert and his merry troupe from Comedy Central moved *The Colbert Report* to Camp Victory, Iraq. The "mission" was named "Operation Iraqi Stephen: Going Commando," and entailed taping and broadcasting the show for one week from amid American troops fighting overseas, the first time an entire nonnews program was presented from a combat zone.[51]

Cable networks are famous for "stunting," the practice of creating some sort of bizarre or unusual programming to grab viewers' attention. Shark Week on the Discovery Channel and an all-day marathon of *Real Wives of Beverly Hills* on Bravo are good examples. Taking *The Colbert Report* on the road then is not out of the ordinary. The choice of location was unusual, but it does fit Colbert's sensibilities.

Anyone who has watched this program is aware that the host is an unabashed supporter of American troops. He helped raise money for the troops through multiple methods during his "stunt" week, all with the Colbert spin. Viewers could provide money to help get school supplies for children of soldiers through donorschoose.org (an organization that helps all schools, not just military ones); buy Colbert's WristStrong bracelets (a takeoff on Livestrong), with the proceeds going to the Yellow Ribbon Fund, helping injured veterans; or download episodes of the show from iTunes.

Does Colbert get something out of this? Definitely. The show got considerable press because it was so extreme. In fact, Colbert shaved his head the first night of the show in solidarity with the troops and because President Obama ordered it (and for full press exposure). Even so, in this case, who benefits? Net-net, you would have to say the troops and their families. They get attention, and money and awareness is raised for charities that benefit them. Moreover, Colbert is not asking you to buy anything (except his WristStrong bracelet), but rather to donate money directly.

Why Does This Matter?

So what's the point? The point is that celebrities bring attention, both for themselves and for the causes that they advocate for—with or without a product attached.

Just as Komen's ability to disseminate pink ribbons influences our perception of reality, so too celebrities blur reality when it comes to which charities can and will get attention. For example, if a charity can get one celebrity, that's great. But what if they can get two or ten or twenty? Is St. Jude with its magnifying glass and multiple celebrities a more important charity than the local cancer hospital because Jennifer Aniston and Antonio Banderas and Robin Williams are attached? Or, is it really more important because it is connecting to an increasing number of retailers like Target and Gymboree and Brooks Brothers and dozens of others?

And is the opposite also true? What about the celebrity who endorses multiple initiatives, like Heidi Klum and Beyoncé? Which of their various charities are more worthy? How do we know?

Unfortunately, smaller and local causes are lost in the bright lights of Hollywood celebrity or hidden behind consumer product messages. Those charities that simply don't appeal to advertisers—ones that can't be prettied up for the cameras or those that affect the elderly or the poor, for example—will be sorely underfunded or simply ignored. Alzheimer's disease, likely to be one of the most debilitating ailments for the nation over the next several decades due to the aging of the baby boomers, is not one with marketing appeal, nor does it have a happy ending, and that is why we do not see it included in the examples here.

Why should this concern you? Because marketing makes celebrities more important than the social causes they are touting. And because caring—real, true caring—becomes secondary to product sales. Hyper-charities and charitainment hinge on the belief that buying more stuff will have a profound effect on the world. Marketers are trying to move you in a direction in terms of what you buy, but not changing that fact that you should and will buy. We can see this in the first sentence of the (RED) "Manifesto": "As first world consumers, we have tremendous power. What we collectively choose to buy, or not to buy, can change the course of life and history on this planet." Thus, promotion-based— no, market-based—compassion lulls us into believing that we are being socially responsible, when the sad fact is that we are abdicating our social responsibilities to the market.

4

The Consequences of Co-opting Compassion

Thus far we have looked at specific consequences of attaching a charity to a product (or a charity to lots of products): (RED) isn't raising as much money for charity as consumers might suspect; breast cancer is ingrained in our minds as the leading killer of women, which is not the case; and any number of consumer products have attached themselves to causes with little or no money actually going to the charity.

We have not yet, however, examined the cumulative social impact of connecting causes to market forces. The consequences are considerable: (1) less funding for charities, and therefore fewer services to those that desperately need them, (2) more burdens on individual consumers, rather than on governments, nonprofits, or the private sector, where more significant inroads can be made, and (3) funding of charities based on their marketability, rather than on the needs of society as a whole. But this just scratches the surface. There are also concerns about ethics and morality and our own shutting down to caring because the promotion of causes has become just one more tool in the marketer's arsenal.

In the preceding chapters we looked at why consumers, businesses, and charities have embraced and responded to the marriage of consumerism to compassion. This chapter not only examines the fallout, but also digs into the economic and social constructs that help explain why as a culture we have bought into this concept. Neoliberalism, the belief that the market is better than the government as a purveyor of services of all kinds, is one such theory. Another important factor is our changing ideas of citizenship; we are citizen-consumers—not participants in a democracy—who can express their political selves through product purchases.

Let's begin by looking at the big picture and asking: what has the interrelationship of compassion with consumption wrought?

CONSEQUENCES FOR CONSUMERS AND CAUSES

Individual Solutions Don't Solve Collective Problems

To date, few have written about the consequences of co-opting compassion. Most writing on the topic has viewed it through the lens of business, with a particular emphasis on teaching corporations how to best implement a cause-related marketing (CRM) or corporate social responsibility (CSR) campaign. In addition to the "nuts and bolts" of implementation, writers have presented the pros and cons of cause-related marketing. The plus side is that marketers have an inexpensive way to improve their reputations, as well as generate *and* quantify incremental sales, while philanthropic groups receive much needed funding and volunteers. The downside is the creation of questionable partnerships—environmental groups bedding down with oil companies, for example. Good or bad, the ultimate goal of such texts is to promote the integration of philanthropy into the corporate structure. This is done, however, without evaluating the long-term or social implications associated with doing so.[1]

One important exception to the numerous pro-business, rah-rah writings is a 2009 article by Angela Eikenberry, a professor of public administration, titled "The Hidden Costs of Cause Marketing," which explains many of the social costs associated with cause-marketing campaigns, what she calls "consumption philanthropy":

> Consumption philanthropy individualizes solutions to collective social problems, distracting our attention and resources away from the neediest causes, the most effective interventions, and the act of critical questioning itself. It devalues the moral core of philanthropy by making virtuous action easy and thoughtless. And it obscures the links between markets—their firms, products, and services—and the negative impacts they can have on human well-being.[2]

"Individualized solutions" place the burden of solving society's ills on the backs of consumers, a pattern we've seen again and again in the marketing programs we have looked at thus far. Buy Diet Coke to alleviate heart disease; buy a dishwashing liquid and help the environment; donate a dollar when you go to the movies and raise money for cystic fibrosis. These campaigns work on the theory that if every person does a little bit, it all adds up to make a big difference.

This may be true—up to a point. When it comes to fund-raising, certainly, if lots of people each give a dollar, you ultimately have a lot of money. The Giving USA Foundation reports, for example, that charitable donations by individuals totaled $227.4 billion, or 75 percent of total U.S. giving, in 2009.[3] The same year, the *New York Times* noted that while billionaires and expensive fund-raisers receive massive publicity for their good works, it is the "little donor" who really makes a difference. "We are deluded by the attention paid to the large contributors in our country," says Wendy Smith, author of *Give a Little: How Your Small Donations Can Transform the World.* "Small checks coming through the mail are the bread and butter for most organizations."[4] Individual giving was nonetheless flat in 2009, after declining in 2008, while corporate giving was up almost 6 percent during the same period. Though not specifically stated by the Giving USA report, one has to wonder if the trend is tied to funds raised through consumer purchases. Changes in donation patterns are discussed further below.

According to *Conservation Magazine,* it also appears that there is quantifiable evidence that if we as individuals do our little bit for conservation, we can have an impact on the environment. A group of scientists led by Thomas Dietz at Michigan State University looked at seventeen small changes that individuals can make to reduce their carbon footprints. This list includes things from routine car maintenance to thermostat setbacks to line-drying your clothing. These researchers found that we could reduce greenhouse gases by more than 7 percent—the same amount produced by all of France—by making these alterations (and not everyone in the United States has to make all the changes; the authors assumed, for example, that only 15 percent of people would make the effort to carpool everyday, though 80 percent would switch to low-flow showerheads, a one-time action).[5] That's good. In fact, it's great. However—and here's the underlying problem—making the environment a personal issue draws attention away from the reality that the detrimental effects of industry vastly outweigh those of individuals, singly or as a group. This becomes fully evident when you consider that carbon emissions need to be reduced by 75 percent worldwide according to current scientific consensus.[6]

Obfuscating the responsibility of institutions and cheering on individuals to make a difference is not limited to marketing circles. Numerous TV shows, particularly environmental programming around Earth Day in April, bombard us with suggestions about how one little thing we do can make a big difference. NBC Universal, majority-owned by the cable operator Comcast and parent company of NBC, USA Network, Bravo, MSNBC, and many other channels, has green week programming every year at this time under the tagline "Green is Universal," with green-leaf logos on the bottom third of the television screen. Companywide programming includes ideas for how to reduce your carbon footprint. For example, Alison Sweeney and Bob Harper from *The Biggest Loser* tell viewers to use Brita filters instead of bottled water for the sake of the environment (note that this is both helpful tip and blatant product placement).[7] In another example, the Sundance Channel—which has a long-standing environmental stance because of its founder, Robert Redford—offers a lineup of green shows, including a recent addition called *The Lazy Environmentalist,* which teaches people how to "be green" without having to work at it. Most recently, Discovery Communications launched Planet Green, a network devoted to all things environmental, suggesting countless ways to introduce sustainability into one's life. While there is nothing wrong with promoting this programming or these types of ideas, there are concerns about marrying a cause (the environment or any other social cause) with a celebrity and entertainment, an idea discussed at length in chapter 3. More important here, marketing and entertainment are by definition about focusing on the individual. They cannot help but present individual solutions. Because of this, ways in which industry and government might assist in providing a solution are not presented. Because the media are so ubiquitous (the only things most Americans do more than watch TV are sleep and work) and so powerful as a source of information, our concepts of the best way to solve problems become skewed. Even in Vice President Al Gore's *An Inconvenient Truth,* the quintessential ecology film, solutions are presented as individual and personal—driving less, changing lightbulbs, and so on. If the only tool you have is a hammer, everything looks like a nail, the old adage says. In this case, if every problem is about the individual and the market, every solution looks like a product purchase.

Often, consumer-based and individualized solutions are not the most effective. Let's take the example of plastic bags. Americans use an estimated 100 billion plastic bags annually. As we all know by now, plastic bags have been catastrophic to the environment, polluting oceans and endangering marine life. This is in addition to being a petroleum-based product. A market solution to the problem was for stores to start selling reusable bags. In response, many people started carrying these totes, but not all, because most stores continued to offer plastic bags. For San Francisco lawmakers, that wasn't good enough. In 2007, San Francisco was the first city to ban the use of plastic bags altogether. While there were concerns about the reaction to this regulation, the predicted consumer backlash never materialized. More important, city officials estimate that approximately 150 million plastic bags per year are being eliminated. In June 2010, a stronger bill—requiring consumers to bring their own bags or pay for 40 percent recycled ones—passed in the California State Assembly.[8] This could eliminate *19 billion* plastic bags annually. While there are no statistics on how many Americans religiously carry reusable bags, if we estimate it to be 10 percent (the percentage of so-called cultural creatives), this would eliminate ten billion bags—about half of the number achievable through legislation. In this case, a political and not a market intervention makes the biggest impact.

Plastic bags are one small example. Hunger, cancer, homelessness, and any number of other social problems have underlying causes that require governmental intervention. "Trying to end hunger with food drives is like trying to fill the Grand Canyon with a teaspoon," Joel Berg observes. "Because local charities cannot possibly feed 35.5 million people adequately, and because their efforts rarely enable people to become self-reliant, this belief that charity does it better than government only ensures hunger will persist in America."[9] The same idea can be applied to the environment, homelessness, and so on. CRM in particular, rather than helping, diverts our attention away from fundamental solutions in favor of curing the symptoms. Symptoms can be solved with short-term solutions; structural change cannot.

The Civil Rights Movement is illustrative of the difference. As we are well aware, until the mid-1960s, African Americans had few rights in the United States—they were hamstrung in their ability to vote through much of the South, their children attended second-rate schools (at best), and in many places they couldn't share a bathroom, drinking fountain, or lunch counter with a white person. The visible symptoms of these restrictions included poverty, homelessness, and hunger. As it is today, feeding the hungry was a necessity. However, the problem wasn't at its base lack of food; it was the fact that most African Americans lacked access to jobs providing a living wage. The only way to change that was to change social policy—an act that took endless political will, years of protests, and, unfortunately, the lives of many innocent people. Compare that to what is happening now forty years later—Beyoncé and Heidi Klum suggest, instead, that we buy Hamburger Helper and Diet Coke!

As Derrick Jensen asks,

> Would any sane person think dumpster diving would have stopped Hitler, or that composting would have ended slavery or brought about the eight-hour workday, or that chopping wood and carrying water would have gotten people out of Tsarist prisons, or that dancing naked around a fire would have helped put in place the Voting Rights Act of 1957 or the Civil Rights Act of 1964? Then why now, with all the world at stake, do so many people retreat into these entirely personal "solutions"?[10]

We are victims of "systematic misdirection." We have been taught to substitute consumption for political acts.

Favoring Some Charities over Others

The more marketable a cause, the more attention it gets, and the more funding it receives. This makes no sense as social policy. Think of this in terms of breast cancer, the cause célèbre, versus heart disease, which actually kills most women. Or of diarrhea, an easily and inexpensively treatable symptom that kills 1.5 million children annually in developing countries, but unfortunately lacks market appeal. Dehydration kills more children than AIDS, malaria, and measles combined.[11] Is this less important than sending antiviral drugs to Africa because a slew of celebrities say so?

Key elements that contribute to successful campaigns relate to corporate marketing objectives. First, initiatives that generate significant funding are highly correlated with the need to appeal to women, who account for 83 percent of consumer purchases. Thus, the most popular sponsorship categories are those that this demographic most cares about: breast cancer (68 percent), education (62 percent), children's welfare (60 percent), the environment (57 percent), and poverty (50 percent). These issues stimulate strong emotions in the target audience and motivate them to purchase through guilt, identification, or a belief that they are doing something worthwhile. It is also why you are less likely to see campaigns around men's issues, such as prostate cancer—a complaint that comes up again and again in the popular press.

CSR campaigns also appeal to the wealthy groups known in market research as "Influentials," those in the know and most likely to influence other people's purchasing decisions, and "Millennials," the children of the baby boomers, who are currently in their twenties and thirties. These groups are populated by thought leaders who set trends for consumer products. They are especially appealing to marketers because they are most likely to propagate word-of-mouth advertising, particularly through online venues like blogs and social networking sites.

Larger nonprofits are more appealing to corporations than smaller groups, for a number of reasons. First, the bigger nonprofits produce their own events, which corporations can tie into, thus reducing their promotional costs. Second, because both the corporation and the charity partner have PR capabilities, their ability to generate press attention substantially increases, which again reduces promotional expenditures. In addition, corporations may be given access to clients, personnel, and donors associated with the nonprofit, all of whom are prospective customers.[12]

Finally, corporations favor noncontroversial charities over those that are politically charged. Thus, education is a popular cause. For example, Visa tied in with "Reading Is Fundamental" during the 1990s. Currently, Procter & Gamble's Always and Tampax brands support education for girls in Africa, and Target uses its credit cards to support local schools, a fact increasingly promoted in its advertising. Upromise has created a network of close to 70,000 affiliates, plus more than 350 online retailers, to raise money for people to attend college.[13]

The push to appeal to particular targets and attract celebrity talent ignores important charities and obfuscates real issues. Charities that don't appeal to women and do not have stars attached are likely to be ignored. Obviously hardest hit are local and smaller charities. And, again, while selling products and raising money may provide some financial benefit for a limited period of time—so-called symptom relief— they do not address core problems. For example, funding breast cancer research is commendable; ignoring inadequate health care for women is not. Raising money for African girls to attend school is heartwarming; ignoring the number of high school dropouts in America is not.

Even if consumers are not, marketers are well aware that focusing on the environment, star power, and hypercharities is detrimental to smaller causes. "Americans will only support so many good causes, and celebrity attention for green initiatives and CRM is likely hurting second-tier CRM causes such as crime, local concerns, and international concerns, like poverty in Africa," the marketing research firm Mintel notes. "If consumers are faced with a decision between two competing CRM campaigns, it seems likely they will choose green or health initiatives over these second-tier ones."

Misleading Consumers: Logo, Licensing, or Endorsement

An area of increasing confusion is the use of charitable logos and certification seals on consumer products. Some of these are legitimate ways for us to know that a product is in fact fair trade or environmentally friendly. The confusion lies in the difference between licensing and endorsement; while they both entail a monetary transaction, one also implies a recommendation of the product's usage.

Licensing is one of the most popular means of generating income for causes, in part, perhaps, because it is a fairly simple operation. The charitable organization gives its logo to a company, which puts it on its product. Martha Stewart's putting her name, and sometimes likeness, on products from kitchen towels to sheets to paint for Kmart is an example of this in the for-profit segment. Stewart licenses Kmart to use her name in exchange for a percentage of the profit on sales of these products. It works the same way in the not-for-profit sector. In this instance, credit cards are the item of choice. So, then, when you use a World Wildlife Fund Visa card, for example, the cause gets a percentage of each transaction.

Licensing agreements, however, are rarely based on independent testing or reviewed by the nonprofit. It is simply a monetary transaction. In a well-known example, the American Cancer Society (ACS) had a $6 million licensing agreement with SmithKlineBeecham to put its logo on NicoDerm nicotine replacement patches.[14] In and of itself, that might not have been an issue. But the NicoDerm advertising claimed that ACS and NicoDerm were "partners in helping you quit." This led to a lawsuit being brought by several attorneys general, who claimed that the promotion of this product misled consumers into thinking that the American Cancer Society was instrumental in developing the product, which it was not. SmithKlineBeecham settled the case and was required to run $2 million in advertising to rectify consumer confusion.[15]

Endorsements, on the other hand, entail a recommendation. They connote that the company using the logo has undergone testing in order to earn the "seal of approval." The Good Housekeeping seal of approval—and now its Green seal—are good examples here. In addition to meeting the requirements for the original seal, environmental products must undergo an additional round of testing. According to *Good Housekeeping*'s web site:

> In evaluating a product for the Green Good Housekeeping Seal, we take a comprehensive, holistic approach, evaluating and verifying data related to a product's environmental impact, including its composition, manufacturing, packaging, and distribution. We look at the reduction of water use in manufacturing, energy efficiency in manufacturing and product use, ingredient and product safety, packaging reduction, and the brand's corporate social responsibility. We want to make sure the product is safe to manufacture, distribute, maintain, and use.[16]

Unlike a logo placed on a package through a licensing agreement, this Green Good Housekeeping Seal provides consumers with the assurance that the product has been tested to meet environmental standards.

Hearst Communications, Inc., publisher of *Good Housekeeping*, is not, of course, the only business to do this type of analysis. Items marketed as "organic" have to adhere to specified governmental requirements. Nonprofits also provide certification. For example, Rainforest Alliance, an environmental organization, teamed up with Naked Juice, a product of PepsiCo. This partnership ensures that juices containing bananas are from Costa Rican farms certified by the Alliance to be sustainable businesses with good working conditions. Whether provided by *Good Housekeeping*, the federal government, or Rainforest Alliance, we have come to trust these seals, and research shows that they positively influence our purchase decisions.

But how is a consumer to know if the logo is a logo or a "seal of approval"? The answer is, we can't.[17] There is little government regulation in this area, and numerous ethical issues have to be considered in relation to thousands of consumer products. The most egregious example of this is the use of the Sierra Club logo on bottles of Clorox GreenWorks products. Clorox approached the environmental group to endorse its new earth-friendly products in exchange for financial compensation. Sierra Club's corporate accountability committee knew the deal was a conflict of interest, but signed on anyway and tried to justify it to members. "Then–executive director Carl Pope defended the move in an e-mail to members, in which he claimed that the organization had carried out a serious analysis of the cleaners to see if they were 'truly superior.' But it hadn't. Jessica Frohman, co-chair of the Sierra Club's toxics committee, said, 'We never approved the product line,'" *Utne Reader* reports.[18] Sierra Club's stamp of approval works not only for

GreenWorks, but for Clorox, which, as discussed earlier, is repositioned as "it's not as bad as you think" bleach. The bottom line is that it is illegal for a nonprofit to endorse a product. But how likely is it that consumers are stopping to notice the difference when they see the logo of an environmental group that they trust? Research suggests that this in very unlikely. Amanda Bower and Stacy Grau found "no significant difference in perception of nonprofit endorsement between licensing agreements and explicit approval . . . the presence of an explicit seal of approval statement was not necessary for consumers to assume a seal of approval; the mere presence of a nonprofit logo was enough to infer endorsement."[19]

In the end, this hurts both the consumers and the nonprofits. Consumers are confused by misleading information and competing messages—which is unlikely to change in the United States, given the number of interest groups putting out a plethora of definitions. (The United Kingdom is doing a much better job of this in terms of carbon-footprint labeling.)[20] U.S. nonprofits that take the much-needed endorsement funding may find themselves sued when promotion by the corporation suggests an endorsement and not a partnership.

Compassion Fatigue, Charitable Backlash

The proliferation of cause campaigns has had negative effects on charitable giving overall. In the short term, scholars have noted that cause-related marketing hinders further philanthropy—either through reduced financial giving or limiting volunteering—because consumers see their cause-related purchases as donations.[21] More broadly, there is concern that consumers have begun to suffer from "compassion fatigue." This term, originally applied to stressed-out caregivers, is now being attached to consumers, because shopping for a cause has become so ubiquitous. "It is not difficult to imagine cause-related marketing campaigns interjecting themselves into the millions of purchase transactions that take place each day. In response, people may simply tune out and say 'no' because they cannot process each and every request, or because they believe they have already donated enough," Matthew Berglind and Cheryl Nakata observe.[22] Thus, the ultimate outcome may be that cause campaigns desensitize us to real problems and trivialize serious concerns.

These campaigns become charitable wallpaper—it's there, but we just don't see it. Should this trend continue, corporations may no longer see the value in cause marketing, because it does not provide a point of product differentiation. Right now, cause campaigns are an expected part of doing business, but there is nothing to say that companies won't walk away from this form of marketing if it does not bolster the bottom line. The devastation for the charities is incalculable.[23]

The possibility that corporations have already begun to turn their backs on big-name cause campaigns is evident in the new marketing concept of microsponsorship.[24] Whereas with cause marketing, you buy a product and a percentage of the sale goes to the cause, with micro-sponsorships, companies fund local pet projects. Pepsi Refresh is the leading example of this kind of marketing. For this campaign, Pepsi bowed out of the 2010 Super Bowl (usually a $20 million commit-ment) and instead put that money aside to give to people with "good" ideas. Anyone with a concept for a project with "positive impact" could submit a proposal online, where people would vote for the best ideas. Every month, Pepsi awards up to $1.3 million. On the plus side for causes, smaller projects get funds they might not otherwise have access to (the same argument that's made with hypercharities, but these small organizations would never be able to compete). Moreover, from a broad social perspective, these campaigns make more sense, because they are funding projects on the ground, where people are interacting with people, and a real difference can be made. On the plus side for marketers, they get to interact with consumers via social media and get free marketing research. Some even claim that these campaigns are more about research than anything else. They increase companies' social media presence and enable companies to create extensive databases of those coming to their online sites, as well as their Facebook pages, Twitter feeds, and so on. As consumers tell marketers what is important to them through their projects and their votes, they provide important information about how marketers can tailor their messages to them.

Each new campaign asks us to believe that the market has our best interests at heart, or at least the interests of the charity being served. However, as we pull back the curtain to see what corporations and char-ities are really doing with the money we have so generously donated, we begin to also see that reality and expectations are not always aligned. The questionable practices of CRM campaigns have already been dis-cussed, but a number of high-profile philanthropic scandals will help to underline this point. The money donated for Hurricane Katrina victims was reportedly spent ineffectively if at all, and five years later, the region remains devastated.[25] In a similar vein, Wyclef Jean's Yele

Haiti Foundation faced allegations that donated funds were used to personal advantage.[26] In yet another example, the nonprofit Kiva, a leader in promoting microfinancing around the world, came under scrutiny when David Roodman, a blogger at the Center for Global Development, "outed" it for not being as transparent as implied. While www .kiva.org invites donors to support small local businesses around the world—a bakery in Peru or a dairy in Kenya, a marketing tool that builds a feeling of connection between the giver and the receiver—in reality, Kiva funnels donations to banks, which give the money to these local entrepreneurs.[27]

Corporations Hold the Purse Strings (Whoever Pays the Piper Picks the Tunes)

Undergirding all the issues surrounding cause marketing and its brethren is the inequitable power relationship that exists between charities desperate for money and corporations that donate it. This imbalance forces a situation such that corporate concerns will always take precedence over the cause and its operations. The unintended consequences of this are manifold and include

- exaggerated perceptions of corporate generosity
- misleading consumers about the relationship between the cause and the corporate partner
- shifting in giving
- tarnishing the cause's image
- variable duration of relationship
- shifting of a cause's activities
- reduced overall giving[28]

Issues like these are not empty concerns. We've seen several instances (and we'll see several more) of corporations overstating their largesse. Caps—limiting corporate donations to a fixed sum no matter how much money is generated by consumer purchases—are common. As we continue to buy products in the expectation that funds are going to a cause, we really don't know if that is the case or if they are filling the coffers of the marketer because the cap has been reached. Moreover, the balance between marketing and charity most often tips in favor of promoting the product. Like (RED) spending millions of dollars to make a small percentage of it back, American Express spent $6 million on the Statue of Liberty campaign (cited as the first successful cause-marketing campaign) to make $1.7 million for the charity. It is numbers like these that lead us to believe that these campaigns are about marketing and not about making a difference.

Contributing to this exaggerated appearance of beneficence are the vague descriptions companies use to describe their donations, such as the commonplace use of misleading and unquantifiable phrases like "a percentage of the purchase price" and "a percentage of the profits." A more straightforward approach is to promote a company's total dollar contribution. Anne Klein, for example, says in its advertising for a pink ribbon bracelet, "you are helping AK Anne Klein donate $50,000 to The Breast Cancer Research Foundation." This, again, brings up the issue of caps (what happens if people buy more bracelets than the $50,000 limit?) and more pointedly, why are consumers helping them donate when you can donate yourself and receive the tax benefits of doing so? Corporations are beginning to realize that consumers are, or will be, getting wise to these conceits. Komen, as discussed, has pushed its sponsors toward transparency. Smart marketers are more candid in their pronouncements. A recent Oakley sunglass ad came right out and declared "Purchase YSC [Young Survival Coalition] edition eyewear and Oakley will provide $20 to the cause."

More important than these deceptions, however, is the ultimate fallout: reduced funding for less "popular" causes and finally less money for charity overall. Prominent charities get more visibility and thus attract an increasing roster of sponsors. This leads to shifts in charitable giving toward the largest nonprofits. Giving patterns also change because a campaign may simply be ineffective, or, worse, consumers reduce their charitable giving because they perceive that the cause is already adequately funded. Further, the interrelationship between charities and corporations affects giving patterns. One way this happens is if the charity's image is tarnished because of a corporate connection; this can lead to increased skepticism on the part of consumers about CRM campaigns and again less financial support. One of the most troubling issues with this structure is that as nonprofits become increasingly tied to corporations through joint marketing initiatives, the less likely they are to rock the boat, not wishing to disrupt their funding. Charities thus change their priorities to fit the goals of the corporation. Because they don't know how long the relationship with the corporation will last, there is pressure on causes to do what corporations want them to, because they never know when the alliance—and the funding, volunteer assistance and promotion—might end. Real reform becomes less likely to occur, because a corporation may be willing to fund a health clinic but not to fight for universal health care. The first provides corporate goodwill; the second, political headaches. The bottom line, then, is that funding is reduced and causes become unable to provide much-needed services—the worst possible scenario. This is the price we are paying for easy compassion.

WHY NOW?

Believing in the Magic of the Market

Over the past 25 years, people around the world have come to put their faith in deregulated free-market capitalism, the so-called neoliberal school of economics. The liberal school of economics—the theory's precursor—is based on the ideas of Adam Smith, who is famous for his 1776 work *The Wealth of Nations* and for coining the phrase "the invisible hand of the market." The idea behind this ideology is that a free-flowing market—one without government regulation—is the best means for growing a nation's economy.

Liberalism remained in vogue until the stock market crash of 1929 and the subsequent Great Depression. Leading up to the crash, the gay days of the Roaring Twenties—a time not unlike the boom-boom 1990s and early 2000s—stock prices climbed, employment was high, and emotions ruled the market, with everyone ebulliently believing that the only direction the economy would move was up. That was until the market suddenly and precipitously dropped, when they became just as suddenly fear-stricken, and then depressed. "It was an event that was driven by a real change in people's psychology that [led] them to be very optimistic and positive in the 20s and then negative in the 30s," the Yale economist Robert Shiller says.[29]

Awareness that emotions contribute to the movement of the markets led to the rise of the economist John Maynard Keynes. Keynes advocated regulation of markets to counteract the bubbles that would inevitably be created by the whims of emotion. In addition, he called for full employment, something that could only be achieved with the "interference" of the government. President Franklin D. Roosevelt's New Deal reflected this thinking, and the idea that the government could improve the common good was generally accepted at that time. Unfortunately, Keynes never solidified a precise mathematical model and his theories lost favor when advanced quantitative methodologies prevailed in the field of economics.

The decline in Keynesianism in conjunction with the rise of globalization, facilitated by advanced technologies, led to an updated version of Adam Smith's ideas. Neoliberalism expands the invisible hand beyond a country's borders and advocates policies that will facilitate trade among nations, allowing for the free movement of goods and the ability to acquire cheaper resources, with the ultimate goal of maximizing profits.

Elizabeth Martinez and Arnoldo Garcia of CorpWatch, a nonprofit that advocates corporate accountability, summarize neoliberalism's agenda roughly as: letting the market rule; cutting public expenditure on social services; deregulation; privatization; and "changing perceptions of public and community good to individualism and individual responsibility."[30]

We've seen all of these occur since the mid-1980s, when Wall Street became as fashionable as Hollywood and MBAs proliferated. Some corporations grew larger than many nation-states and had increasing visibility, not only in their hometown headquarters but also around the globe. As these international corporations became wealthier and more influential, governments around the world became institutions viewed as a means to facilitate profit making through tax cuts and corporate incentives. Because government reduced taxes, particularly on the wealthy and businesses, governmental attempts to improve the life of the middle and working classes have been stymied. Instead, it has become up to individuals to fend for themselves with limited public aid. Under neoliberalism, this is framed as advantageous to the individual as well as society as a whole. "Neo-liberal theory is disdainful of government assistance as interference in people's private lives. People, the argument goes, should devote their attention to self-improvement through the market instead of depending upon the government. In neo-liberal theory, an absence of government social programs will spur the work ethic, productivity, innovation, entrepreneurship and growth of a society," Inger Stole writes.[31]

The current recession, reckoned almost a second Great Depression, has brought these ideas into stunning relief, and the fallout has bordered on disastrous. A deregulated financial system is what nearly crippled the economy. Before and after this debacle, the increasingly wealthy upper class and the businesses that support it were serviced hand and foot by the government: first in the form of reduced regulation, and then through government largesse in the form of bailouts and continuing tax relief. While it is true that the economy expanded and the market provided some increased prosperity during the boom years of the Internet, those gains have all since disappeared—plus some. We now have the highest unemployment rate since the Great Depression, and it is likely worse than reported because so many people have been out of work for so long that they are not accounted for in the official unemployment figures. Many of those who have jobs have had to take considerable pay cuts and fewer benefits in order to keep their jobs. When these jobless and underemployed people seek aid, it is now unlikely that the government is there to assist them.[32]

Nonprofits and the public sector must fill in the gaps, because we have "outsourced compassion."[33] Just as corporations have outsourced jobs, our government has given the job of caring to someone else—first, the nonprofit sector, then, through it, the consumer marketplace.

Since the time of President Ronald Reagan and his leading economist, Milton Friedman, the United States has moved responsibility for the needy out of the purview of the government and into the nonprofit sector. Unlike the government, however, philanthropists are not stand-alone players. Instead, nonprofits and business interests are closely aligned. In the 1980s, these relationships existed through corporate funding of nonprofits (philanthropy as opposed to strategic philanthropy), corporate participation on nonprofit boards, and, finally, foundation funding.[34] By the 1990s, the interactions between these players changed so that their interests would be synergistic—the nonprofits get money and the corporations generate revenues, while solidifying their reputations as good corporate citizens.

Drawing our attention to pro-social campaigns draws our attention away from the devastation of neoliberalism. Emotional marketing campaigns open our hearts to donate to the next big cause or PR leads us to cheer on billionaires who are donating half their wealth to charity. Most disturbing is that an increasing number of people are expecting less and less from government, while taking more and more of the burden on themselves—individualism being a key aspect of neoliberalism. In 2010, researchers learned that only 30 percent of consumers in the United States believe that "the government should be doing the most to support good causes." This was down dramatically from 41 percent only the year before. At the same time, expectations that "people like me" should be doing the most to help causes increased by 8 points to 23 percent of the population. And, 74 percent "believe brands and consumers could do more to support good causes by working together."[35]

Meanwhile little attention is paid to why consumers have to support so many charities to begin with or the fact that generous tax breaks are what enable the wealthy to pick and choose the causes they wish to support. For example, Henry Kravis, well known for buying out distressed companies, donated $100 million to the Columbia Business School to construct new buildings for this institution—certainly not what Bill Gates had in mind when he suggested that the wealthy should support institutions of learning to improve our educational system. Also not taken into consideration is that while the government is accountable for its programs; private-sector firms are not. We can only know if our donations are being spent as we expected if these organizations choose to tell us.

These issues are further complicated by the complex and changing definitions of a corporation, what its rights and responsibilities are to society, and how that affects the lives of individuals. "The recent controversy over the wisdom of bailing out our country's megacorporations has revealed that the role of corporations in our lives is incredibly complex, and no one of the current legal theories of the personhood of corporations, standing alone, is sufficient to give us a completely satisfactory picture of the corporation and its place in our society," Susanna Ripken notes.[36] Companies may be defined through a multiplicity of frames, she points out: they are either legal constructs, defined as "artificial people"; or they are associations based on mutual agreement among the individual human constituencies that compose the corporation and interact with it; or the corporation is a person—a "real entity"—and the human beings that relate to it are incidental, because the corporation goes on no matter who the players are that run it.

How we view corporations affects how they are regulated. If, for example, the corporation is a legal construct, then the laws that created it should be framed to have it work in the public interest. If it's an association, then the law is based on private contracts. The prevailing theory since the turn of the twentieth century has been that the corporation should be regarded as a real person. This affords corporations legal rights and protections in terms of property rights and liberty rights—constitutional protections—like those afforded to individuals. The 2010 *Citizens United v. Federal Election Commission* case addressed this interpretation of personhood. The Supreme Court decided that corporate political campaign spending was a form of free speech and therefore protected by the First Amendment.[37] With this decision, corporations were given an even more powerful voice in public issues.

While the law humanizes corporations, CSR frames them as moral players. Avon cares for women with breast cancer, and Procter & Gamble cares about girls in Africa. It is also true that CSR reports remain in many cases just so much PR, and cause campaigns are often the equivalent of slapping a pink ribbon on a package. In putting a caring face on corporations, we have come to embrace them as benevolent beings having the power to make positive change—more so than the government. According to 2009 research by Waggener Edstrom Worldwide, 60 percent of American consumers "say businesses are in the best position to impact social issues, as opposed to government," which only 14 percent of respondents picked as being the institution to tap for providing social support.[38] Trickle-down economics has become trickle-down caring.

The Industry of Innovation

Given our reliance on the market for all matter of goods and services, it was inevitable that an industry would be created around cause-related marketing and corporate social responsibility. One of the leading names in the field is Carol Cone, formerly of Cone Communications, noted earlier. The other is a more controversial figure, Dan Pallotta.

I saw Dan Pallotta speak at Columbia University promoting his 2008 book arguing for the corporatization and deregulation—the neoliberalizing—of nonprofits. Titled *Uncharitable: How Restraints on Nonprofits Undermine Their Potential,* "[i]t is about freeing charities—and all of the good people who work for them—from a set of rules that were designed for another age and another purpose, and that actually undermine their potential and our compassion."[39] Pallotta sat on the stage that May evening in 2009 looking far less powerful than the image those words project. In fact he looked fidgety and uncomfortable, as if he was waiting for someone to pick on him. You can't blame him. He's been the punching bag in the fight around charitable promotion for the past decade.

As the founder of Pallotta TeamWorks, he is best known as the man who created the multiday AIDSRides and Breast Cancer events. He is also known as the man who charged lots and lots of money to companies and organizations to help execute these fund-raising events—$300–$350,000 per city, plus expenses. These reportedly exorbitant charges led to Pallotta being sued and summarily dropped by organizations that used his services, reportedly because of questionable fees and a tendency for Pallotta to grab the spotlight for himself.

When he spoke at Columbia, Pallotta's argument—one that I thought had some validity—was that charities, unlike for-profit ventures, are evaluated based on a model that says the organization should keep costs to a minimum no matter what. Charities are assessed in terms of their ability to have limited administrative costs, because donors want to ensure that their money is going to the cause, and not to line the pockets of the promoters. Web sites like charitynavigator.com, the leader in overseeing charitable spending, assess the health of organizations based on how much money goes to charity rather than overhead—the thinking being that the lower the overhead, the better-run the organization. But Pallotta gave an example that argues against this thinking: if I have a bake sale and I sell $10,000 worth of brownies and have no overhead, I have zero administration costs. If I put an ad in the *New York Times* and pay $75,000, I can attract thousands of people and perhaps raise $22 million. Which is better, $10,000 with no overhead or $22 million with some percentage of costs?

His point is a good one, and one that seems to have influenced the field, because Charity Navigator is revamping its ratings to evaluate effectiveness and not simply finances.[40] However, it wasn't the ad in the *Times* that people were opposed to. It was the fact that Pallotta TeamWorks got paid $350,000 no matter what happened at the event. Because of this and other facts not made public, TeamWorks was shuttered in 2002.

The initial success of Pallotta and the continuing success of Cone Communications were surely instrumental in the growth of an industry around cause marketing, corporate social responsibility, and social innovation. It's not that these marketing services didn't exist before; they did. However, they were primarily public relations initiatives with the goal of maintaining or improving the corporation's reputation. Now, they exist to get more causes in front of us and to teach businesses how better to do that while making money themselves

Here is a broad outline of how this business is constituted: marketing companies that provide services from strategy to PR to advertising and so on make up the bulk of this new industry. Many of these organizations are within larger marketing holding companies. These include OgilvyEarth, part of Ogilvy & Mather, one of the old-line agencies started by legendary ad man David Ogilvy, and Saatchi & Saatchi S, a division of the international communications conglomerate and famously run by the former Sierra Club wunderkind Adam Werbach. Aside from these large firms, there are smaller companies like BBMG and The SOAP Group and What on Earth Is Going On.[41]

Trade associations, conferences, and publications have sprung up to serve these marketing professionals.[42] The two largest organizations are the Cause Marketing Forum (www.causemarketingforum.com), which provides information about campaigns and holds an annual meeting and awards presentation, and the CSR Wire (www.csrwire.com), a wire service for social-responsibility activities. Another major player, though with a focus limited to environmental issues, is Sustainable Life Media, which runs ongoing workshops and online seminars called "webinars." There is a growing list of publications in this area. For business professionals, there are the *Corporate Responsibility Magazine* (www.thecro.com) and *Business Ethics: The Magazine of Corporate Responsibility* (http://business-ethics.com). And now there are two publications for consumers: *Ode,* which is for the more ardently philanthropic among us, and *Just Cause Magazine,* an electronic publication and community web site that "looks at the causes that unite us, and the good that can happen when we work together."[43] I would also include *Fast Company* in this list, because of its commitment to doing good. Its mission statement reads: "We believe that work isn't simply a paycheck: It is the ultimate expression of a fully realized self. We believe that a company's obligations extend far beyond its bottom line and its shareholders—to a wider constituency that includes employees, customers, suppliers and the community," practically the definition of social innovation.[44]

Marketing companies most strongly perpetuate the ideology of individualized responsibility. The following example demonstrates how entrenched this is:

> Do One Thing—DOT: Saatchi & Saatchi believe that sustainability is driven from consumers-up, not companies down, and the heart of [our work] is to inspire people to make the best choices for themselves and for the planet.
>
> Each person is encouraged to choose one thing to pursue regularly. It can be anything from cycling to work or doing laundry with cold water. We call this DOT—Do One Thing. One person's DOT may stand alone, but connect a billion DOTs together and you'll see a movement of change happening.[45]

This is a nice sentiment from Adam Werbach and the folks at Saatchi. But will it make a difference? Not really. And that's because the problems are being evaluated within a marketing paradigm, a framework that must inevitably also lead to increased consumption and the overuse of resources.

What is heartbreaking in all of this is that there is undoubtedly a very serious commitment to making a positive difference in the world, particularly among those involved who are committed to social innovation, as opposed to straight CRM. I've talked with many of them, and they are truly inspiring, passionate, and really smart people. That is not the point. The point is that as more organizations come into being to support cause marketing and CSR, and the more they are able to make money doing it, the more entrenched these practices become. As Albert Einstein famously said, "No problem can be solved from the same level of consciousness that created it." I can't think of a more perfect example of where this idea applies.

Scalability: Giving In or Giving Up

Sustainable products and those with a legacy of being organic or ethical are appealing acquisition targets for large corporations, because they provide two important benefits. First, the product is a proven success, developed at someone else's expense and by someone else's hard work. Second, the products bring their mythology with them, and it is hoped that that ethical image will rub off on the larger organization. "The ethical equity often can spread across an entire range of products, even if only a small percentage of products actually meet ethical standards," according to Packaged Facts.[46]

Acquisitions of independent firms are increasingly common and are expected to continue as multinationals look to improve their images and expand their product offerings. Some famous examples include Ben & Jerry's, acquired by Unilever in 2000; Stonyfield Farms, now part of Groupe Danone (makers of Dannon yogurt); Tom's of Maine, bought by Colgate-Palmolive in 2006; and Burt's Bees, acquired by Clorox in 2007. Founders of such firms tend to be the driving force behind them. The vision and control they instilled in the company when it was privately owned are often lost when they become part of a larger entity—the reason why so many are accused of selling out. The argument founders make is that they did not sell for the money but for the ability to be able to scale up the business, that is, they could never become big enough to make a difference on their own. For example, Tom's of Maine's sales were approximately $45 million at the time it was sold to Colgate; today they are estimated to be five times that amount. In an interview with the *San Francisco Chronicle,* Tom Chappell justified the need for a corporate strategic partner. "We were becoming aware that remaining an independent company was going to be very high-risk," he said. "We needed to bring the business to scale, and we just weren't doing it at a pace that was fast enough to catch up with the phenomenal growth going on in natural products."[47] Without a partner, Tom's could not get the distribution it needed, particularly in the most important player—Walmart.

In 2008, Coca-Cola bought a 40 percent stake in Honest Tea. Seth Goldman, the company's founder, explained the positive impact of this deal not just for his company, but for the planet and the people who help grow the ingredients for his product:

> I believe in what we're doing and what we're selling. When we sell a bottle of tea that's grown organically and often with fair trade we're doing a good thing for the ecosystem, for the people who picked the tea leaves and for the people who drink the tea who are getting a healthier product.
>
> If you believe that, then you have a responsibility to sell as much of it as you can. Buying 2.5 million pounds of organic ingredients, as we do, is a notable thing, but it doesn't change markets, it doesn't change the landscape of agriculture in tea fields. When we go to 25 million pounds, then you'll start seeing some of the larger suppliers say, "Wait a minute, we're going to have to change things. We can't use chemical pesticides and herbicides—we have to find a way to grow the leaves and our business in harmony with our environment."
>
> And when we look at consumers, selling 30 million bottles is good. But if you think about what happens when we get to 300 million or 3 billion bottles, then you start changing the diet of people in this country and have a huge impact. I firmly believe a partner like Coca Cola can help us achieve that.[48]

That sounds reasonable. But it also rings hollow when you compare it to the reaction of Yvon Chouinard, founder of the outdoor clothing and gear firm Patagonia, who told a consultant that he would not consider selling the company, because the money he earned from it enabled him to aid the planet. The consultant pointed out that if he sold Patagonia, he could donate far more than he was doing as its owner, but Chouinard realized that even if this were true, it would be a one-time contribution and not a long-term sustainability strategy.[49]

Scalability came up again and again in my discussions with people in the field. It raises many questions for companies that want to make a difference. Should they stay small and true to their values? Won't they lose their responsibility initiatives if they sell to a larger company? Won't greater size provide the added value of making your more ethically produced product widely available, with all that that entails?

The sector's response is B Corp certification. B corporations—recognizable to consumers through their symbol of a B in a circle (instead of the C in a circle)—are required to meet a number of guidelines in order to be certified. The Certified B Corporation web site explains that they are unlike traditional responsible businesses because they:

- Meet comprehensive and transparent social and environmental performance standards
- Meet higher legal accountability standards
- Build business constituency for good business[50]

Launched in 2006, there are now over two hundred B corporations. Most are companies you've never heard of. The main exception to that is Seventh Generation, one of the eighty-one founding members.

B corporations are not just about certification, however. They are about creating a new economic sector that takes social and environmental issues into account. Legal implications include preferential tax treatment and recognition by states. In October 2010, Maryland became the first state to enable companies to incorporate as "benefit corporations," for-profit companies that are required to benefit the public in some way other than profit.[51] This protects business owners from shareholder lawsuits if they make a decision that puts the environment or the community ahead of generating profits. B corporations retain their values and mission even if the company is sold, because by law it becomes a wholly owned subsidiary and cannot be transformed into a corporate division of the larger acquiring corporation. This allows the company to maintain control over its policies and practices and retain its B Corp status, as long as it is recertified every two years.[52]

Given the entrenched belief in the market, this is the closest thing I've seen to combating its inherent tendency to put profits before people and the planet.

The Rise of the Citizen-Consumer

Words change their meaning. Think about the word "friend." What does that really mean today? If you "friend" me on Facebook, are you really a friend or just a "Facebook friend." Is friend a noun or a verb or both? Do people have to meet face-to-face to be friends? Is time a factor? However you answer these questions, it is certain that your definition of "friend" is different from how it was defined fifty years ago.

Two words specifically related to our discussion are morphing considerably in their connotations: citizen and consumer. Rather than becoming more fully defined individually, they have given rise to an unexpected hybrid: the citizen-consumer. "The hybrid concept implies a social practice—'voting with your dollar'—that can satisfy competing ideologies of consumerism (an idea rooted in individual self-interest) and citizenship (an ideal rooted in collective responsibility to a social and ecological commons)."[53] This convergence of philosophies suggests that we can express our civic concerns and practice our politics through the purchases that we make.

Purchasing with purpose is not new. The grape boycott of the 1960s and the lettuce boycott of the 1970s come to mind as obvious examples of expressing one's politics. Boycotting manufacturers that use sweatshop labor—think Nike or a tearful Kathy Lee Gifford—is more recent. Today, however, boycotting—not buying—has increasingly been replaced with what is called "buycotting"—buying (usually much more pricey stuff) with a political motivation. Also known as ethical consumerism, critical consumption, and moral economics, among other things, buycotting has the advantage over boycotting of being exceedingly positive and easily practiced. It is not just for the activist but for everyone.

We are demonstrating our politics in the marketplace in part because we have become less civic in the traditional sense—that is, protesting in the streets, voting in elections, or working on local community boards. As a culture, we are "bowling alone" according to the Harvard sociologist Robert Putnam, who famously decried the disintegration of family, community, and our democratic structure because we are more isolated, with far less social capital, than preceding generations.[54] At the same time, perceptions of shopping have changed vis-à-vis politics. Buycotters will pay a premium price for goods because of the cause attached. "Proponents of buycotting see these premiums as pure political expression: citizens' parting with money to refine the world. Some even argue that cash-voting goes further than ballot-casting: we buy, and thereby incentivize producers, every day; but we vote far less often."[55] Shopping is presented as a more efficient, and more persistent, form of political statement—an idea that ties in nicely with neoliberalism.

Cultural critics have traditionally seen consumer culture—a world of buying stuff, where individual satisfaction is optimized—as subordinate to political engagement—putting the needs of the whole, the commons, over the needs of the individual. Consumer selfishness and political selflessness are perceived here as conflicting.[56] According to the sociologist Michael Schudson, "The inferiority of consumer behavior seems to be either that consuming is self-centered whereas political behavior is public-regarding or public oriented, or that consuming, whatever its motives, distracts people from their civic obligations. . . . It is high time to put both of these notions in the trash rather than the recycling bin."[57] Schudson claims, rather, that consumer choice is political (boycotting or purchasing fair trade or environmental products) and politics are very much like the consumer marketplace, because people vote for their personal self-interest. He goes on to suggest that politics is messy—sitting in endlessly boring meetings, debating with people about putting up a much-needed traffic light, for example—while shopping is, well, fun. He, and others, have advocated for making politics more satisfying by making it more like the consumer experience, make it sexy and appealing and a source of pleasure. The historian Lawrence B. Glickman agrees. Writing about "boycott mania," he notes:

> The fact that so many Americans are not only ardent consumers but avid consumer activists suggests that they see consumption not only as a private pleasure but as a public good. At a time when cynicism about the political process is at an all-time high—not least because politics has itself become increasingly commercial—the enduring appeal of consumer activism is that it promises citizens, in their capacity as shoppers, a kind of power and responsibility that seem largely unavailable through conventional politics.[58]

I have fundamental issues with this thinking, not least because research hasn't determined the underlying reasons why consumers make the purchases that they do. Much of the research on why people buy cause-based products uses surveys, a method that does not allow for understanding the cause-and-effect relationship between CRM and its effect on the purchase decision. Alternatively, research has not accounted for brand preferences and already established purchase intentions as part of the decision process.[59] So, for example, if you buy the romaine lettuce in your supermarket and it has a pink ribbon on it, did you purchase it to support breast cancer or because you couldn't buy the brand you like without the ribbon? Do people buy hybrid cars because they are environmentally conscious or because of the status a Toyota Prius—the top-selling hybrid—confers?[60] Or, going back to the Dawn example, is it because consumers think they are being civically minded, when in fact they are simply buying a consumer product and contributing to the corporate bottom line? This final point concurs with the conclusions of the researchers who discovered the spillover effect. "Our results suggest that actions of CM [cause-marketing] firms should be looked on with some skepticism by consumers and government officials—while the firms may be helping with charitable causes, they are also using CM to increase their own prices and profits," they say.[61] And this was written by two business professors, certainly a group not known for being anti-corporate!

The sociologist Josée Johnston put the citizen-consumer hybrid to the test using Whole Foods Market (WFM) as a case study. As you likely know, WFM is the world's largest purveyor of natural foods. It promotes its environmentally friendly stance throughout its stores and in its marketing materials, which use the tagline "Whole, Foods, Whole People, Whole Planet." In addition, 5 percent of after-tax profits are donated to charity, and caps are placed on executive salaries. Through numerous store visits and analysis of marketing materials, Johnston examined how products were physically positioned in the store, as well as the marketing language used to entice consumers to buy. The overall message being presented is one of health and happiness on a personal level, while contributing to sustainability and social justice for the wider society. While this is a nice sentiment, it does not fully reflect reality. First, this message is pitched to the affluent, conscientious "lifestyles of health and sustainability" (LOHAS) demographic. Whole Foods Market's upscale operation is sometimes derisively dubbed "Whole Paycheck." The prices in WFM stores exclude many who might like to take advantage of the healthy alternatives they have to offer. Second, the marketing is presented in such a way as to "maximize consumer pleasure and alleviate guilt of mass-market consumerism." This obscures the inherent contradictions of ethical consumerism, a point addressed more fully below. Third, by making citizenship part of consumption, citizenship becomes voluntary. Traditionally, we would think of our citizenship responsibilities as obligatory, but ethical consumption reframes them as something we can choose whether or not to participate in. Fourth, while the WFM store as a brand and everything in it are presented as being politically correct, that is not true. Many products are not organic and may even have been flown in from around the world—Chilean sea bass being one example. Finally, in the end, WFM marketing is more about the individual's health (framed as a civic action) than it is about social justice or sustainability for the planet. "Rather than meeting the requirements of consumerism and citizenship equally, the case of WFM suggests that the citizen-consumer hybrid provides superficial attention to citizenship goals in order to serve three consumerist interests better: consumer choice, status distinction, and ecological cornucopianism," Johnston concludes.[62]

While Schudson suggested we should be making politics more appealing, what has happened instead is that politics has become immersed in the market—almost completely undifferentiated from it. Simply being socially minded and environmentally conscious without acting on those impulses has become the norm. Margee Hume provides a compelling analysis of how Gen Y expresses sincere concern about the environment, but that concern is rarely translated into actions—even very simple things are left undone, never mind grand political actions. Hume specifically looked at environmental issues to understand this cohort's level of compassion: few recycled or used environmentally friendly transportation or had water-saving devices or grew any of their own food. Worse was that all the candidates studied had more than four electronic devices, which were updated regularly, with the older versions simply thrown away.

You can hardly blame them. More than any other cohort, Gen Y was raised immersed in the culture of marketing and media. Ease and immediate gratification are practically part of their DNA. This is not to say that they are not compassionate. It's that they don't know how to express that compassion—except, perhaps, through the market. Hume's prescription to correcting this group's lack of sustainable initiatives is of the "if you can't beat them, join them" variety. She suggests that sustainability be marketed like other consumer products:

> The strategies and social change impetus must show how easy, fashionable and "cool" it is to create a sustainable world. . . . Messages disseminated to capture Generation Y's attention must appeal to their self-interests and idealism. . . . Social change campaigns need to [show how] . . . poor practices and excessive consumption will damage the world and its people. This group needs to be informed that . . . sustainable practice is required [of them], with sustainable practice designed and articulated as simply and conveniently as possible. This group will not seek out change if it is not cost-effective, convenient and self-serving.[63]

Could the articulation of consumer language applied to politics be any more enmeshed? So much so that doing good has to be "cool" and "convenient" and "cost-effective"?

In sum, what passes for politics is decidedly passive. In the supermarket, it is about allowing the producer to decide what charities you can or cannot support. Online, politics amounts to little more than the click of a button. Turning caring for the whole into buying for the individual depoliticizes issues—the topic tackled at the beginning of this chapter. "Is it a sign of how corroded citizenship has become that shopping is the closest many of us are willing to come to worrying about labor laws, trade agreements, agriculture policy—about good old-fashioned politics?" Anand Giridharadas asks.[64] Unfortunately, the answer is yes. Thinking of ourselves as citizen-consumers (and shouldn't it really be consumer-citizens, to put the emphasis where it belongs?), and never as participants in a democracy, traps us in the struggle of one versus many. Nothing has demonstrated this more clearly than the fight over universal health care. In any other industrialized nation on the planet, health care is a given. People should not have to die because they cannot afford to see a doctor. But so many Americans are so self-absorbed that they can't see that taking care of their neighbors *is* taking care of themselves, because long-term if this problem isn't fixed, it will affect us all.

This concept of the citizen-consumer is a loaded one, and one that needs to be parsed and examined thoughtfully, not accepted blindly. My thinking is more in line with that of the feminist philosopher Kate Soper, who believes that philanthropic consumption should be an entry point to politics and not the political endgame.[65] Participating in boycotts—and now buycotts—is a good first step. They serve to call attention to public issues and raise funds. But, as Glickman notes, boycotts have not led to social change, and to my mind buycotts, by and large, lead to more promotion. However, this is not to say that consumer activism beyond boycotts can't make a difference; it obviously can. In the 1960s, Ralph Nader took on corporate capitalism and forced automobile manufacturers to make safer cars, and in 1995, Greenpeace famously stopped Shell Oil from sinking a storage platform in the North Sea, the "Brent Spar" incident. But this was not buying. It was grassroots activism used to push the government and corporations to protect the public safety.

I don't want to condemn any action that helps, even in some small way. Raising money to help alleviate suffering and providing advice for improving the environment are laudable goals. Moreover, cause-related marketers will argue that they are not trying to save the world. They are trying to increase awareness, generate some funding, and perhaps drive volunteerism. Fair enough. However, we must not let short-term market solutions depoliticize issues by putting a pleasant face on complex problems requiring long-term responses. Consumption is not a new form of citizenship, and not every problem can be solved by a trip to the mall. The alternative is also true. "I don't pretend that not buying much (or not driving much, or not having kids) is a powerful political act, or that it's deeply revolutionary," Derrick Jensen says. "It's not. Personal change doesn't equal social change."[66]

Moreover, while I don't believe we can make politics "fun" (except for happy, Rachel Maddow-y policy wonks who love that sort of thing), I believe we can appeal to people's own self-interest. Certainly, in this time of need, any means for increasing happiness that doesn't cost anything is a godsend. Increasingly, we are seeing research attesting to the benefits of volunteering. It's good for your health; it will improve your job prospects; and it has been proven to increase happiness. The PR message about this has gotten out, but the marketing effort behind it has not. Here's an idea: instead of motivating people to march in the streets for a dollar a mile, the goal should be to sign their friends up to commit to a certain number of hours of volunteering for each mile walked. Imagine that: thousands of people spending their time to improve the world—and they get happier and healthier to boot.

Someone recently said to me, "There is a difference between social action and social justice," and I believe that that's the real point here. Yes, we as individuals should do what we can to make the world a better place. Recycle, buy organic, volunteer, and vote. That's social action, and these things can be done within the marketplace construct.

Social justice is much bigger than that, and it can only be achieved when we think beyond ourselves. Social justice involves big issues like the environment, health care, and education. It leads us to ask bigger questions, such as: What ingredients or chemicals are in the products we buy and are they contributing to illness in us or our children or the planet? Could we find a way to live without cars and create more open spaces? And was anyone's life made worse so that I could have this probably unnecessary consumer product?

These are not easy questions, and they don't have easy answers. But they deserve our consideration. If we have been so indoctrinated by the market that we can't resolve them for our neighbors' sake, let's at least think about reinventing the world for the sake of our children and our children's children.

5

Shopping Is Not Philanthropy. Period.

When I was growing up in the 1960s and 1970s, I'd visit my Great Aunt Rose on the upper west side of Manhattan. She was your typical New York grandmotherly type—she cooked five different meals when my family came over so that everyone would have their favorite food. She constantly fawned over my sisters and me, saying, "I don't understand why there isn't a line of men outside your door!" And she always slipped a little cash or a check into your pocket before you walked out the door. There was one way in which Aunt Rose was very atypical: in the foyer of her one-bedroom apartment sat—without fail—a crate containing Mountain Valley Spring Water. She had those huge green glass bottles delivered to her apartment (and returned to the company for refilling) month after month, year after year. We all thought it was ridiculous—paying for water, come on!—and this little quirk became a running (though loving) joke among the relatives.

The joke, of course, turned out to be on us—the bottled water industry became a $5 billion annual business in the United States alone. And Aunt Rose lived to be 102, although I don't think it was just because of the water.

There's a big difference, though, between how Rose bought water and the industry as we know it today. First, drinking bottled water has become commonplace, if not "common sense." This is so even while there is no research to support that bottled water is better for you, and in many cases tap water is the superior alternative. Second, there has been a proliferation of providers from Coca Cola to the Kabbalah Centre offering varieties from spring water to flavored water, from flat to·fizzy. All of these players have contributed to this category quadrupling in the past twenty years. In 2008, Americans consumed 50 billion bottles of water, which now costs more than gasoline, is sourced from aquifers that may be halfway around the world, and is mostly packaged in petroleum-based plastic. To cite just one example, half a pound of greenhouse gas is produced for every one-liter bottle of the most popular imported water brand, Fiji.[1]

But even for the most successful products, eventually the tide will turn and sales will begin to slow. The water industry faced its first sales declines in 2008, with U.S. consumption down by one hundred million bottles and $200 million.[2] This was in part caused by the recession and in part due to increased awareness of the destructive practices associated with this now commodified product. In response, two strategies emerged—both cause-related. One is to make the bottle "better." Coca-Cola, for instance, has created a PlantBottle that is 70 percent petroleum-based and 30 percent made from sugarcane (only available in the West, according to the label, which I found confusing because I wasn't sure if it meant the western·United States or the Western world),[3] and Naya, a new brand on the market, claims that it uses only 100 percent recycled bottles. The alternative strategy connects bottled water purchases to a cause—most often that of providing water to so-called Third World countries. While there are several companies that implement this tactic, one that may come to many people's minds is Ethos Water, acquired by Starbucks in 2005 and distributed through its many outlets.[4] If you go to the Ethos Water web site, the opening splash page states: "Our mission is helping children get clean water," which refers to donations of 5 cents in the United States and 10 cents in Canada from the sale of each bottle going to water projects in East African and Indian communities that grow coffee and tea. The site explains that the company is committed to raising $10 million, initially with the expectation that this would be fully realized by 2010. This date has had to be extended, because sales dropped with the recession, and Ethos has only distributed $6.2 million thus far. There has been considerable controversy over this brand, because the label misled consumers to believe that Ethos was a charity and not a consumer product. The label in the United States (but not Canada) was redesigned to reflect that the purchase triggers a 5 cent donation (not a $1.80 one, the entire purchase price). Given the redesign—or should we say the truth—you have to wonder whether that revised consumer knowledge contributed to the decline in sales. Moreover, if the goal of the company is to raise $10 million, will it put itself out of business once that goal is achieved? It doesn't say so in Ethos's materials, but I tend to doubt it.

Both of these strategies—appearing environmentally correct and raising money for charity—make perfect sense from a business perspective. From a social perspective, however, they miss the mark. That's because cause marketing isn't about marketing causes. It is about attaching a cause to a consumer product for the purpose of creating profits for the manufacturer. What happens to the cause is secondary, except in terms of what it can do to further the goals of the corporation. This occurs because most managers and executives have been trained and are "bonused" to be concerned about the next quarterly financial statement. This myopic perspective hinders them from thinking about the consequences of their actions beyond the short term and their own four walls. This remains the driving force behind business, whether the followers of Milton Friedman are willing to admit it or not.[5] It was also evident to me based on conversations I had with social innovation practitioners—their clients really want to implement these strategies, but when push comes to shove they don't have the time or the inclination to create the significant changes needed. Some companies have, but they are in the minority. The Dow Chemical Company, for example, "incorporated sustainability objectives into compensation models, reviews, and other management processes, including a requirement that all newly promoted business unit managers review their units' sustainability plans with senior management within 90 days,"[6] a good example of social innovation and not simply window dressing.

If water companies were really concerned about water and the environment, they would stop putting it in bottles. Given the recent hit to corporate pocketbooks, people are increasingly realizing this. The first bottle backlash occurred in 2007, when upscale San Francisco restaurants stopped offering bottled water, providing filtered tap water instead. The same year, news stories "outed" Pepsi's Aquafina and Coke's Dasani bottled waters as being filtered tap water—even though the labels, particularly Aquafina's snow-capped mountains, suggest it is more naturally sourced. By 2008, consumers were implementing alternatives to commercially packaged bottled water, such as employing reusable plastic bottles, switching to tap water, or simply eliminating this item from the family budget to reduce household spending. But this downward trend isn't stopping this product category from expanding.

According to the marketing research company Packaged Facts, "the slowdown in bottled water sales will continue, even as bottled water marketers are attempting to make their products more ethically correct and their packaging more environmentally friendly . . . some [new] marketers are . . . positioning their bottled water brands on the very basis of ethics."[7]

Positioning (that is creating an identity for a brand in the mind of the consumer) as ethical and environmentally friendly isn't actually being ethical or good for the planet. Instead of looking at pictures of lush, verdant landscapes and faraway natural springs on the labels of plastic water bottles, we should be addressing the questions these products generate by their mere existence. Wouldn't we all be better off just not using bottles to begin with? Wouldn't water from the tap save us money, improve our health, and be carbon-neutral? And, with all the money we save, couldn't we send, say, half to countries that need to improve their water systems, particularly in light of the information that it is estimated that by 2030, two-thirds of the world will be without potable drinking water?

As long as we continue to address problems from a consumer mind-set, we'll never begin to ask these questions, because marketing is designed to frame the answers through a narrative of fulfilling personal, individual beliefs about happiness through consumption—an idea that is at odds with being magnanimous and sustaining resources. In chapter 4, we examined why we have been led to think that the market is an acceptable mechanism for solving social issues. This chapter looks at why the consumer marketplace is not, and really never could be, a means to improve our lives on the planet.

CONSUMER BEHAVIOR IS ABOUT INDIVIDUAL NEEDS, NOT SOCIAL GOODS

When we act as consumers, we are not looking to right the world's wrongs. We are looking to fulfill our personal needs. Remember, this is why marketers are connecting causes to products in the first place; they want us to buy more stuff. The way that many of them do this today is by providing charitable meaning to a product through branding—Dove soap is about self-esteem, Whole Foods is about fair trade—and we want those attributes and beliefs to rub off on us.

Buying a product is very often a split-second decision, where we make choices for reasons we aren't even aware of. And, though we might not be conscious of it, consumer behavior has recognized steps—ones that do not inherently include stopping to think about saving the world along the way.

This is how it works: When we decide to buy a product, the first step in the process is realizing that we need something, that is, our current state of being is not what we would like it to be—I'm thirsty and I want a drink; I need to get to work every day and public transportation can't get me there. Once we become aware of this, we begin to look for products that will fulfill our recognized need. Before we purchase the product, however, we might have to find out some information about it. Applying this to the car example, you would search out information by asking your friends what they like about their cars, going online for prices and safety ratings, and ultimately taking a test drive. Once you've looked at all the different makes and models, you need to evaluate your alternatives—one is a little more expensive, but it gets better gas mileage; another is a bit sportier and comes with the GPS system already installed. You make your decision, you purchase the car and, hopefully (from the marketer's perspective), you then go out and tell everyone how much you love your car. In sum, then, the consumer decision-making process is about recognizing a need, gathering information about products to fulfill that need, evaluating alternative options, purchasing the item, and finally any post-purchase behavior, such as telling friends or blogging that you hate it.

Now, let's apply that model to a recent cause campaign.

In the summer of 2010, McDonald's ran a campaign for its Happy Meals with the tagline "The simply joy of helping." The commercial focused on a number of really cute kids laughing and playing and looking for "hope" in Happy Meal boxes. One after another they said, "I can't find it, I can't find it." The voiceover (in a child's voice) says, "You can't see it there [visual of the box], but you can see it here [visual of a Ronald McDonald house] because every time you get a Happy Meal or a Mighty Kids Meal some of the money goes to Ronald McDonald House Charities to help lots of kids and families." The related print ads were targeted at moms, because Happy Meal consumers are, of course, too young to read. Under the headline "Mommyisms: insights from mom to mom," the ad shows a big picture of a woman holding her daughter, who is holding a Happy Meal. (Smaller pictures show the product, a Ronald McDonald House and presumably a sick child with his father.) The copy reads in part: "The Happy Meal she loves now helps families be closer to the ones they love. And that makes every trip to McDonald's® even more special for me." Teeny-tiny type running up the side of the page adds: "McDonald's donates 1¢ per Happy Meal sold, at participating McDonald's® beginning June 25th."

So where does this promotion fit into the decision-making process? Advertising comes into play during the information-gathering step and becomes a factor when we begin to evaluate alternatives. Where should we go eat today—Burger King, which is promoting a movie with its kid's meal, or McDonald's, because its Happy Meal gives money to charity? Mothers can use the contribution to the Ronald McDonald Charities as justification for purchasing the Happy Meal. However, Mom is not the only person involved in this purchase decision. Kids have also seen the cause message and nag their mothers to take them to McDonald's—not just because of the food but also because they can help other less fortunate children, and anyone with kids knows they like to be "little helpers." And children today influence more than 70 percent of food and beverage purchase decisions, so it's not surprising that they are integral to this campaign.

But—and this is the key issue—*what don't we think about* when we are thinking happy thoughts about Happy Meals? First, we are unlikely to focus on the lack of nutritional value of these products. While much has been made of this in the press, and McDonald's has countered with creating "healthier" alternatives, the reality is that some of us (or more likely a lot of us, based on the numbers) give in to the ease of fast food, even if our kids opt for eating the French fries over the sliced apple now included with all Happy Meals. We are not thinking of the social (and personal) good of healthy eating; rather, we are contributing to the poor health of our children. Now, certainly, McDonald's alone cannot be blamed for the rising obesity rate among America's youngsters. However, it is a contributor, not only because of the food but because of the image portrayed in McDonald's commercials—a world where kids can eat their product and still maintain a healthy weight. Second, we don't stop to ask how much money is going to the Ronald McDonald House. If you knew only a penny was going to charity, would that be enough to motivate you to change your purchase decision? McDonald's obviously doesn't think so. After all, the commercial doesn't scream, "One penny for charity, one penny for charity." Finally, what about the (usually) plastic toy in the Happy Meal? This package of food for kids is all about making mealtime fun. A crucial part of that is the toy. When we are focused on fun (because by the time we've purchased the product, we've forgotten about the charity and how many calories we're putting on our hips), do we ask ourselves how long before the plastic toy ends up in the garbage and then later how long it will live in the landfill?[8]

Because cause campaigns have become so ubiquitous, multiply this experience by millions of purchases of everything from plastic toys to gas-guzzling cars to pollution-causing shampoos, detergents, and dish-washing liquids. When shopping, a few people might think: "I'll buy a Ford because it supports breast cancer research," or, far more likely, "I'll buy this shampoo because it's good for the environment." The cause becomes one of a set of elements that are assessed along with the color of the car or the anti-frizz factor in the shampoo. And, just as every little bit helps when it comes to the charity, every little bit hurts when we use charity as justification for buying products that may be harmful to ourselves or the planet. Because the marketing leads us to believe we are doing something good, we don't question whether or not we really are.

Let me be clear here: consumers—that is, you and me—are not dupes. While early communication theories suggested that the masses could be brainwashed by the media, more recent audience-reception theories suggest otherwise. The media, while a powerful influence, are not the only source of information in our lives. Moreover, there is simply no amount of marketing that will get you to buy a product that doesn't perform the way it is supposed to. This does not negate the fact that *marketing does work*. Otherwise, why would American marketers spend more than $180 billion a year on it? It works on us as individuals because companies have spent hundreds of millions of dollars in research to understand how and why we use the products we do. This is a psychological process meant to pinpoint individuals' deepest wants and needs and desires. We would be foolish to underestimate the impact of this industry.

BUYING, WALKING, OR RUNNING FOR CHARITY IS MORAL ROBBERY

One of the reasons why I was drawn to corporate social responsibility as a topic of study is that I was trying to understand why I had such an issue with combining shopping with monetary donations. When I looked at the definition of philanthropy, I began to realize the answer. According to dictionary.com, philanthropy is the "altruistic concern for human welfare and advancement, usually manifested by donations of money, property, or work," and the *Oxford English Dictionary*'s definition 1a is: "Love of mankind; the disposition or active effort to promote the happiness and well-being of others." Two important aspects of philanthropy are lost in these transactions tied to consumer purchases: heartfelt concern for others and intentional work to improve the human condition. Both of these actions have to do with our living our ethics, perhaps even expressing our spiritual nature. Giving money is not philanthropy without the accompanying acts of kindness and justice, which, one hopes, will build character, increase compassion for others, and develop a sense of morality.

Shopping to trigger charity, however, both negates our ability to strengthen our moral core and motivates us away from philanthropic acts. "Spend and send"—spend money, send it to charity—is easy; it may in fact be *too* easy. When writing a check, you decide who it should go to and why you care enough to give your hard-earned money to that cause. When you volunteer, you give of yourself while interacting with others to make the world a better place. Shopping not only eliminates these moral acts, it also gives us the false sense that we've already done our good deed, our mitzvah. Since when did buying green products or a pink blender or a can of Coke do any of those? Simply buying a product that you would have bought anyway doesn't lead you to any type of moral decision. Of course, you might choose a socially responsible product over one that has a questionable reputation, but there is no sacrifice or effort associated with having done so.

So, too, the proliferation of cause-related marketing "may diminish the compunction of individuals to act magnanimously toward others without expectations of return."[9] If time and time again, when you give you get, it becomes ever more difficult to dissociate the one from the other. Think of Pavlov's dogs: every time the bell rang, they expected food—bell-food, bell-food. Even when the food was not there, the dogs continued to salivate with the expectation that food was coming. If every time we give, we expect to get something in return, we'll be disappointed when it doesn't happen, which is likely to lead to decreased giving. We become prone to giving only where it makes us feel good—thus eliminating any compunction toward self-sacrifice. Morality derives from a sense of duty, according to Immanuel Kant. What duty is there in buying an overpriced baby stroller or a Tory Birch puffer jacket?

Finally, corporate philanthropy allows us to distance ourselves from the beneficiaries of our "largesse." Under the glaring lights of a supermarket brimming with 30,000 products or more, it is easy to avoid thinking about hunger and want and homelessness.

Ease and detachment not only distinguish the act of purchasing, but also the marketing associated with consumer products. For example, let's examine a Starbucks (RED) commercial. The ad is in red and white type (either white on red or red on white). No pictures of dying people in Africa, no baristas, just the words

What (if)
We're not separated from everyone else
But connected?
What (if) what we do to another, we do to ourselves?
What (if) when we help someone else, we help ourselves?
What (if) when we save someone else's life, we save our own?
What (if) just part of our purpose here, is not me, but we?
Should we give it a try?
It doesn't take a grand gesture.
It's actually a lot EASIER than you think.
Starbucks is partnering with (RED), and during this holiday season,
    five cents from every (STARBUCKS) exclusive DRINK you buy will help
    save lives in Africa.
Not sure if you noticed, but there are a LOT of Starbucks out there.
It'll add up.
Lots of lives can be saved.
You & Starbucks.
It's BIGGER than coffee.[10]

The copy is about making charity easy. It also makes the consumer feel important ("It's BIGGER than coffee"), implying that the purchase is not just about having an expensive hot drink but also about having a larger social impact. Moreover, the language is pretty blatantly religious—"when we help someone else, we help ourselves," "our purpose"—these are ideas that we readily associate with scripture, but here have been used to connect morality to consumption. The concern with this, as Angela Eikenberry suggests, is "in the absence of people's active and effortful moral engagement, corporations and their profit-driven needs set the tone for acceptable ways of being philanthropic. As a result, people's genuine benevolent sentiments are co-opted for profit, and their care is reduced to a market transaction."[11]

Focusing attention on the doer instead of the receiver doesn't apply only to Starbucks purchases. As noted in chapter 1, Livestrong bracelets do the same thing. Another example is the way in which walkathons and similar athletic events are promoted. While not specifically sales transactions (though they are sponsored), and raising money is certainly a focus, improving the health and athleticism of the participant is equally in evidence in these campaigns. In their study of the Avon Walk, Heidi Edwards and Peggy Kreshel found the participants walked for personal needs: for some, it was to help fight the disease because it affected themselves or a loved one, but for just as many it was a way to build self-esteem by adopting a healthier lifestyle.[12] Taking this idea further is the Leukemia & Lymphoma Society's Team in Training, the largest charity-based training program. If you go to the website (http://www.teamintraining.org), you see people in running gear and swimming attire. The copy says, in part, "You'll get more help than with other charities, gyms, online training programs or sports clubs. . . . We set your training regimen. We advise you on nutrition and injury prevention. We hold weekly team workouts to encourage one another and stay on track." A coach for endurance athletes is quoted as stating that one of the reasons why this trend has gotten so popular is because "gym culture's gotten boring."[13] Another reason is that women see working out as an indulgence and connecting physical training to charity gives them license to take the time for themselves. Either way, the time and effort becomes about the "athlete," not the affected.[14]

The recent launch of Donna Karan's fragrance pureDKNY embodies these ideas of consumer over charity. The ad takes up two pages, with one side being the typical beautiful blonde woman in a white dress. The copy reads "a drop of vanilla sourced from Africa, a drop of goodwill. pureDKNY supports local communities by taking small steps to help make a difference. pure and simple." When you turn the page, the ad continues on the back. It has four flaps that can be pulled open. They read: pure responsibility, pure difference, pure gift, and pure scent. Pure responsibility explains that the packaging is environmentally friendly; pure difference ambiguously explains that DKNY is partnering with CARE to empower women (showing pictures of women from Africa); pure gift tells purchasers that they will get a $25 gift card with any purchase when they buy at Nordstrom, and a gift from *Real Simple* magazine; and pure scent allows you to sample the fragrance and see the pricing. Thus, you've spent a lot of money in a very upscale store to send some small percentage to charity and you get two gifts to boot. Sounds decidedly selfless and character strengthening, no?

Whether consumption philanthropy strengthens moral character or not, proponents have espoused the notion that cause marketing is beneficial because it makes donating money easier. This might have been true at one point, but as causes have become more married to products, and as companies need to find ways to create community with consumers, companies are asking for more and more action on the part of customers. Known as "two-stage giving programs," these campaigns ask consumers to buy a product and then perform an additional act. It is this second action that triggers the donation. Some examples include

- Yoplait Save Lids to Save Lives—For every lid that consumers send in, Yoplait donates 10 cents to Susan G. Komen. This entails buying the product, eating the yogurt, cleaning the lids, putting them in an envelope with a stamp, and sending them back to the company.

- Dawn dishwashing liquid—purchase the product and $1 goes to help wildlife, but only after you input a code online.

- Any of the walk-, bike-, or race-a-thons—all of which require extensive hours of physical training, in addition to signing up friends and family to donate. This is particularly true of events like the Avon Walk, which requires at least $2,000 in fundraising per person. I'd also include Lee National Denim Day, which doesn't require athletic training but does ask participants to enlist others to donate money.

There are campaigns that do make giving easier. In Scandinavia, customers of the Danish retailer Coop can donate money to charity when they return their recyclable bottles. Instead of taking the cash back for themselves, they can push a button and their refund will be given to charity.[15] In the United States, Target's education campaign is a good example. In this case, when you use your Target credit card, 1 percent of the sale goes to a school you designate. You have to go online to do that, but it only has to be done once. However, Target's campaign is the exception. Most campaigns at minimum ask for a purchase, and now companies are asking for more than that—not because it will engender charity, but because it requires the consumer to be more fully engaged with a product.

The reality is that these things are more difficult than sitting down and writing a check, and they are not the most effective ways to raise funds. The best way to give to a cause, according to Ken Berger of Charity Navigator, is to donate directly to the charity.[16] That way you know that every dollar (or close to it) is going to the cause. And, now with online checking and the ease of automatic payments, we can set up a payment schedule so that our favorite charity receives money from us on a regular basis. Continuous support and ensured cash flow are the argument for campaigns like (RED). With that argument eliminated, there is little need to purchase coffee in paper cups, electronics that will be out of date in a year, and clothing that will be given away with the change in the season.

While some (but as already noted, not all) of these campaigns help causes by providing much-needed funding, they come with strings attached: they are not the most efficient, they focus on the giver and not the receiver, and they separate us from opportunities to be truly compassionate, caring, and philanthropic.

SUSTAINABLE CONSUMPTION IS AN OXYMORON

The hypocrisy of sustainable consumption is stunning, and stunningly in evidence. My favorite example of this is from *O, The Oprah Magazine*. Every month, Oprah creates her "O List" of favorite things for her readers to buy. In April 2009, the magazine had the "Green O List," which contained nine "environmentally correct" consumer products. These included sunglasses made from recycled plastic, a Vizio flat-screen TV (which uses less energy than traditional LCDs), and $325 pillows made from organic cotton and printed with azo-free dyes that don't release carcinogens. As the piece proclaimed, "Think of them as a politically correct sofa makeover."[17] The only "environmentally correct" item on the list was arguably a biodegradable container with soil and seeds for growing your own herbs.

Our inability to rein in consumer purchases has become a joke. "I buy too much stuff," no less than Jeff Hollender, the founder of Seventh Generation and occupier of a 5,000-square-foot house (!), is quoted as saying. "A friend of mine challenged me to go for 30 days without buying anything new. I said, 'That's a great challenge, I'll take you on. But I'm going to start next month, because the new MacBook Air is coming out.' Then next month, for the iPhone, and I realized I just endlessly put off making the commitment because consumption had become such a part of my life."[18] It's only sad that this is no laughing matter.

Social critics have been writing about the environmental impacts of the consumer culture for decades. Vance Packard, author of *The Hidden Persuaders* (1957), a seminal study of advertising, was writing about this over half a century ago. In another important book, *The Waste Makers* (1960), Packard pointed out the social, environmental, and economic degradation brought about by planned obsolescence. Following in Packard's analytical footsteps is Sut Jhally, professor of communication at the University of Massachusetts and executive direc-tor of the Media Education Foundation (MEF). Never one to mince words, Jhally writes: "Simply stated, our survival as a species is depen-dent upon minimizing the threat from advertising and the commer-cial culture that has spawned it." Writing from a Marxist perspective, Jhally explains that under industrialized capitalism, commodities have to be sold to perpetuate the economy. Once the problem of mass pro-duction was solved, the issue of selling had to be managed, which occurred through the medium of advertising. "Indeed there has never been a propaganda effort to match the effort of advertising in the 20th century," Jhally says. "More thought, effort, creativity, time, and attention to detail has gone into the selling of the immense collection of commodities than any other campaign in human history to change public consciousness." Moreover, our media industries exist as a delivery system for marketers; it's not about creating entertainment for us, but for aggregating eyeballs for advertisers.

But it's the message that is most telling: every society has its happiness story, the myth of how to achieve personal satisfaction. In consumer cul-tures, happiness is achieved through the consumption of objects provided by the marketplace. Unfortunately, the question that is not asked is, Is this true? Do objects make us happy? Most surveys from as far back as the 1940s tell us no. Rather, it is close personal relationships and connection to community that most contribute to that state of being, something the market cannot bestow.[19] "The marketplace cannot provide love, it cannot provide real friendships, it cannot provide sociability. It can provide other material things and services but they are not what makes us happy." And, this can't help but perpetuate itself: we look to the market to make us happy, it can't make us happy, so we buy more stuff to try to get happy—a perfect cycle of addiction. That addiction has led to a hole in the ozone layer, a radical depletion of the environment, and a fight for natural resources—a state that is likely to pit nation against nation, as the second Gulf War and its fight for oil readily attest.[20]

In the same way that the concepts of citizen and consumer are at odds, so, too, the ideas of sustainability and consumption do not mix. They are opposites—a yin to a yang. They cannot be combined, and wishing and hoping won't make it so, even when it's packaged as con-vincingly as it is with Whole Foods, or when electronics like the Kindle are promoted as environmentally friendly.

Tied into the hypocrisy of sustainable consumption is the situation in which the company is not only providing the solution, but also creating the problem, what Eikenberry calls "market blindness." Marketing is part and parcel of this because its function is to get you to look at what the company wants you to look at—our detergent gets your clothes cleaner—while minimizing or obscuring attributes that are less desirable—bleach is bad for the environment.

A recent example of this offense is Coca-Cola. In response to concerns about the use of plastic bottles and looking for a way to reduce costs, Coca-Cola has redesigned its bottle to be stackable. During transport this saves fuel, because it reduces the amount of air (and therefore weight) being shipped. Sounds great, right? Sure, it does. But it's still made out of plastic, and aluminum could be used, which is completely recyclable. Or we could go back to the water example at the beginning of the chapter. Pepsi introduced the Aquafina Eco-Fina bottle in 2009. This bottle contains 50 percent less plastic, eliminating 75 million pounds of plastic per year and 20 million pounds of cardboard, because this packaging is no longer needed in its 24-packs of water. If you go to Coke's Dasani web site (www.dasani.com), for example, a plant grows from the bottom of the page, which when fully formed has the Plant-Bottle coming out of the stem where a flower might be. This draws our attention to the environmental aspects of the packaging, while never addressing that one of the key reasons that people around the world are dying from lack of water is because the water is being stolen by industry.

In October 2009, Coca-Cola took out a one-page ad in the *New York Times* to promote what the company was doing to help Americans live more balanced lives. To that end, Coke was providing "knowledge" (calorie counts would be displayed in the front of the packaging), "portion-control options" (90-calorie cans), and a "school guideline" (removed full-calorie options from schools). The ad ends with the line: "We know there's more to be done. With each step, our goal is to help make everyone's lives a little happier." The ad then directs readers to www.livepositively.com. At first glance, the site seems to provide useful information on links labeled "Balanced Life" and "You & Your Family." Unfortunately, it's more about Coke products and Coke-sponsored Olympic athletes than about promoting a healthier lifestyle.[21]

Coca-Cola is not the only offender in this regard. Nestlé, maker of Pure Life water, asks consumers to go to its web site nestle-purelife.us to "get involved and receive money-saving coupons!" While there, you are asked to pledge that you will switch one sugary beverage a day for water, thus helping reduce obesity (again an individual solution). Nestlé also sponsors the Great American Cleanup, an environmental and community initiative of Keep America Beautiful, and its Eco-Shape Bottle uses 30 percent less plastic than other half-liter bottles. In short, Nestlé is a shining example of implementing almost every element of responsibility in a half-hearted way.

But plastic bottles are not the only area where this occurs. You might remember the example of Avon from chapter 1—a company that raises considerable funds for breast cancer yet the effects of its products have raised health concerns. I'd like to say that Avon is the exception, but unfortunately, it isn't. In 2009, Stacy Malkan, co-founder of the Campaign for Safe Cosmetics, looked at how young girls are indoctrinated to want an expanding array of cosmetic products from the time they are five or six years old, with products like the Hannah Montana Backstage Makeover Set and hair straighteners targeted at seven-year-olds, with the starting age in salons hovering around ten. With nail polish, makeup, and hair products comes corresponding exposure to toxic chemicals, a situation whose impact we can't completely calculate, though one that seems to be associated with the early onset of puberty. Because of chemical changes in the brain connected with puberty, girls lose out on a few additional years to master complex skills such as playing an instrument or learning a language. This is only the beginning. "Girls who enter puberty earlier are at higher risk for breast cancer and depression, and are more likely to engage in high-risk behaviors such as drinking and unprotected sex." One girl found that her beauty regimen contained more than one hundred chemicals, including a number of carcinogens and dozens of hormone-disrupting chemicals. Remember, we are not talking about grown women here, but young girls, whose bodies and brains are nowhere near fully formed.[22] We should not be so quick to congratulate the cosmetics companies for their support of women when they do so much damage to little girls.

But it doesn't stop there. Given the longevity of breast cancer causes, promoting "pink awareness" to girls is an obvious next step for cause-related marketers if they want to continue to grow. Since mature women have been dealing with this issue for decades now, the only place left to go is a younger target audience. Peggy Orenstein points to retail campaigns that "support the cause," like Save the Ta-Tas T-shirts and companies like Project Boobies and Save Second Base.[23] These irreverent, sexualized approaches to breast cancer have both questionable positive applications in terms of increasing awareness and fund-raising and decidedly negative effects in terms of setting women back about fifty years by reducing them to a body part, suggesting it is the most significant aspect of their being. What this makes abundantly clear is that what happens in marketing generally is beginning to happen here: as people have seen it, heard it, bought the T-shirt, the market has had to ratchet up the noise to get our attention. But to what end? As Orenstein notes, "the number who die has remained unchanged—hovering around 40,000—for more than a decade."

The primary form of corporate hypocrisy is what is called "greenwashing"—when corporations mislead consumers about how environmentally friendly they or their products are. However, while we know greenwashing exists, most of us are unaware of how pervasive it is. The Canadian company TerraChoice Environmental Marketing reported in 2009 that greenwashing was involved in 98 percent of the more than 2,200 green products reviewed, from children's toys and baby products to cosmetics and household cleaners. The abuses included:

- Highlighting environmental bona fides on one aspect of the product while downplaying a more serious concern
- No evidence of marketing claims to being "green"
- Using vague or misleading terms such as "all natural"
- Creating fake certifications or claiming certification when the product had never been assessed[24]

Marketers hawk us products based on their being sustainable, but there is often little evidence that they actually are. Moreover, there is little being done to rectify this deception. In 1998, the Federal Trade Commission (FTC) issued a "Green Guide," but over the past ten years, the FTC has reportedly taken legal action for violations against only three companies.[25] The agency began to revise its guidelines in 2008 and only completed a new draft version by October 2010. The new Green Marketing Guides make several suggestions for marketers, such as recommending that they avoid unqualified claims like "eco-friendly" and specify how a product is renewable. However, these are only recommendations. They are not law, and the FTC has limited ability to enforce them, except under section 5, which prohibits "unfair and deceptive practices," the same regulation used to regulate misleading advertising generally, such as overblown weight-loss claims. Web sites like green washingindex.com and Greenpeace's www.stopgreenwash.org do a better job of educating consumers.[26]

Green marketing—never mind greenwashing—is fundamentally flawed. We are asked to make behavioral changes, but these are still rooted in consumption, whether the product is environmentally friendly or not, and as we've just seen, usually they aren't. The idea of consumption reduction can't even be considered within this framework. As Ken Peattie and Sue Peattie explain, any gains achieved through innovation over the past twenty years have been offset by an increase in consumption: thus, for example, while organic food consumption is up, so is use of convenience meals, with their eco-unfriendly packaging. Homes may be more energy efficient, but energy usage is up because of the increased number of homes and home appliances. True sustainability requires (a) becoming more aware of the full life cycles of products (including their use and disposal), (b) meeting as many as possible of our needs and wants through "non-purchase-based behaviors," and (c) reducing consumption, not as a product benefit, but for the environment's sake.[27] I heartily agree these solutions would be a positive step. However, before they can occur, there has to be a fundamental shift in our thinking, a move away from the cornucopian notion that there is a never-ending basket of resources.

MARKETING FOR CHANGE

Not all marketing is tied to a product or has sales as its objective. Social marketing seeks to change negative social behaviors and maintain established positive habits. Change might be accepting a new behavior (e.g., wearing a helmet while bicycling), modifying a current behavior (e.g., eating more than five fruits and vegetables a day), or abandoning an old behavior (e.g., quitting smoking). Such marketing has been used for decades and has contributed to reducing cigarette smoking, encouraging seat-belt use, and designating a nondrinking driver if we go out for cocktails.

Alan Andreasen, professor of marketing at Georgetown University's McDonough School of Business and executive director of the Social Marketing Institute, points out that if social marketers are going to have a significant impact, they must understand how social problems arise. There is competition for attention and resources. Problems that rise to the top have been focused on through the process of agenda setting. In media, when we talk about agenda setting, we are talking about the idea that the media don't tell you what to think but do tell you what to think about. Whatever is on the front page of the morning newspaper will drive the conversation for the day. Social issues are also driven by agendas. These are the public agenda (what we believe is important as determined by public opinion polls), the media agenda, and the policy agenda (what politicians see as important). These three types of agendas influence one another. Where social marketing can have considerable impact is through campaigns that motivate media gatekeepers to want to promote action toward a solution by providing coverage of an issue or free media space to public service announcements.[28]

If the Internet has taught us anything, it is that we do not have to leave it up to politicians or marketers to drive the public agenda. Like the women who founded Mothers Against Drunk Driving (www .madd.org), communities can create their own organizations. They can help motivate policymakers to pay attention, and the latter can impose tariffs, increase or decrease taxes, and require labeling. They could, for example, ban the advertising and promotion of products that target children under 12.[29] Americans may have difficulty imagining this, but think of the effects a policy like that might have on education, family relationships, and obesity. Communities can also act as competitors against an initiative. "It may be that they oppose the initiative's goals, believe it is too high on the social agenda, think that other issues are more important, judge the proposed solution is impractical, believe the leaders of the initiative to be misguided or evil, or, in extreme cases, believe that the initiative or its objectives (e.g., "a woman's right to choose") are just plain bad for society."[30]

Social marketing has been effective in creating positive social changes. But, we have to be cognizant of the fact that these campaigns are not what we primarily see or the ones that are significantly funded. Their goal is to change behavior. Most campaigns exist to continue moving us in the direction in which we are already going. We might hope that the new ways of marketing will bring more people to care about good works, but given marketing's history, it is far more likely that these campaigns will simply give us one more reason to feel good about buying overpriced consumer goods. The ultimate consequence of merging profits and purpose is to further desensitize us to those less fortunate, while doing little to engage us in meaningful altruism. Shopping is not a virtuous act; by definition, it is a selfish one.

6

Can Companies Make a Difference?

Flying into Colorado, I kept wondering what to expect. I'd known about LOHAS (Lifestyles of Health and Sustainability) for a long time, but this was my first trip to Boulder for its annual gabfest.[1] Was this just another New Age movement? Did LOHASians walk the walk or just pay lip service to social innovation? After years of researching and analyzing all that business had been doing—much of it, unfortunately, ineffective and self-serving—I was beginning to lose hope. Happily and fairly quickly, my fears were assuaged. I began to see real innovation, real commitment. I even dared to feel a sense of optimism. The usual suspects were there—the "lifestyle media company" Gaiam, "super responsible" juice vendor Odwalla, and Seventh Generation—but so were Frito-Lay, General Mills, Coca-Cola, and S.C. Johnson. When major companies like these attend conferences like this, perhaps making the world a better place is no longer a business niche but a business necessity.

If LOHAS has been seen as a New Age movement, it's because many of the baby boomers who embraced Eastern philosophies and non-traditional metaphysics in the 1960s are now more concerned about health (they are aging) and sustainability (they are concerned about their children and grandchildren). Unlike the New Age expos I'd attended in my youth, however, this was no thinly disguised bazaar for healing stones and questionable potions; it was earnest, smart, and very much business. To be sure, there was a certain level of what we used to call the crunchy-granola crowd. But the bottom line was about how business can help the wider world, not about how individuals can develop themselves and then (perhaps) heal the world.

The full extent of this event's purposeful attitude was made obvious by the keynote speaker: the futurist and best-selling author Faith Popcorn, whose consultancy firm Brainreserve, she said in her presentation, works to "deliver future-focused Consumer Insight through the Trends that explain and predict consumer behavior." Popcorn is famous for, among other things, coining the term "cocooning" (snuggling at home in the 1980s, when we had no money), alerting McDonalds to be ready when the "smoking police" started looking for a new target, and recommending that Coca-Cola bottle water (okay, so she needs to repent for that one). And, when it comes to predicting trends, Popcorn has been spot-on, with the *LA Times, Fortune,* and the *Wall Street Journal* putting her accuracy rate at at least 90 percent. All this to say the woman knows what she's talking about.

The time for LOHAS is now, Popcorn told us. Several trends lead to this conclusion. Consumers are looking for transparently safe products; anxiety about the future leads them to embrace brands that project optimism; a questionable healthcare system has led them to look for ways to take personal responsibility for their well-being; our fast-paced lives lead us to want more clarity from product companies; and ways to interact with the natural world and our inner world are replacing mindless consumption. These consumer trends are interacting with broader social trends that have us moving from a focus on "Me" to a focus on "We." Because we've lost faith in cultural pillars—ethics, economics, and the environment—and have rejected excess (a sure sign of self-involvement), Popcorn explained, we have moved toward "communities of common interest" and seek spiritual purpose and an increased standard of ethics and compassion. All of this means that consumers want "brands that inspire, inform, elevate and connect."

Traditional LOHAS brands are becoming mainstream (Stonyfield Farms, WhiteWave Foods, Seventh Generation) and mainstream brands are implementing LOHAS-style ideals like Higher Purpose (Dove's Campaign for Real Beauty or fair trade products), green (Tom's of Maine or Visa Green card), transparency (Timberland's "nutritional label" on footwear), or community commitment (Campbell's urban renewal project for Camden, New Jersey, or Apple fixing Chicago's subway system). In sum, Popcorn predicts that every consumer is becoming a LOHAS consumer.[2]

Researchers from the Natural Marketing Institute (NMI), a research company that specializes in LOHAS trends, later presented statistics to support Popcorn's assertions. Major corporations have implemented sustainability initiatives, most notably:

- General Electric generated $18 billion in sales of its ecomagination products in 2010, invested $1.5 billion in cleaner R&D, and reduced greenhouse gas emissions by 30 percent. According to the *Harvard Business Review,* GE's ecomagination initiative allowed "CEO Jeff Immelt not just to reposition the company as an energy and environmental solutions provider but to build a green aura into the GE brand."[3]

- Bank of America has invested $10 billion in climate-change projects. In 2010, the Bank of America Tower in Manhattan became the first commercial skyscraper in the United States to achieve Leadership in Energy and Environmental Design (LEED) Platinum certification.

- Ford launched its Fusion hybrid, the most fuel-efficient U.S. midsize sedan, in 2009, and the hybrid electric Focus in 2011. The Ford Escape plug-in hybrid will be in car showrooms in 2012.

Moreover, some product categories like compact fluorescent light bulbs (CFLs), hybrid cars, and energy-efficient appliances can no longer be considered fringe, because more than 70 percent of the purchasers of these products are mainstream consumers; organic food and natural cleaning products are close behind, with nearly 60 percent of product purchases made by mainstream consumers.

The 80/20 rule of thumb in marketing is that 80 percent of sales come from 20 percent of customers. When it comes to sustainability, that number has now been turned on its head, according to NMI.[4] Since 80 percent of consumers now consider themselves more or less "green," manufacturers must take environmentalism into account. Looking more broadly at LOHAS, which includes health as well as sustainability, NMI segments the market into five groups, three of which sign on to LOHAS to some degree. At 19 percent of the market, true LOHASians care about the environment, personal health, and lifestyle, and are the heaviest purchasers of socially responsible products. "Naturalites," who resemble LOHASians attitudinally, especially as regards personal health, but are limited by income, make up 15 percent of the market. Trend-conscious, price-sensitive "drifters" looking for "easy green" constitute another 25 percent. This adds up to 59 percent of consumers who consciously purchase products that are good for themselves and the environment.

The Shelton Group, a marketing company specializing in sustainability, supported these findings. Based on survey data and focus groups, it, too, came to the conclusion that green has gone mainstream. Suzanne Shelton, president and CEO of the Shelton Group, presented two additional important insights. First, consumers know less about what constitutes green than most producers think (which leads me to question whether we really are green, or if we've simply deluded ourselves into thinking we are). For example, most consumers did not know whether a product might be organic but not sustainable, and most consumers think "all natural ingredients" or "100% natural" are the best labels indicating that a product is green. And, second, consumers are skeptical. They believe that claims exist to appeal to them and to improve the company's reputation. This last claim is something that came up again and again at LOHAS. While not particularly earth-shattering—you are probably skeptical about product claims—the fact that researchers are consistently coming up with this conclusion and putting it in front of marketers suggests that using unsubstantiated claims as a marketing tool is likely (hopefully?) on the wane.[5]

The next section looks at a few companies that are embracing social innovation to promote the values of sustainability, health, and social justice, a credo some people are now calling "philanthrocapitalism." Happily, because this trend is taking off, there are far too many to list them all here, and we'll have to limit ourselves to some of the most innovative. These fall into three types: companies created to make a profit, but more important, to make the world a better place; companies that embed responsibility throughout their organizations; and companies that are retrofitting as LOHASian.

First, however, I want to tell you about an inspiring morning at the LOHAS forum. The second day of the conference began with a boy named Alec Loorz. A few years earlier, at the age of twelve, he had seen Al Gore's documentary *An Inconvenient Truth* and felt moved to do something. He contacted Gore and asked if he could be a presenter for the Climate Project, the Powerpoint presentation derived from the film. Gore told him he was too young, but that didn't stop Alec. Instead, he started Kids vs. Global Warming (http://kids-vs-global-warming.com/ Home.html), a nonprofit that teaches young people what they can do to stop climate change. In 2008, Gore relented; Alec is now the young-est presenter for the Climate Project. He speaks at schools around the country and organized the iMatter March, a million-kid march to show concern about the planet, which was scheduled for Mother's Day 2011. The mission was revised to allow additional participation. In all, 150 marches, in thirty-three countries, had occurred by the fall of 2011. Watching Alec present at the LOHAS conference, I felt like running out and signing up everyone I knew to support him in his efforts. It was easy to be drawn in by his charisma, passion, and commitment. His concern was heartfelt in a way that we sometimes forget when we get older.

Alec was followed by Deborah Szekley, founder of Rancho La Puerta and Golden Door Spa, now in her late eighties, who spun a wonderful tale about her life as a spa owner, diplomat, and philanthropist, and the many lessons she had learned. Szekley did this by explaining how she manages her daybook. At the end of the week, she stops to assess how she spent her time—what was good, how time could be better spent, and what was a waste of time. She made the following recommendations for visual cues to see where your time goes: highlight in red what you did for your health, use green for what you did to encourage growth or what you did to challenge yourself, underline in blue those things you can delegate to others, and finally use your favorite color to highlight time spent with family, friends, and for fun. In this way we can come to make our time our own and put into balance the things in our life that have the most value. Szekley's final recommendation, simple yet profound, is to close your office door twice a day, in the morning and the afternoon, and take a tea break. This is not time to sit at your computer and play solitaire. It is a time to sit with what you have experienced, reflect on how your day is going, and process the world around you. "It is about owning your time, owning your mind," Szekley said.

I see these presentations as two ends of the spectrum—boldly going out in the world with the passion of youth, and calmly assessing the world with the wisdom of age and reflection. The companies examined below embody both of these perspectives, which is what enables them to make a difference with passion, yes, but also with wisdom and thoughtfulness.

WHEN PROFIT IS NOT THE ONLY GOAL

Newman's Own, Inc.

A growing number of consumer companies don't simply measure success in terms of profit. The corporate DNA of some embodies social good, though profit is obviously a necessity. Many of these companies resemble the stalwarts in this area, like Ben & Jerry's or The Body Shop (both of which were sold to larger multinational conglomerates, with mixed results),[6] or the newer entrant Seventh Generation. Smaller companies of this kind that you are likely aware of include TerraCycle, an eco-friendly company that creates products such as messenger bags and toys from recycled materials collected by schools and community groups to raise money, and Life is good, Inc., mentioned earlier, a clothing company whose foundation "helps kids overcome life-threatening challenges such as violence, illness and extreme poverty" and is supported through product sales, speaking fees, and annual festivals.

While most of these companies combine charity with profit, there is one unique business that exists solely to make money for charity: Newman's Own, Inc., founded by the late actor Paul Newman, which donates 100 percent of its profits, after taxes "for educational and charitable purposes." Since 1982, this totals more than $300 million.

As the brand mythology goes, Paul Newman and the writer A.E. Hotchner had the tradition of giving homemade salad dressing to friends for the holidays. This became the basis for the company's line of food products in the early 1980s. Newman and Hotchner started the company not knowing exactly what they were doing. When they generated nearly $400,000 in profits the first year, they decided to give it away "to those who need it." Since then, the company has expanded beyond salad dressings into pasta sauces, salsa, popcorn, and ready-to-eat cereal, among other things. With a full-time staff of twenty-eight people, the company keeps costs down by using third-party manufacturers.

The original line has no artificial ingredients or preservatives and is "all-natural," something considered a breakthrough in the 1980s. In 1993, Nell Newman, Paul's daughter, launched Newman's Own Organics. In 2001, this division was spun off as a separate company.

Charitable donations are managed by the Newman's Own Foundation. "During the 2006–2008 period, approximately 25% of the grant money went to support human services, 22% to education, 16% to health, 16% to arts and culture, 8% to environmental and humane causes, 10% to other causes, 2% to international affairs and 1% to emergency relief."[7] Paul Newman's pet cause was the Hole in the Wall Camps for kids with life-threatening illnesses, which he started in 1988 (the outlaws in *Butch Cassidy and the Sundance Kid,* one of Newman's most successful films, are called The Hole in the Wall gang). There are now eleven camps throughout the world, and tuition is free. The Newman's Own Foundation has also implemented an outreach program for children who can't leave the hospital.

The downside of celebrity has been discussed, but Paul Newman exemplified the value of recognition and the power of a well-placed phone call. In 2001, Newman called Bill Ford, chairman of Ford Motor Company, and asked for refrigerated trucks to help deliver food to rural America's hungry. This led to an alliance with Feeding America, and eighty-two trucks have carried an estimated 125 million pounds of food to thirty-eight states. Newman also helped form the Safe Water Network, which funds water projects around the world (notably this is funded in conjunction with the PepsiCo Foundation). Perhaps Newman's crowning achievement was helping to found the Committee Encouraging Corporate Philanthropy (CECP), which urges greater commitment to corporate giving. Today, CECP has more than 175 CEOs or chairpersons among its members, in companies from Aetna to Zurich Financial.[8]

Paul Newman seems to have been driven by a profound personal belief in what is right, ethical, and just, a character trait seen again and again in the leaders of the most forward-thinking companies. What is also true of these men and women is a deep sense of humility. After receiving an Oscar in 1984 for his humanitarian work, Newman decided never again to accept an award for his philanthropy. In fact, he marked that resolve by burning his tuxedo in a ritual bonfire.

But every coin has two sides, and critics have noted two concerns in regards to Newman's Own. One person pointed out to me that prior to his death, all the profits of Newman's Own went to Paul Newman, who in turn took the charitable donations as a tax deduction. While she seemed to think this was a major issue, I see it as a minor point. What I do take issue with is the blurring of the mission of Newman's Own with Newman's Own Organics. The latter is a for-profit company. It does not donate all its profits to charity, but rather must, according to its web site "pay a percentage of its sales of products for the benefit of Newman's Own Foundation."[9] I doubt many consumers know the difference.

As we have seen throughout the book, companies like Newman's that were created with a mission have an easier time integrating social innovation. Happily, more and more such companies are being launched. Mobile Accord, for example, is the company behind mGive, a platform that allows charities to collect donations via text donations. "Our goal was always to use mobile devices to make a social impact," its founder James Eberhard says.[10] Or, in another example, Me to We Style, a clothing company that calls itself a "social enterprise," creates apparel for the socially conscious consumer. Its products are organic and sweatshop-free, and 50 percent of profits go to Free the Children, "the world's largest network of children helping children through education," which includes building schools, providing health care, and improving sanitation in Kenya, Sierra Leone, China, and Sri Lanka. "Our mission at Me to We Style is to empower consumers to make purchasing decisions that lead to a better life for people around the world."[11]

Social Innovation in Action

Clif Bar and Company

Chapter 2 outlined the principles of social innovation—doing good is embedded in the company, which entails incorporating ACTS (authenticity of product and cause, customization for consumers to choose the causes they want to support, transparency of operations even when done wrong, and sustainability of the planet and the bottom line). We looked at Chipotle as an example of this. Clif Bar and Company, the maker of Clif and Luna Bars, is another. This company is in the enviable position of growing while other products in the category are in decline. The company now has annual sales of $200 million. It adheres to a set of guiding principles that it calls its 5 Aspirations:

- *Sustaining our Planet.* Keep our impact on the environment small, even as we grow. (Clif Bar uses 70 percent organic ingredients and recycled packaging and has both a staff ecologist and a sustainability manager on the payroll.)
- *Sustaining our Community.* Be good neighbors. Give back to the community. (Clif Bar has teamed up with TerraCycle and other community fund-raisers, including a traveling film festival by and about women, "Lunafest," which raises funds for women's issues.)
- *Sustaining our People.* Create a workplace where people can live life to the fullest, even from 9-to-5. (Clif Bar has an on-site gym and subsidized organic salads.)
- *Sustaining our Business.* Grow slower, grow better, stick around longer.

· *Sustaining our Brands.* Make what people actually need. Never compromise quality.[12]

Because Clif Bar is in the health business (not the food business—there's a difference), the work it does supports that mission. One of the really cool things it does is help local communities put on more eco-friendly events. Beyond demonstrating community commitment, support for local events ties back into the company's environmental stance, because Clif Bar helps producers make their events more earth-friendly by providing them with a checklist on everything from how to recycle to promoting sustainable transportation to serving organic food—all with applicable web site information about how to implement these planet-friendly objectives. From the products to the packaging to the events it supports, this company projects a singular image of commitment to people and the planet, while successfully producing profits.

Eileen Fisher

If you are female and of a certain age, I don't have to tell you that Eileen Fisher produces high-end, comfortable clothing. What you might not know about Eileen Fisher is the number of innovative things it does, both in and outside of the company.

I first learned about these at a CSR conference at New York University's Stern School of Business in 2008, where Susan Schor, Eileen Fisher's chief culture officer, told students, executives, and academics that the company gets eight or nine hundred résumés when a job becomes available. After she laid out the company's vision and its culture of support and nurturance, it was easy to understand why this is so.

Employees are genuinely and generously supported, not only in terms of their livelihood but also in terms of their health and well-being. This is because Eileen Fisher's philosophy is if "we take care of ourselves, we'll have more energy and creativity to bring to our work. We strive to develop a culture that encourages staff to integrate self-care into their workday: 'to stop, to stretch, to breathe.'" Employees can receive up to $1,000 reimbursement for wellness purchases (health club memberships, exercise equipment, acupuncture). A similar amount is available for education, not as reimbursement for MBA classes but to fund whatever employees want to learn for themselves, be it things like dance or meditation or pottery. A massage therapist is available on-site, as well as yoga classes, personal training, and reflexology. In 2005, employees were given company stock, and in 2008, Eileen Fisher did so well that they got eight and a half weeks' salary as a bonus.[13] As they do at LOHAS, company meetings begin with a short period of meditation, a point that stuck with me. While this sounds utterly hippy-dippy, imagine what your work life would be like if everyone stopped to calm themselves for just a moment before diving into a meeting.

Benefits also accrue for women outside the company. Under the social consciousness tab on its web site, the company outlines its commitment to sustainability (use of organics, explanations of why its products are eco-friendly, in no small part because of their long usability, and a list of ten things consumers can do to "make a difference," such as go organic, simplify, and re-use), human rights (the company is committed to SA8000, workplace standards on issues like child labor and health and safety in its factories around the world), and efforts to support women in leadership positions, including grants for women starting their own businesses. Finally, the company demonstrates its commitment to the community through volunteerism, matching grants, and in-store events that support local nonprofit partners whose mission is aligned with Eileen Fisher's.

Alternatively, companies have taken the strategy of creating a separate line of products whose purpose is to raise money for charity. Some examples include Philosophy Cosmetics ("Shop for a Cause" products support breast cancer, PBS, and the Christopher and Dana Reeve Foundation, among others) and LUSH Cosmetics (Charity Pot Body Lotion: "Every penny that you pay for a pot, excluding the tax, goes to grassroots charities all around the world"). These are not organizations that are using these products as loss leaders as in the case of the Slatkin lighter, discussed earlier. This is also not like (RED), because the product and the cause are integral to the corporation. The best example of implementing this strategy is MAC's VIVA GLAM lipstick.

MAC VIVA GLAM

MAC Cosmetics was founded in 1984 by two Canadians, one a beauty salon owner, the other a makeup artist. They opened their first store in the United States in 1991. The two Franks (as the owners were known) created products meant to withstand the long days and hot lights of a professional photo shoot. The intensity of the product and their connections to the fashion and entertainment industry led to the company's growing popularity. Estée Lauder had acquired a controlling interest in the company by 1994 and bought the remainder of it in 1998.

Also in 1994, at the behest of company employees, MAC Cosmetics began a campaign to support people affected by AIDS and HIV, which had a significant impact in the fashion industry.[14] The MAC AIDS fund supports men, women, and children affected by HIV/AIDS globally. Unlike other charities that fund research, this foundation pays for education and support for those living with HIV/AIDS. This fund is supported through the sale of a single item—VIVA GLAM lipstick. "Every cent of the selling price of M·A·C VIVA GLAM lipstick and lipgloss is donated to the M·A·C AIDS Fund," MAC Cosmetics' web site says.[15]

VIVA GLAM's inaugural advertising campaign featured the model and drag queen RuPaul. Since then the campaign has featured cutting-edge pop culture icons including Fergie, Mary J. Blige, and most recently Cindy Lauper and Lady Gaga together in a single ad. The 2010 ad's headline read: "From our lips: You know you've got a sexy voice . . . Use it! Let's talk about how to keep your love life safe, seductive and satisfying. Just between us girls." Combining an older pop icon with a new star tipped its hat to the reality that AIDS and HIV is not just a young person's disease. Nor is it only a gay man's disease, an idea that dominates public opinion. The message presented is that women of all ages must take responsibility for their sexual health and think about who they are kissing and where it might lead. Thus far, 11 million VIVA GLAM lipsticks have been sold, raising more than $160 million. This is the only product that MAC advertises. All other promotion is word of mouth.

This initiative does everything right from the perspective of social innovation. The cause is related to an industry affected by the product, the campaign is embedded in the corporate culture—employees initiated it but also benefit from information and education provided, and finally, the source of funding is unambiguous—buy a lipstick, the money goes to help people afflicted with HIV/AIDS. When the Lady Gaga lipstick sold out (as it did almost immediately), people naturally bought other products instead. But it did sell out, and in so doing, enabled the company to continue its efforts "to make a difference on the ground where it matters most," which has always been the goal, according to MAC AIDS Fund's chairman, John Demsey.

These companies show that it is possible to be successful—really, really successful—while embracing the values of sustainability and social justice. Such success can be achieved in multiple product categories.

RETROFITTING TO THE NEW REALITY

The companies examined thus far were established with positive social goals as part of their strategic missions. Many older organizations created at a time when generating the highest return for shareholders was the only consideration are now reassessing the way they do business. This has been the hardest category to analyze, because it is all too easily assumed that these organizations are entrenched in the old ways of doing business. Also, they are so large that it makes you wonder whether they really can turn things around. However, a number of them have. GE came up in more than one conversation as a company that has reimagined itself and made substantial changes. A company better known for its defense contracts and polluting the Hudson River in New York than for its environmental stance, GE repositioned itself under the name ecomagination and now has executed a number of innovative projects, including a $200 million challenge to find the best ideas for creating a smarter power grid. GE developed the Watt-Station—an electric vehicle charger. It reduced companywide energy use by 37 percent and committed to spending $5 billion on research and development for "cleaner technology" over the first five years of ecomagination, spending it hopes to double over the next five years. Finally, GE has a charitable campaign that is imaginative and well integrated into the message of the company. Visitors to its web site are asked to tag pictures on Flickr for water, light, or air and, of course, then tell their friends through social media that by simply uploading a picture, they can make a difference. Photos trigger donations to one of three organizations—charity: water (water), Practical Action (wind), and d.light (light—this organization is discussed below).[16] Certainly, this is not the company I remember from when I worked at NBC (a division of GE and now primarily owned by Comcast, with a 51 percent stake in the company). Compare this to McDonald's, another company that came up in a number of conversations. McDonald's can take credit for teaming up with Greenpeace to create a moratorium on illegal deforestation, creating a number of sustainability initiatives, including recycling cooking oil for biofuels, using some recycled materials in its packaging, and working toward sustainable agriculture, but I'm not ready to give the company a medal given its deceptive advertising and its continued promotion to children. Moreover, whereas a companywide commitment and belief that runs throughout the organization are typical of companies that have embraced social innovation, this isn't yet the case with McDonald's, although the company may be evolving in that direction.

Below, we'll look at a few examples of companies that are further along in realigning their operations in concerted efforts at social innovation.

Interface Carpet

What usually drives successful responsibility initiatives is the commitment of someone with almost superhuman persistence. We might even call it "getting religion," because it tends to be the case that the person driving the initiative must become evangelical in his or her pursuit of innovation. No company illustrates this better than Interface Carpet.

Anyone who has worked in the area of sustainability has heard the story of Interface Carpet—a company that for twenty-one years made flooring materials without any consideration for what that product might be doing to the environment. I first read about Interface when I began doing research for this book, and its name came up in almost every book about sustainability as an example of an environmentally disastrous company rethinking what it did to become one of the most sustainable companies in America. This sea change came about under the direction of the company's founder, Ray Anderson.

Interface began as Carpets International in 1973 and was renamed Interface about ten years later. The company produced both flooring and carpeting and grew over time through a series of acquisitions both in the United States and internationally. Carpet has been targeted as being particularly bad for the environment because of its high petroleum content and the amount of waste that ends up in landfills, because it has traditionally not been recycled or made recyclable.

In 1994, the company began to hear from its customers "what are you doing for the environment?" Initially, this didn't bother Anderson, but it did hit home with some of his employees, who were at a loss as to how to respond. People in the research department put together a task force made up of employees from around the world to evaluate the company's environmental stance and find a way to respond to customer concerns. The leaders of the task force asked Ray Anderson to come to the meeting to provide an environmental vision for them. The problem was that he had none. Around the time Anderson realized this, Paul Hawken's book *The Ecology of Commerce* landed on his desk. Anderson says reading this was an epiphany. He decided "unless we can make carpets sustainably, perhaps we don't have a place in a sustainable world. But neither does anybody else making products unsustainably." He realized that he was plundering the planet, taking resources that did not belong to him but to everyone, every creature.[17]

Since then Anderson has spoken to groups big and small, inside his company and out, preaching the message of sustainability.[18] Interface's web site notes his vision: "To be the first company that, by its deeds, shows the entire industrial world what sustainability is in all its dimensions: People, process, product, place and profits—by 2020—and in doing so we will become restorative through the power of influence."[19] Interface understood this to be a systems approach—an ecological approach, if you will. It has culminated in Mission Zero, the goal of which is to have the company not take anything from the earth that is not sustainable by the year 2020.

Sustainability occurs along three perspectives at Interface—reducing its footprint, finding new ways to create its products, and engaging the culture in order for these things to occur. Highlights (and these are just a few of them) include

- Eight of nine Interface manufacturing facilities operate with 100% renewable electricity.
- Interface's "Just" product line uses sustainable materials handwoven in India on wood frames certified as sustainably harvested.
- Interface provides transparent product information through its environmental product declarations (EPDs), the first company in the industry to do so.
- Through its "ReEntry" program, Interface has been able to recycle carpeting, diverting more than 100,000 tons of material from landfills.

If you have any doubt about the need for sustainability or the heartfelt motivation of Ray Anderson, watch the YouTube videos in which he speaks of his vision.[20] These are well-produced corporate messages, certainly, but the sincerity that emanates from the screen simply cannot be faked. I challenge you to walk away from those videos unmoved.

Walmart

I know this choice is going to be controversial. I didn't really believe it either, but Raphael Bemporad of the brand innovation studio BBMG told me to take a second look. I said, "Come on. Really?" And he showed me some of the work Walmart had done. The example that stuck with me was the redesign of its gallon milk jug. The new milk containers had flat tops and ridged sides to facilitate stacking and reduce shipping costs. The problem was that consumers didn't like the new milk jugs. They didn't know how to pour the milk without spilling it all over the place. Instead of walking away from the project as a failure, Walmart put salespeople in stores to show consumers how to use the container. Okay, that's good. But I asked Raphael, "How can you support Walmart? Don't you get push back from people, particularly given your reputation as a sustainability and social justice guy?" He said that he did, but that part of his job in working with Walmart is to help its management understand the criticism and to find ways to solve the underlying problems. That's why one of the projects he was working on was an employee-rewards system similar to WhiteWave's social innovation program Values in Action, or VIA, discussed in chapter 2.

Because Walmart is so big, it can influence sustainability objectives up and down the supply chain. So it isn't just about Walmart; it's about everyone that Walmart does business with. This has a ripple effect on Walmart's competitors, who are also putting pressure on their suppliers. Those who shop at Walmart are offered an increasing array of more ethically appropriate products, thus increasing demand for those products and, one would hope, reducing demand for those that are more harmful.

Can we be cynical and frame this all as a marketing ploy to reposition Walmart after years of bad press for everything from union-busting to mistreating women to destroying Main Street USA? We could, but that doesn't bring us any closer to solving any problems. So let's suspend judgment for a moment and look at what Walmart is, perhaps, doing right.

When we think about the repositioning in terms of the triple bottom line—people, planet, and profits—we must realize that, being Walmart, the primary focus is going to be on the last of these. That's okay. The issue isn't how we get to a more sustainable planet; it's that we get there. And no matter what you might think about Walmart, the reality is that it is the world's largest retailer—with just over $400 billion in annual revenues—and what it does has considerable impact throughout retailing and manufacturing. Walmart has implemented sustainability initiatives because they save it money, and that is exactly how it is promoting them to its customers.

Walmart has added more ethically appropriate and environmentally friendly products to its offerings. In the food category, it has added organic and locally grown products, fair trade and Rainforest Alliance certified coffee, and eggs from cage-free hens.[21] Because of criticism from environmental groups that the company was greenwashing and using "industrial" organic producers, as well as tepid response, from consumers, organic has been limited primarily to dairy products. In terms of household products, Walmart leads the industry in promoting the use of energy-efficient light bulbs and concentrated laundry detergent, causing suppliers GE and Procter & Gamble to innovate in their product lines.

Realignment of Walmart's business strategy began in 2005. Its CEO at the time, H. Lee Scott Jr., saw sustainability as a means to improve the company's profits and aid a sagging reputation after much negative publicity about labor issues and a negative environmental record. In 2006, *Fortune* magazine reported that the push toward environmentalism came from the Walton family, founders of the store and owners of 40 percent of the company.[22] One of them was also on the board of Conservation International, which did a yearlong assessment of the company, determining that Walmart was the largest private user of electricity in the United States and identifying waste, that is, ways for the company to save money. Sustainability 360 is the company's blueprint for sustainability. Over the long term, the goal is to use 100 percent renewable energy, produce no waste, and sell only sustainably produced goods.[23] These goals are grouped under one of three areas: facilities, packaging, and logistics. In this last area, the company was able to improve its transportation strategy to the point where it increased its vehicle fleet's efficiency by 38 percent, reduced costs by $200 million, and cut GHG emissions by 200,000 tons annually. Goals also include reducing 30 percent of the energy use in its stores, and while some stores have already achieved this, older stores have yet to be retrofitted to improve efficiencies. *USA Today* reported late in 2010 that the company has "barely made a dent in the goal" of being 100 percent reliant on renewable energy.[24] However, it also noted that Walmart continues to expand the use of wind and solar energy, as well as introducing new technologies, such as fuel cells, in more stores around the world.

Walmart has expanded its sustainability initiatives to its suppliers, an important requirement being that they reduce packaging—an aspect that would be measured. The company held a summit with 250 CEOs to outline how it would be holding its suppliers accountable for their carbon footprints, while also providing these companies with information on sustainability. Overall, the goal was to reduce packaging by 5 percent in ten years. Packaging was an important focus, because it has "a significant ripple effect. Improved packaging means less waste, fewer materials used, and savings on transportation, manufacturing, shipping, and storage." Cost savings are expected to be in the billions of dollars. Launched in 2008, Walmart's Sustainable Packaging Scorecard is an assessment tool that was created in conjunction with leaders in the packaging industry. Through this scorecard, Walmart and its suppliers can know how much progress is being made. Currently, the card contains information on 300,000 items sold in Walmart stores. The company has also worked with academics, suppliers, and environmental groups to develop a universal sustainability index for consumers, which would be similar to nutrition labels but, rather than vitamins and carbohydrates, takes into account social and environmental issues surrounding a product throughout its life cycle.[25] Like the carbon label in the United Kingdom (see chapter 4), the expectation is that as this label becomes more widely used, it will move companies toward creating more sustainable products. Walmart's rating is more expansive, however, requiring companies to focus not simply on one or two sustainability issues but on a product's social impact in its entirety.

Social innovation extends to Walmart employees as well. In 2007, the company launched the Personal Sustainability Project, a plan whereby associates pick an unsustainable aspect of their lives and find ways to make it better. Associates could also commit to myriad actions, including eating healthier food, recycling, quitting smoking, and getting involved in their communities. (This project was instituted under the direction of Adam Werbach, who took considerable heat for working with Walmart. You can see the same idea on Saatchi & Saatchi's Do One Thing blog, which Werbach manages.) Again, the environmental impact is considerable—associates have eliminated three million pounds of recycled plastic alone. In its 2009 "The State of Green Business" roundup, GreenBiz lauded Walmart for "engag[ing] its employee base [and] helping them connect personal and corporate missions to make a difference for their own health and the health of the planet."[26]

Are there elements that we can criticize in this plan? Absolutely. Critics have already complained about the misrepresentation of organic farms. Working conditions at Walmart seem to remain questionable, as a recent story in Gawker asserted. However, these were simply postings by mostly disgruntled ex-employees and not a systematic representation of employee satisfaction or lack thereof.[27] While we know that Walmart is enacting these programs to save money, it may also be installing the rating system to forestall governmental environmental standards.[28] I consider neither of these serious offenses. Finally, however, a point made by Heather Rogers, author of *Green Gone Wrong: How Our Economy is Undermining the Environmental Revolution,* did make me pause. Because Walmart is constantly expanding into new stores it may also be true that any environmental savings the company accrues is eliminated through expansion.[29]

Procter & Gamble

I have decidedly mixed emotions writing about Procter & Gamble. Some of its initiatives are interesting and innovative. Others are just so much window dressing. According to Packaged Facts, the company spends more than $100 million annually on social responsibility. The umbrella name for its initiatives is "Live, Learn and Thrive," whose goal is to aid disadvantaged children worldwide. According to the P&G web site, it has helped improve the lives of more than 300 million children. Pur water purifying packets, for example, are an important part of this initiative, which helps bring clean drinking water to thirty countries (more on that in a minute). Another example is a straightforward cause-marketing campaign: buy Pampers and the cost of a tetanus shot is donated for babies in Third World countries. P&G also has a sustainability program under the name "Future Friendly" (www.futurefriendly.com/Challenge.aspx). This campaign is consumer-focused, providing tips for reducing energy use, saving water, and reducing waste (all through buying P&G products). However, the only reason I even knew about this campaign is because a student of mine was working on it. Given P&G's marketing prowess, one has to wonder why this is not more broadly promoted if it really had a stake in the game.

The truth is these initiatives are not all done for philanthropic purposes. Corporate philanthropy enables P&G to open new markets for its products, particularly in areas of the world where its brands and products are not in common household usage. Protecting Futures, for example, is a program where feminine hygiene products are given to school-aged girls in the developing world. The theory behind this is that by providing these products and building school restrooms, teenage girls will not miss out on school. What this promotion does as well is build brand recognition for Always and Tampax among a potential customer base. It also informs the company about distribution channels and consumer habits in a market where it does not yet have entrée.

There's something sort of smarmy about these campaigns. They don't feel particularly innovative, and they reek of doing good because it's good for the corporate bottom line. (Dare I remind the reader here that Dawn dishwashing liquid is a P&G product? And please don't get me started on why I think their "Proud sponsor of moms" campaign is just a bunch of blowing smoke.) But since this chapter is about what folks are doing right, I really do like P&G's "Loads of Hope" promotion, which is why I bothered to include P&G here at all. For this promotion, launched in 2009, the company tied sales of Tide laundry detergent to helping victims of natural disasters. This sprang organically out of the company in 2005 after Hurricane Katrina and was only turned into a promotion in 2009.

The Tide Loads of Hope program sends mobile laundromats to devastated areas where residents have no other means of getting clean clothes. Using energy-efficient washers and dryers, the trucks and vans are able to wash more than 300 loads of laundry per day apiece. "We wash, dry and fold the clothes for these families for free," and they've done so in six cities, including cities devastated by Katrina like New Orleans and Baton Rouge. From a marketing perspective—and to a limited extent even from a social innovation perspective—this campaign works. It fills a need few people ever think about. P&G tapped into what it knows best—laundry—and partnered with the nonprofit Feeding America (again!) to further the mission. But, as with Hamburger Helper, consumers need to buy specially marked packages of Tide and enter the code at a web site in order to generate funds for the campaign. This technique of fund-raising—which as we can see is quite popular—falls flat. How much money goes to the campaign? Why do consumers need to buy the product? And more recently, why should they (or would they want to) buy a vintage Tide T-shirt?

I knew the theorist turned sustainable-marketing expert John Rooks of The Soap Group (http://thesoapgroup.com) liked this campaign as well, so I asked him about what worked and didn't work from his perspective. First, he said that it wasn't scaled enough. And when I thought about it, he's right. It's P&G, so why have they only been to six cities? Secondly, "They should have gone after being neighborly," the much-tattooed Rooks said. "Remember when you used to borrow a cup of detergent from your neighbor. That would have been the message that would have more value and would bring people back to that state. As opposed to it's the little things that add up to make a difference." This is a strategy that is much overused, Rooks noted. But even given these issues, the campaign works, for two really good reasons, he said: "It's so stinkin' on brand and it solved a problem."

Something else that P&G implements is strategically on target. P&G created Pur, a low-cost powder for purifying water. Initially, the product was a commercial failure. However, the product proved its value after the 2004 tsunami in Sri Lanka. Since that time, according to the *Wall Street Journal,* the company has committed to a twenty-year plan that introduces Pur into the forty countries with the highest infant mortality rates, at a rate of two countries per year. Under the leadership of A. G. Lafley, P&G's CEO, the company began by introducing Pur into Haiti and Uganda, and he has committed to making this product both a commercial and a humanitarian success.

Bob Gilbreath, chief marketing strategist at digital marketing agency Bridge Worldwide, and former P&G brand manager for Mr. Clean, told me that P&G is doing an internal audit to ensure that each of its brands has a purpose, with the umbrella theme Touching Lives and Improving Life:

> Each of their major brands has gone through a process to identity their purpose—"here's why we exist." It's a higher level thing, rather than product benefits and maximizing profits. It's about having some kind of positive impact on consumers' lives around the world. It's early. It's going to take a while to change the whole thinking, but the money that used to go to the CSR report is increasingly going toward marketing or at least being tied together with what the brands are doing.[30]

Let's hope that as P&G moves forward with this process, the initiatives look like Loads of Hope and the Pur campaign and not the self-serving Always promotion.

A Cautionary Tale?

Frito-Lay, a division of PepsiCo and a $12 billion business, decided to jump into the social fray with its SunChips product. Frito-Lay controls almost 60 percent of the snack chip category, according to the company. In addition, the company has implemented environmental initiatives through both PepsiCo and its Frito-Lay division. For example, in 2008, Frito-Lay began using solar power in its Modesto, California, plant to produce its SunChip product. At the same time, the company reached almost 97 percent re-use rate of its shipping cartons, saving approximately five million trees annually, and it redesigned one of its factories to use solar energy and biofuels, as well as recycle solid wastes ("such as sending potato peels and cornhusks to livestock farms for use as feed"). If successful, this will reduce electrical and water consumption by 90 percent and reduce GHG by between 50 to 75 percent, and the hope is that the plant will be a prototype for other factories.

Where SunChips made the most publicized move toward sustainability was in the creation of its 100 percent compostable packaging, launched on Earth Day 2010. You may remember the advertising: a dark blue SunChip bag on a pile of dirt with time-lapsed photography showing the bag disintegrating over a fourteen-week period. When the bag was fully gone, a flower grew out of the earth. I remember my friends and colleagues in the field saying how cool they thought this was—what a breakthrough!

Our enthusiasm was a bit premature. Opening the bag turned out to be irritatingly noisy, and optimum conditions were needed for it to break down completely. Moreover, there seems to be dispute over whether the bag is compostable (meaning that in addition to breaking down, it also released nutrients into the ground, which is how it was promoted) or simply biodegradable. What Frito-Lay probably should have realized is that whatever people say, ultimately, they buy what is convenient, which trumps the environment every day of the week. Sales of Sun Chips dropped by 11 percent, and eighteen months after its introduction, the bag was pulled.

In February 2011, a revised SunChip bag was introduced. With a new adhesive but the same compostable material, opening the bag was significantly quieter and in line with the noise made by other bags in the category. Particularly interesting was that the company had to promote the quiet nature of the bag rather than its compostability when the product was relaunched. Since then, it has turned to promoting its "all natural ingredients," which has very limited validity.

INNOVATING AT THE BOTTOM OF THE PYRAMID

Alternatively, corporations can make a difference in people's lives while being true to the bottom line by creating products and services that serve what is known as Bottom of the Pyramid (BoP), the four billion people who are the poorest of the poor, living on less than $2 a day. BoP is rapidly becoming a field unto itself. Like social innovation, it requires that the work be part of the company's core business; unlike SI, it is not any part of a CSR initiative. The obvious example of this is microcredit or microfinancing, where banks lend small amounts of money to people in impoverished communities so that they can create small local businesses. Perhaps the best-known of these operations is Kiva.org, where visitors to the site loan money (they do not donate it) to aid small businesses around the world. (As discussed earlier, there are marketing issues, but the donating aspect of the site is sound.)

Microfinancing is not the only form of Bottom of the Pyramid enterprise. Some large companies have entered into this market, and an increasing number of them have had success in doing so. This management strategy was popularized by the late C.K. Prahalad, who urged in his book *The Fortune at the Bottom of the Pyramid* that we see the poor as consumers seeking value, just like anyone else, and not as fringe members of society. The multinational Unilever, which produces everything from Hellman's mayonnaise to Dove soap, is a case study in Prahalad's book. Unilever created Project Shakti in India. Local women take out loans through microfinancing, and Unilever provides them with products and the training to sell them. What makes this process different from other markets is that products are manufactured in much smaller unit packages—usually single-serving sizes of things from shampoo to aspirin to tea—to reduce the cost to the consumer, who may only have enough cash to be able to buy on a daily basis. For Unilever, it means smaller profit margins per unit, but this is made up for by significantly higher volume. The advantages are many: employment for local women who sell Lifebuoy soap and other products at what is the equivalent of a Tupperware party,[31] access to much-needed products for consumers who traditionally pay a "poverty penalty" (premium pricing due to "local monopolies, inadequate access, poor distribution, and strong traditional intermediaries"), and in this case, improved health through better distribution of soap and an advertising campaign that promoted the necessity of washing hands to reduce the incidence of diarrhea, a major cause of death, particularly in small children, and lost wages due to sick days for adults.[32]

BoP is increasingly an area of interest for smaller companies and the focus of conferences at leading business schools. This tends to be what people think of when they use the term "social enterprise" or "social entrepreneurship," as opposed to some of the other terminology we've discussed thus far. (Some would limit social entrepreneurship to only those who are not seeking profit.) At Harvard's Social

Enterprise Conference, there is an annual "Pitch for Change," a competition where students give an "elevator pitch" for their company in hopes of winning seed money and consulting time with industry specialists. I found these pitches smart and thorough (as much as they could be in a short period of time) and created to solve problems on the ground. The winners in 2010 were the telecommunications company Ruma (www.ruma.co.id), which provides microfranchising opportunities in Indonesia, where cell phones are widely available, but retailers of prepaid minutes are centralized in large cities; Angaza Design (http://angazadesign.com), a company that provides a solar-powered lighting and charging system that enables communities in East Africa to improve their lives through more efficient and less expensive forms of lighting; and DrinKup (http://e.younoodle.com/startups/drinkup), which took the audience prize (the populist award). DrinKup is also a microfranchise company, which rents water-filtration systems to local entrepreneurs, who learn how to collect, clean, and sell drinking water in their communities.

A company that is already making a difference through its products is d.light, which provides solar-powered lighting products in Third World countries, as Angaza Design is also attempting to do. Co-founded by Sam Goldman, a former member of the Peace Corps and a Stanford business school grad, the goal of d.light is to replace kerosene lamps with solar-powered lights. In many rural areas around the world where electricity is unavailable, kerosene is used for lighting. This is bad for a number of reasons—the light is not particularly good, the kerosene is expensive, and, worse yet, it is highly flammable, leading to untold tragedy. Goldman realized that establishing a business as opposed to a charity was the only way to reach the millions of people he wanted to help. The mission is simple: "Enable households without reliable electricity to attain the same quality of life as those with electricity. We will begin by replacing every kerosene lantern with clean, safe and bright light."[33] Thus far, d.light has delivered 1.7 million lamps.[34]

A single strategy will not fit every problem. The for-profit models of microfranchising are not conducive to children's education, for example, as several critics have noted. It is easy to raise money for enlightening children (who doesn't want to do that?), but the program may be compromised in order to get the necessary funding.[35] However, as we are seeing, microfranchising businesses created around solving a problem and run by passionate (and compassionate) leaders are a welcome alternative to First World overconsumerism.

DON'T DO WHAT DOESN'T WORK

Most of us have heard the old saw by now: the definition of insanity is doing the same thing over and over again and expecting different results each time. Just as we need to stop eating ice cream and thinking we're going to lose weight, so too companies should stop creating cause-marketing campaigns that neither build consumer trust nor fundamentally fix a social concern. As one of the slides I saw at a conference so aptly put it:

MYTH: YOUR CSR CAMPAIGN IS WORKING

The reality is that most of us are skeptical. We think that sustainability is about marketing rather than about improving the environment. A third of us don't buy green products because we don't believe the environmental claims, and two-thirds don't believe the media when they report on environmental issues. Not only this, but fewer than 10 percent of consumers even remember CSR campaigns from major corporations like J&J, Walmart, GE, P&G, S.C Johnson, Target, or Toyota according to NMI. All of this would suggest that throwing money at these initiatives simply doesn't make any sense.

What does make sense is actually being a good company, not going around screaming about it. Interface Carpets—truly one of the leaders in this field—has the right idea: get caught doing something good. In this age of interconnectedness, people will find the good companies—if they are there in the first place.

What that means is that companies need to connect to consumers through what is important to them—something companies know how to do very well. Yes, we want our clothes clean (and you'd better be able to do that first and well), but we also want to know that you're not killing the planet and ruining the water system or degrading your employees when you do it. Companies need to create their brands around a mission, but the mission can no longer simply be about product attributes. It has to be about benefits to the world that relate to the product. It doesn't make sense to work toward hunger relief if you are a clothing company. And for goodness sake, tell the truth. Companies have been rewarded for admitting it when they are wrong. Getting caught in a lie will only get you in trouble.

As we've seen from the examples in this chapter, businesses organized to effect positive change make far more sense than the vast majority of cause campaigns we've looked at. In the several cases of microfranchising we examined, people are provided with a way to make a living, not just given a handout. Through companies like Newman's Own, a charity (or charities) comes to have a consistent, long-term cash flow. And, finally, environmental changes at the company level have more substantial impacts than what can be generated at the individual consumer level. People (internally and externally), the planet, and profits are all better served under this paradigm.

7

We Are Not Consumers

Call me mother, daughter, teacher, friend, sister, or citizen. What I will not be called is consumer, and neither should you be. If we continue to name—or worse yet define—ourselves by what we purchase, we have little chance, if any, of getting out of the buy-use-dispose, buy-use-dispose cycle of consumer behavior. Thinking of ourselves as "consumers" is a vestige of the age of mass marketing and makes no more sense today than expecting the entire family to sit down together at 8 p.m. and watch an episode of *The Brady Bunch*.

Thankfully, there are inklings that marketers have figured out that this label no longer applies. Coca-Cola's Tom LaForge gets it partly right. He recognizes that people are, well, people and that macro-forces are changing business to be more "human-centric," right-brain-oriented (that is, more holistic), and environmental- and social justice–minded. "Today we have to talk to them [customers] as consumers, environmentalists, community members and citizens."[1] Consumer is still in the mix, but at least it's being recognized as just a small part of who we are and not the sum total of our being.

That change won't come easy is evidenced in a presentation I saw given by the Neighbor Agency (www.neighboragency.com), a marketing firm that works in the LOHAS sustainability space. The opening slide said: "Rewriting the Rules of *Consumer Engagement." The asterisk references Rule 1: Let's stop calling people consumers. But if you are going to stop calling people consumers, you also have to stop calling the process "consumer engagement."

Will companies ever cease branding products and then pushing their meaning on us? Probably not. But, as both of these examples attest, marketers are beginning to think of us as living, breathing human beings and not just "targets," "demos," or "consumers." Doing this may help motivate companies and clients to make more sustainable and more socially conscious products.

Even as companies move to align their businesses with social needs, we must encourage them to extract the social cause from the corporate marketing. This is not to say that corporations shouldn't do good— they absolutely should. In fact, they have to for competitive reasons.[2] What I am suggesting, however, is that the good they do should not be tied directly to product sales. Become more sustainable through better operations management, allow employees to take time off to volunteer, donate products to local causes, hold charity events, whatever makes sense for the company. Just don't make us buy a product in order for that to happen.

We citizens of the world, too, must do our part to change the consumer-focused mind-set. LOHASians have the right idea when they talk about mindful consumption:

> Mindless consumption is buying without considering the impact of the product's production and distribution. Mindful consumption, on the other hand, means assessing a product's lifecycle, not taking more than you need and finding other avenues to self-fulfillment besides accumulation. It means supporting specific types of products and practices that in turn support cultures, worker rights, environments and animal rights.[3]

Taking responsibility for the purchases we make is different from believing we are solving the problems of the world through individual product purchases. The first gives us agency; the second binds us to the whims of the market. By "agency" I mean we take control of our semiconscious buying attitude and demand products that better serve our needs and the needs of the planet. When these purchases reach the tipping point, they will force industry to change the way it does business. This is not theory; it's reality. Think of hybrid cars, compact fluorescent lightbulbs, or organic food. So imagine, then, if we all stopped buying bottled water tomorrow. What would happen? Twenty years ago, we went to the tap when we were thirsty and were fine, thank you very much. We could all do that again now, eliminate billions of plastic bottles, and save money. Or one of my pet peeves: since when did every single tea bag on the planet have to be wrapped in its own individual envelope? Are we all such brewing aficionados? Couldn't we get companies to stop doing that? Or, how about we tell Apple that we're not going to buy another iPad, iPod, iPhone, or iWhatever until it tells us how the new one is more sustainably produced and the one we have is going to be more efficiently recycled?[4]

Denouncing the consumer attitude is not just about the environment. It's also about putting one's money where one's mouth is, whether we are talking about improving our own lives or the lives of other people. As discussed in chapter 6, research confirms that experiences enhance our lives, while things—and in particular buying things—merely give us a momentary high. We are filling our homes with things we don't need and then buying plastic boxes from the Container Store to put them in closets so that we don't have to look at them. Does that make any sense? Better instead—if you can afford it—to go out to dinner with friends at a restaurant, take the dance class you've been putting off, or volunteer at your local botanical garden. Alternatively, try things that don't cost any money but do enhance your life experience, like reading a book from the library, taking a walk with your significant other, or pulling an old, forgotten board game out of the closet.

There's an assignment I give my students: Go without media for a week. Some actually can't make it that far, or are just trying to pull one over on the professor. Most, however, found that their lives were enriched, because they spent more time talking with their parents or significant other, played with their younger siblings or cousins, completed their homework and some extra studying (!), or performed some physical or creative activity that they say they "don't usually have time for," like writing, gymnastics, or painting. Turning off the media, even for one day a week, not only enhances your relationships but also has the added benefit of reducing your exposure to marketing messages—something we could all use a lot less of.

The point is to do what you can, whenever you can, whether we are talking about a company or an individual. A creative example of this is a music video by Sarah McLachlan for her song "World on Fire." Instead of spending hundreds of thousands of dollars creating yet another mindless music video, McLachlan arranged for the costs of production to go to charities around the world. The director and crew donated their time, so labor costs, too, went to charity. The video is shot in a single room, with the artist playing a guitar, without makeup, and with her hair naturally done. Interspersed with this performance are slides with information about the typical costs of producing a video, such as crew, location fees, hair and makeup, and so on. These figures are then compared with the cost of food, education, and medical supplies for more than one million people and visualized with footage (provided by charitable agencies) of those living without basic necessities. The final production cost was $15—the price of a Sony MiniDV tape—and the $150,000 usually spent on a McLachlan video went to eleven charities.

WHAT YOU CAN DO

Thankfully, you don't have to be a celebrity or practice D.I.Y. philanthropy in order to improve the world. In fact, there are plenty of simple things that you can do right now—without purchasing a product. Most of these suggestions are low-cost or no cost. The list below is by no means exhaustive; it is meant to provide information on some of the more interesting groups and ideas I've discovered and to spur you to want to find more.

In creating this list of suggestions, I based the weight of options on the 1-9-90 rule that was developed in terms of how many people actively participate in online forums. The framework posits that 90 percent of people lurk on web sites, 9 percent contribute periodically, and 1 percent are the passionate few most committed to participation. Noopur Agarwal, of MTV's Department of Public Affairs, demonstrated how MTV applies this thinking to its cause campaigns.[5] As an organization with a long-standing tradition of supporting causes from Live Aid to Rock the Vote to its newest campaign, called "A Thin Line," which teaches teens about digital abuse—how to identify it, report it, and respond to it—MTV Networks is well versed in this area. It adapted the 1-9-90 theory to social action in the following way: 90 percent of people will do simpler tasks such as follow, fan, or friend a cause, play a game, discuss the issue, or help a friend; 9 percent will donate money, volunteer their time, or start a project; and the most committed 1 percent will start an organization or a movement.

Here, then, are Einstein's Ten Tips toward a Better World:

1. *Advocate.* We are citizens—of our local communities, of our countries, and of the world. I hope by now that you agree with me that individuals and companies alone cannot solve the problems of sustainability and social justice. We need to do it together with the help of government

and nonprofits, and the reality is that governments are unlikely to do anything about these issues unless we oblige them to do so.

Do we need to march in the streets as we did in the 1960s? Maybe. The key issues of our time from hunger to homelessness to health care cannot be solved without government intervention. But the concerns are so broad, and the need for change so daunting, that the problems facing the world can come to feel overwhelming. Moreover, my fear is that there are so many problems that need to be addressed that no single message will break through. Therefore, the most effective regulation, and the one to advocate for, is a revision of the corporate tax code; this would not only bolster the social safety net, it might also spur corporations to find solutions that are not only socially good but economically efficient.[6]

And since it is unlikely that cause campaigns will stop in the immediate future, advocating for regulation of these initiatives is definitely in order. When companies run promotions, they are executing a commercial coventure, which is regulated at the state level. Only a handful of states require that advertising contain disclosure statements; fewer still require that the advertising specify the level of donation, particularly on a per-unit basis—what most people are likely to want to know. Check and see if your state has these laws in place. If not, advocate for them; if they are, make sure they regulate cause promotions at the per-unit level of specificity. This type of regulation can put the charitable decision back in the hands of the product purchaser. At the federal level, the Federal Trade Commission (FTC) should institute a policy of requiring transparency in terms of promotion. So, for example, if it says $1 on the bottle, then $1 should be donated to the cause—without having a database mechanism attached.

There are numerous ways to take action in addition to organizing a demonstration. Call, write, or e-mail your senator or representative. Volunteer with organizations that do the work that you'd like to see done in the world. Participate in local government. Visit web sites like Green America, formerly Co-op America, publisher of the Green Pages. There is a "Take Action" section on its web site (www.greenamericatoday .org) where you can participate in everything from keeping airlines accountable for recycling to telling Congress to invest in clean energy. The Internet is powerful, too, not just for motivating corporate change, but for advocating for social change. If you have a passion, there is certainly a group that matches it and needs your help. And if there isn't one, you can start one yourself.

In the end, activities should focus on creating frameworks within which corporations will be motivated to conform to what is ethically just and environmentally sound. This can happen at the regulatory level. But it can also occur within the corporation itself. If you work for a company that doesn't have social innovation initiatives in place like WhiteWave's VIA, for example, see if you can start one. Demonstrating that the ideas you generate will save the company money is the fastest way to see them implemented.

2. *Volunteer your time and talent.* You can volunteer your time in a myriad of ways, and I'm sure many of you do. It has become a popular trend during the present recession, not only because of the now well-known health benefits of helping others, but also because it can lead to job opportunities. Whatever reason you have to give of yourself, it has become easier to find something that matches your talents or interests. You can find opportunities through individual organizations, your religious institution, or local aggregating institutions, such as New York Cares (www.newyorkcares.org). Online services such as Volunteer match (www.volunteermatch.org) and Idealist (www.idealist .org) are also helpful for matching you with an organization in need of volunteers. In addition, think beyond the typical volunteer day or single event. Are you a marketer? An accountant? An artist? Donating your talent to an organization in this way can save it expensive fees for these services. Finally, if you are looking to get your teen interested in volunteering, Dosomething.org provides opportunities for young people to get involved, while talking to them in a relatable way.

A slightly different take on this theme is using your skills to create something for charity. One area where this has blossomed is knitting for charity. This idea had its roots in World War II. There are dozens of organizations that accept these offerings and you can find some of them at The Daily Knitter (www.dailyknitter.com/charity.html). My favorite is Project Linus, which provides security blankets for children.

3. *Write a check.* I know that this may not be an option for everyone in these hard times, but it still is and always will be a very good one. Don't feel you have to send $100 or even $50 to make a difference. Just as the Penny Harvest raises millions of dollars in pennies, lots of people writing $10 checks can add up to serious money. Better still is to have the money taken out of your account or charged to your credit card on a monthly basis. That way you won't forget to do it, and the charity gets a steady stream of donations.

A growing number of web sites act as aggregators of philanthropy. They make it easier for many people to donate funds, because, much as with Kiva, you can see small incremental ways in which your donation can be used. Here are some examples that I have found to be both reputable and easy to use:

- Globalgiving.org—Philanthropists, big and small, can come to this site and find more than a thousand "pre-screened grassroots charity projects around the world." It's easy, transparent, and effective. "Since 2002, 219,463 donors like you have given $51,631,694 to 4,572 projects. Wonderful!" www.globalgiving.org says. Wonderful, indeed!

- Donorschoose.org—This web site brings together donors with students who need everything from basic supplies to more advanced teaching tools to musical instruments. Like Kiva for the classroom, each public school teacher posts a picture of his or her class and usually something that represents the needed item. What I love about this site is that you can give a small amount of money and know that you are helping educate a child, in your local community, if you so choose. And you get a thank-you note from the teacher and handwritten notes from the kids if you donate more than $100.

- Two other fund-raising sites that provide individual options for donation are Causecast (www.causecast.org) and Crowdrise (www.crowdrise.com). Causecast combines philanthropy with news and advocacy. It has partnerships with AARP (though the site is anything but old) and the Huffington Post. Crowdrise is celebrity-driven (it was created by the actor Ed Norton) and takes a tongue-in-cheek, let's-have-fun approach to charity. This is an incredibly smart strategy, because much of the research suggests that making philanthropy (or even politics) fun is the only way to sustain the giving audience. Even ABC News has gotten on the bandwagon—this time in a good way. ABC created "Be the Change. Save a Life" (http://saveone.net/filter/action#840847/Take-action), a broadcast and online initiative that provides a wealth of options for taking action.

What you want to avoid like the plague are the so-called giving malls. These sites are the e-version of cause marketing. The way they work is like this: you shop on your favorite sites but you access them via e-giving mall sites like iGive.com. These mall sites try to sell you with the line "You Shop, They Win! Help your favorite cause for free." However, they take a significant fee off the top, thus reducing the effectiveness of your donation.

4. *Know where your money is going.* You work hard for your money, and the money you donate should work hard too—not for the organization, but for the people in need. Charity Navigator (www.charitynavigator.org) is the largest charity evaluator in the United States. Before you donate any money, search this site for information about the breakout of expenses based on three elements: program expenses (the actual work), administrative expenses, and fund-raising expenses. The World Wildlife Foundation, for example, spends only 6 percent of its revenue on administrative fees and 12 percent on fund-raising, which leaves more than 80 percent of money donated to do the work of saving the environment around the world.

Conversely, the Magic Johnson Foundation, which supports minority children with college scholarships, helps fund community HIV/AIDS programs, and creates community centers in underserved communities, is listed as one of the charities drowning in administrative debt. The numbers are 49.8 percent for administrative expenses, 0.2 percent for fund-raising, and 49.9 percent for program expenses.[7] That's less than fifty cents of every dollar raised going to do the charitable work—the "program expenses"—while the same amount of money is spent simply to run the organization, and presumably that's mostly salaries. Not all celebrity organizations spend so much on expenses. The Elton John AIDS Foundation, which has a long-standing reputation for educating people about HIV/AIDS, as well as providing direct care and support, spends less than 14 percent of its revenue for administration and fund-raising, leaving 85.9 percent of funds for helping people with AIDS.

Another site where you can find information about charities is Guide Star (www.guidestar.org). This site is not as user-friendly as Charity Navigator and requires a membership fee for premium information. However, if you have the time and you are an information junkie, this site might be just right for you. You can also find giving ideas and analysis at the Charities Review Council (www.smartgivers.org) and the American Institute of Philanthropy (www.charitywatch.org).

I recently saw a billboard for the Michael J. Fox Foundation. It said, "We don't just fund research. We fund results." That is a good mantra to bear in mind when deciding what cause you will be funding. After all, we don't want to give money just to give money; we give money because we want it to make a difference.

5. *Get educated. Get inspired.* As Marxist scholars have lamented for decades, there are consequences to separating the information of where and how a product is created from the object itself. In doing so, objects come to seem magical—they simply appear. We know that's not true, but we usually don't have the time (or don't take the time) to find out the backstory. Until marketers make the story—that is, create a brand narrative—that is transparent about what it is and how and where it was made, it is incumbent upon us to take the initiative to educate and inspire ourselves to make better choices.

A great place to learn about the life cycle of a product is at a site called the Story of Stuff (www.storyofstuff.com). The activist and writer Annie Leonard made a twenty-minute film and put it online in 2007. Expecting to attract other activists and environmentalists, she thought perhaps 50,000 people would view the film. There were 50,000 viewings in four hours, and now the film has been viewed more than twelve million times.[8] Based on this success, Leonard created spinoffs like "The Story of Cosmetics" and "The Story of Electronics."

Two other sites that provide helpful information are TreeHugger.com and care2.com. The first is brought to you by the same people that bring you the Discovery Channel. TreeHugger is the "leading media outlet dedicated to driving sustainability mainstream." Because of this philosophy, the site combines news, ideas, and product information. Stories are classified in categories such as Cars + Transportation, Fashion + Beauty, and Business + Politics. For those looking to act on their newfound knowledge, there are places to interact with others (forums, games, pop quizzes) and a section for taking action ("How to go green," "Green Buying Guide"). Care2 has a similar setup, though its breakdown of topics is more extensive, and overall the site is more user-friendly. In addition, the site rewards you for participating by giving you "butterfly points." These points can be redeemed by donating to charities at www .care2.com, much as with the micro-donor sites we've already looked at.

Bar none, my favorite web site is www.ted.com. Started as a conference on technology, entertainment, and design twenty-five years ago, TED (the acronym stands for Technology, Entertainment and Design) has become a cutting-edge biannual event for thought leaders in a broad range of areas. Artists, world leaders, teachers, writers, chefs (and, okay, Bono) are given eighteen minutes to "give the talk of their lives." The best talks from the conferences are made available online. With over

700 talks to choose from, there is certainly something that will move you to think, or better yet act. And because they are all under twenty minutes, this is something anyone can do—even during a lunch break.[9]

6. *Donate for free*. Sounds ridiculous right? But in the age of the Internet, innovative organizations have come up with ways for you to interact with web sites (at no expense to you other than time) and good works get done around the world. The best example I have found for this is www.freerice.com, which has the dual aim of providing free education and helping to end world hunger by providing free rice to hungry people.[10] The concept is simple, but brilliant. Children (or you, in fact—the site suggests that even corporate CEOs can benefit from the education) go to the site and answer multiple-choice questions. For each question that is answered correctly, ten grains of rice are donated to the United Nations World Food Programme, the administrators of the site. Sure, you're thinking, "what can ten grains of rice do?" With twenty-two countries helping to answer questions, over the past five years, over ninety-one billion grains of rice have been donated.[11]

Similarly, MTV, which has supported numerous initiatives from voting to the environment, has created an online simulation to help college students understand the underlying issues around the conflict in Darfur and the human suffering it causes. This was done in conjunction with Reebok's Human Rights Fund and the International Crisis Group. While tying what looks like a videogame to a tragedy may be offensive to some, it is also a very effective way to help young people understand the issues affecting Darfur, as well as drawing them to the "Darfur is Dying" web site, where they can find out how they can take action.

On the other hand, stay away from social media fund-raising sites like www.SocialVibe.com. Not only is this web site slow and utterly confusing, but it asks visitors to endorse a brand while promoting a cause. The press release for the site's launch lets you know exactly where the emphasis lies: "Get the Vibe: SocialVibe.com Empowers Consumers to Get Sponsored, Do Good."[12] SocialVibe forces you to watch advertising for a sponsor before you have to decide—really quickly—where you want to donate your "money" (it puts a timer on your donations of sixty seconds). In turn, you are supposed to share your charitable causes with your friends through various social media. The more you share, the more brand "perks and points" you earn. Points are turned into funding for your selected charity; perks translate into "one-of-a-kind travel experiences, high-end gadgets and access to exclusive events" for the social networker. This is the very essence of online philanthropy done wrong.

Better—particularly for young people who are more facile at this than I am—are sites that help you set up a social media site for a cause that you care about. You pick the nonprofit, you set up the fund-raising page, and then ask your network of friends and family to donate. It's just like what Avon does for breast cancer, but you get to control the choice of charity. Causes.com, started with Napster's founder Sean Parker, works under this framework. Check out www.ecobonus.info, too. Eco-bonus is an online version of the old S&H Green Stamps. Now, though, instead of trading your stamps in for toasters, you can save them up to purchase eco-friendly products or donate the points to charity.

7. *Be a microlender.* Kiva (www.kiva.org) has harnessed the power of the Internet to turn individuals into microlenders.[13] Partnering with existing microlending institutions, Kiva attempts to match you with an entrepreneur of your choice. Simply go to the site, review the profiles of various small business people around the world, and select the one that you feel moved to support. Microfinance partners distribute the loan, and they may also provide training to increase their chance of having a successful business. Loans usually last six to twelve months. Over that time, lenders can receive updates on repayment, as well as how the business is faring. When the money has been repaid, you can use it again to support another organization, donate to Kiva to help with operational expenses, or simply keep the money. Thus, if you select this last option, other than the opportunity cost of the money, this donation has cost you nothing.

As discussed earlier, there are issues in terms of Kiva misrepresenting the direct aspect of the lending process. But, at this point, it has addressed this problem, while ensuring money goes where it is needed. So I say give a Kiva account as a bar mitzvah gift (an increasingly popular trend) or a Christmas gift, or use it as a learning tool to teach younger children about money, philanthropy, and how the rest of the world lives.

8. *Buy one, and one goes to charity.*[14] One example of this that we've discussed is the TOMS One for One campaign. TOMS Shoes (www.tomsshoes.com) will donate a pair of shoes to a child in need for every pair of shoes purchased. Since 2006, tens of thousands of shoes have been donated to needy children in Argentina and South Africa. Soles4Souls, which works a bit differently, is even more effective. For every dollar you donate at www.soles4souls.org, a pair of shoes goes

to someone in need. If you don't have $50 for a pair of TOMS, you can achieve the same effect for $1. You can also donate new or gently used shoes by dropping them off at a local business that partners with Soles4Souls for this purpose. These donations have the added benefit of reducing some of the 300 million pairs of shoes Americans toss out annually.

A product that will be launched imminently (it doesn't have a name yet) also works under this rubric. This yet-to-be-named product produces water from air. While the technology to do this has been around since the 1950s, it has only now been developed for home and office use. I saw an office prototype (it looks like a water cooler you might see on the Jetsons) when I met with George Alvarez, CEO of Immerse Global, which has been developing this mystery product with Stanford University over the past four years.[15] He explained that the filtering system his company developed produces five gallons of contaminant-free water per day (the home version will produce two gallons per day) and is environmentally friendly because it reduces the need to tap into global water supplies and eliminates the need for bottles. It is also energy-efficient, because it moves into idle mode when not in use.

When I met with Alvarez in his New York office, he explained the philanthropic aspect of his company: "There are two things going on. Number one, when a consumer buys this product, we want to send one overseas. It's like a TOMS Shoes [operation]. It's one to one. It's not the same [water filter] model, it's sturdier. But the issue is about just getting water to them. So we're going to do that one-for-one." He also explained that the company was developing a sand filter in conjunction with Rice University to eliminate arsenic from contaminated water. "So like in Bangladesh, there is a lot of water but there's arsenic. This removes the arsenic." In addition, the company will pay for people to go to a doctor or a clinic to get treated for arsenic poisoning. As Alvarez noted, "no one else has ever done that." This is all theoretical, at this point. Even so, that this thinking is out in the business environment is more than heartening, it's inspiring.

9. *Learn from our children.* Instilling values and compassion into our children usually appears near the top of the list of parental duties. Introducing kids to volunteerism and charity often occurs through the combined efforts of parents, schools, and religious institutions. One example we've all likely seen in one form or another is the campaign of collecting small change from a large number of people—a practice that helps children see that everyone can do something, and even a

little help can make a difference. You likely see or remember this from Trick or Treat for UNICEF, a program that started in the 1950s. In New York City public schools, there is a similar annual event called the Common Cents Penny Harvest. By collecting pennies, the charity was able to raise more than half a million dollars in the most recent school year. Every penny goes back into the community, with grants going to "women's shelters, animal rights organizations, community gardens and senior centers." You can replicate a penny harvest in your own home. Empty your pockets and put your change in a jar when you come home. At the end of the month, the family comes together and decides where the money will go to. This is as easy as buying a T-shirt, less expensive, brings the family together to discuss their values, and the ultimate impact is more immediate and dollar for dollar is more efficient.

There's another important reason why you should bring kids into the conversation about doing good—it can help motivate you. According to the Shelton Group, parents and kids discussing charity, health, and environmental topics is influential in leading to behavioral changes in both. (If you've ever smoked cigarettes and then have a kid come home after they've watched a movie on how bad smoking is, you know exactly what I'm talking about.) The Shelton Group discovered that 68 percent of those who had conversations with their children about energy and water conservation, global warming, or chemicals in foods, among other things, modified their behavior and buying habits.[16]

While you are at it, it's never too early to instill an anticonsumer mentality into your kids. I started telling my daughter that advertising lies when she was about four. That's effective. But if you want more information, PBS has a great site called "Don't Buy It" (http://pbskids .org/dontbuyit) that helps kids understand how they are being manipulated by commercial messages.

For older children, a great site is Best Buy's @15 (www.at15.com), which is set up to empower teens to drive the content. "On this site you'll find a lot of things to do and people to meet," it says. "But this site is all yours. It's up to you to build it. You can *say what you think*. You can make a difference. You can *decide where we donate our money*. Your opinions and ideas will inspire and make a difference."

@15 works for a couple of reasons. First, it provides the platform and then gets out of the way. Second, the issue with teens is not that they don't want to do anything; often it's that they don't know how. This site provides that structure.

Tim Showalter-Loch, then Best Buy's senior manager of community relations, spoke at the 2010 Cause Marketing Forum.[17] He noted the obvious business reasons to implement this campaign: the need to differentiate as the company matures; teens' expectation that brands will have a purpose; and the fact that teens are both purchasers and influencers when it comes to shopping at Best Buy, because they tend to be their families' chief technology officers. Best Buy thus seeks to relate positively to teens in their environment. The web site has established relationships with more than two dozen partners, including DoSomething. org, Teens Against Bullying, and Room to Read. "The future is about creating a business that works for social change," Showalter-Loch noted. "Don't just fix your reputation by giving money; do something."[18]

10. *Slow down.* The first step in putting on the brakes is clear: consume less. This is a simple idea, but the benefits cannot be overstated. If you use less, you don't have to work so much—certainly a plus in most people's book. There are, of course, considerable obstacles to this, not least of which is that we may not have control over the number of hours that we work. But working less has to arise from the belief that it is possible, and with the downturn of the economy, some companies have decided that you can.

While capitalist economies are built on the idea that they must grow endlessly, we now know that our planet can't support that. The Canadian economist Peter Victor tried to determine if there might be another way. He created a computer model of Canada's economy in which consumption, productivity and population would cease growing after 2007. Workers had a four-day week, which created more jobs. The wealthy paid higher taxes, the poor got more public services, and a carbon tax was instituted, which gave the government more money and discouraged corporate use of fossil fuels. Based on this model, in a few decades' time, we could see lower unemployment, an increased standard of living, and reduced greenhouse gas emissions.[19] Is Victor right? We can't know that, but simply raising the idea that there might be another way other than growth is, I think, an invaluable first step.

As for us as individuals, turning down the need to work, work, work runs counter to an underlying ideological issue for most Americans— the Puritan work ethic. This was based on the idea that the more you worked, the more God-like you were. Endless work, however, is not the only path to godliness. For if we continue to have relationships that are rooted in the prerogatives of the market, we shall be resigning ourselves and those who follow us to a life of more work in an environment of depleted resources and more strife between those who have and those who do not. This is not righteous, and we do not have to choose this route. We can decide instead to make less money, to buy less, and to live with less. And in the process, we can be sure that rather than simply building profits, we are forming a moral core—for both ourselves and our communities.

Second, it is time to revise the old saying "Think globally, act locally." Let's think locally and act locally. The media theorist Douglas Rushkoff suggests that this isn't about eliminating the global economy, "just that it be balanced by local activity. Computers don't go away, and we don't lose our internet. We can still work in big groups making really complex stuff. We just do it differently."[20] "Acting local" is first of all a matter of voting with your pocketbook: buying things that support what you believe in—like your local community—and thinking twice before buying things that don't. Buying local provides more of a connection to community, while keeping more money in the local market. For example, perhaps $14 of $100 spent at Target stays in the local community, while if you spend the same $100 with a local merchant, $45 may stay local.[21]

Acting local is also a quality of life issue; local stores tend to be more personal, and people are willing to spend more for a more enjoyable experience. This dovetails with the slow movement—slow food, slow money, slow parenting—a trend that counters the McDonaldization of society.[22] We've seen the rise in farmers' markets and struggles against Walmart, the downturn of public schools and the increase in homeschooling. The rise in slow is integral to the rise in local. And the need to slow down may be the means to what could truly make us happy—personal connections and stronger communities.

NO ONE'S PERFECT

We are none of us perfect. One of the funniest pieces of information I remember seeing during my research is that LOHASians are the population segment most likely to watch the *Victoria's Secret Fashion Show*,[23] misogynistic programming I wouldn't necessarily equate with this upscale, environmentally friendly crowd that's trying to improve the world. While amusing, this demonstrates something we already sense: we may in our heart of hearts want to do good and by our actions demonstrate the best we are capable of, but the reality is that most of us can't act, or simply don't.

We don't act because the sad fact is that change is hard. But it is doable, once you change your perceptions and motivation.

I think it would be helpful to remember that the current consumer culture in which we find ourselves has only been in existence for a handful of decades. Someone I talked to who was heavily involved in the LOHAS movement in Europe said to me that "we should just admit that this is a sixty-year experiment gone utterly wrong and pull the plug." While I can understand the sentiment, it is unfortunately unrealistic. What may be possible, however, is to harness the same talent that got us into this mess to get us out. Coming out of World War II, the American public had a thrifty mind-set because of years of living through war and economic depression.[24] To reverse that frugal thinking, Madison Avenue began marketing based on identity and storytelling— the Marlboro Man, new model cars every year, and a TV set in every room. It's time for a new story, a story of community and caring for the planet and, yes, maybe even thrift.

Perhaps advertisers can't or won't make the difference. Perhaps, then, we should look to change the yardstick by which we gauge our success. Bhutan, a small country in the middle of Asia, has the right idea. Instead of measuring accomplishment based on Gross Domestic Product, the Bhutanese evaluate their country's wealth based on Gross Domestic Happiness. Bhutan is also a country that has no advertising. Coincidence? I don't think so.

Notes

PREFACE

1. When the 2010 *PRWeek*/Barkley PR Cause Survey looked at men's responses to cause marketing, 88 percent of respondents said that brands should support causes. These findings are new, so as of now brand companies have not changed from their strategy of targeting women.

2. Edelman press release, "Role of 'Citizen Consumer' to Tackle Social Issues Rises, as Expectation of Government to Lead Declines" (November 4, 2010), 3, www.edelman.com/news/2010/EdelmangoodpurposeUSpressrelease .pdf (accessed July 28, 2011).

3. For cross-cultural responses, see Peggy S. Bronn and Albana B. Vrioni, "Corporate Social Responsibility and Cause-Related Marketing: An Overview," *International Journal of Advertising* 20 (2001): 207–22.

4. Daniel Yankelovich, *Profit with Honor: The New Stage of Market Capitalism* (New Haven, CT: Yale University Press, 2007), 60.

1. VALUE BRANDS . . . THEY AIN'T WHAT THEY USED TO BE

1. The ubiquity of cause-related wristbands led the fake conservative news anchor Stephen Colbert to lampoon this form of philanthropy after he broke his wrist in August 2008. While making fun of this form of charity by creating his own red wristband, Colbert managed to raise more than $170,000 for the Yellow Ribbon Fund, an organization that assists wounded soldiers and their families. See www.eonline.com/uberblog/b57292_Colberts_High-Wrist_Venture_Pays_Off.html (accessed July 14, 2011). Subsequently, Colbert did a brilliant spoof in 2010 on cause-related marketing campaigns generally when he poked fun at a tie-in between KFC and Susan G. Komen, discussed in chapter 3.

2. Lauren Gard, "We're Good Guys, Buy From Us," *Businessweek,* November 22, 2004, 72–74.

3. "THE GLOBAL FUND WELCOMES Product RED: New, Innovative Private Sector Initiative Will Increase Global Fund Resources and Improve Knowledge about the Global Fund among Consumers" (press release, January 26, 2006), www.cosmoworlds.com/product_red-the_global_fund.htm (accessed July 25, 2011). (RED) is reviewed more fully in chapter 3.

4. See Marcel Danesi, *Brands* (New York: Routledge, 2006).

5. T.J. Jackson Lears, "From Salvation to Self-Realization: Advertising and the Therapeutic Roots of the Consumer Culture, 1880–1930," in *The Culture of Consumption: Critical Essays in American History, 1880–1980,* ed. Richard Wightman Fox and T.J. Jackson Lears (New York: Pantheon Books, 1983), 1–38.

6. Douglas B. Holt, "Why Do Brands Cause Trouble? A Dialectical Theory of Consumer Culture and Branding," *Journal of Consumer Research* 29 (2002): 70–90.

7. Hamish Pringle and Marjorie Thompson, *Brand Spirit: How Cause Marketing Builds Brands* (Hoboken, NJ: John Wiley, 1999), 72.

8. There are newer theories that suggest that the brain itself can be stimulated directly to purchase particular products and bypass our thoughts and feelings all together; see Martin Lindström, *Buyology: Truth and Lies about Why We Buy* (New York: Doubleday, 2008). However, since these have not been proven and are not in common usage, they will not be part of this discussion.

9. Bohemian Mix is a group in New York City; Mayberry-ville is a group from Wasilla, Alaska. You can look up your own city or town by going to www.claritas.com/MyBestSegments/Default.jsp?ID=20&SubID=&pageName= ZIP%2BCode%2BLook-up and entering your zip code.

10. Bruce Horovitz, "Alpha Moms Leap to Top of Trendsetters: Multitasking, Tech-Savvy Women Are Expected to Be Next to Watch," *USA Today,* March 27, 2007, 1B; and see also CBS News, "The Powers of the Alpha Mom," www.cbsnews.com/video/watch/?id=2821119n (accessed October 3, 2011).

11. "Wii Would Like to Play" (2008 Gold Effie Winner), http://s3.amazonaws.com/effie_assets/2008/2331/2008_2331_pdf_1.pdf (accessed July 25, 2011).

12. Paul H. Ray, "The Emerging Culture," *American Demographics* 19, no. 2 (1997): 28–35.

13. I had several interactions with BBMG. The first and most substantial was in June 2010, when I met with Raphael Bemporad, principal and chief strategy officer, and Scott Ketchum, creative director.

14. LOHAS in the United States was estimated to be a $209 billion industry by 2006 (www.lohas.com). This category includes products related to personal health, green building, ecotourism, natural lifestyles, alternative transportation, alternative and renewable power, and socially responsible investing. While initially targeted to boomers (who still comprise the majority of LOHASians), the market has expanded to include other demographic segments, notably Millennials, and overall is estimated to be 17 percent of the population ("Beliefwatch: Lohasians," *Newsweek,* June 5, 2006, www.newsweek.com/2006/06/04/beliefwatch-lohasians.html [accessed July 25, 2011]). See the Natural Marketing

Institute web site, www.nmisolutions.com, for more information about this market segment.

15. Monica Emerich, *The Gospel of Sustainability: Media, Market and LOHAS.* (Urbana: University of Illinois Press, 2011).

16. Michael Schudson, *Advertising, the Uneasy Persuasion: Its Dubious Impact on American Society* (New York: Basic Books, 1984).

17. Carrie Heeter, "Program Selection with Abundance of Choice: A Process Model," *Human Communication Research* 12 (1985): 125–52.

18. Randolph J. Trappey III and Arch G. Woodside, *Brand Choice: Revealing Customers' Unconscious-Automatic and Strategic Thinking Processes* (New York: Palgrave Macmillan, 2005).

19. Robert Goldman and Stephen Papson, *Nike Culture: The Sign of the Swoosh* (Thousand Oaks, CA: Sage Publications, 1988).

20. In addition to Danesi, *Brands,* see Douglas B. Holt, *How Brands Become Icons: The Principles of Cultural Branding* (Cambridge, MA: Harvard Business School Press, 2004); Adam Arvidsson, *Meaning and Value in Media Culture* (London: Routledge, 2006); Celia Lury, *Brands: The Logos of Global Economy* (London: Routledge, 2004); *Brand Culture,* ed. Jonathan Schroeder and Miriam Slazer-Mörling (London: Routledge, 2006); James Twitchell, *Branded Nation: The Marketing of Megachurch, College Inc., and Museumworld** (New York: Simon & Schuster, 2005); *Corporate Cultures and Global Brands,* ed. Albrecht Rothacher (Hackensack, NJ: World Scientific Publishing, 2004); and Gareth Williams, *Branded? Products and Their Personalities* (London: V & A, 2000).

21. There is disagreement between marketers and academics and even among academics about the impact of brands and branding, particularly how it relates to identity creation. There is a growing body of literature that suggests that brands are becoming less influential in identity production because consumers find means to resist them, notably through culture jamming. See Holt, "Why Do Brands Cause Trouble?" and Zeynep Arsel and Craig J. Thompson, "Demythologizing Consumption Practices: How Consumers Protect Their Field-Dependent Identity Investments from Devaluing Marketplace Myths," *Journal of Consumer Research* 37 (2011): 791–807. See also Robert V. Kozinets and Jay M. Handelman, "Adversaries of Consumption: Consumer Movements, Activism, and Ideology," *Journal of Consumer Research* 31, no. 3 (2004): 691–704; Joseph D. Rumbo, "Consumer Resistance in a World of Advertising Clutter: The Case of Adbusters," *Psychology & Marketing* 19, no. 2 (2002): 127–48; and Vince Carducci, "Culture Jamming: A Sociological Perspective," *Journal of Consumer Culture* 6, no. 1 (2006): 116–38.

22. Brooke Erin Duffy, "Empowerment through Endorsement? Polysemic Meaning in Dove's User-Generated Advertising," *Communication, Culture & Critique* 3 (2010): 26–43, notes "much of the discourse on user-generated content (UGC) situates it within a framework of either exploitation or empowerment," which parallels the utopian/dystopian arguments that exist in relationship to the Internet generally. For the consumer empowerment argument, see Henry Jenkins, *Convergence Culture: Where Old and New Media Collide* (New York: New York University Press, 2006). For exploitation critiques, see Tiziana Terranova, "Free Labor: Producing Culture for the Digital Economy," *Social*

Text 63, no. 18 (2000): 33–58. On appropriating consumer labor in helping to sell branded products, see Adam Arvidsson, "Brands: A Critical Perspective," *Journal of Consumer Culture* 5, no. 2 (2005): 235–58.

23. Cone, Inc., "2002 Cone Corporate Citizenship Study: The Role of Cause Branding," www.coneinc.com/stuff/contentmgr/files/0/7c6165bb378273babd9 58415d58ec980/files/2002_cone_corporate_citizenship_study.pdf (accessed July 25, 2011).

24. Greg Dickinson, "Selling Democracy: Consumer Culture in the Wake of September 11," *Southern Communication Journal* 70, no. 4 (2005): 271–84.

25. Jeff Greenberg, Tom Pyszczynski, and Sheldon Solomon, "The Causes and Consequences of the Need for Self-Esteem: A Terror Management Theory," in *Public Self and Private Self*, ed. R. F. Baumeister (New York: Springer, 1986), 189–212.

26. Naomi Mandel and Stephen J. Heine, "Terror Management and Marketing: He Who Dies with the Most Toys Wins," *Advances in Consumer Research* 26 (1999): 527–32; Jamie Arndt, Sheldon Solomon, Tim Kasser, and Kennon M. Sheldon, "The Urge to Splurge: A Terror Management Account of Materialism and Consumer Behavior," *Journal of Consumer Psychology* 14, no. 3 (2004): 198–212; Jounghwa Choi, Kyoung-Nan Kwon, and Mira Lee, "Understanding Materialistic Consumption: A Terror Management Perspective," *Journal of Research for Consumers* 13 (2007), www.scribd.com/doc/17238756/ Understanding-Materialistic-Consumption-A-Terror-Management-Perspective (accessed July 25, 2011).

27. Jennifer Lerner in "Mind over Money" (*Nova* transcript), April 27, 2010, www.pbs.org/wgbh/nova/transcripts/3707_money.html (accessed July 22, 2011).

28. Philip Kotler, Hermawan Kartajaya, and Iwan Setiawan, *Marketing 3.0: From Products to Customers to the Human Spirit* (Hoboken, NJ: Wiley, 2010), 4.

29. On *The Secret,* see www.thesecret.tv (accessed July 14, 2011). For more on the blending of the sacred and the secular, see Mara Einstein, *Brands of Faith: Marketing Religion in a Commercial Age* (London: Routledge, 2007). See also Ronald Inglehart and Christian Welzel, *Modernization, Cultural Change, and Democracy: The Human Development* (New York: Cambridge University Press, 2005), on secularization in the broader context of modernization.

30. For information about possessions and sense of self, see Russell Belk, "Possessions and the Extended Self," *Journal of Consumer Research* 15 (September 1988): 139–168; Aaron C. Ahuvia, "Beyond the Extended Self: Loved Objects and Consumers' Identity Narratives," *Journal of Consumer Research* 32(June): 171–84; Banwari Mittal, "I, Me, and Mine—How Products Become Consumers' Extended Selves," *Journal of Consumer Behavior* 5 (206): 550–62; Erving Goffman, *The Presentation of Self in Everyday Life* (New York: Doubleday, 1959); Mihaly Csikszentmihalyi and Eugene Rochberg-Halton, *The Meaning of Things: Domestic Symbols and the Self* (Cambridge: Cambridge University Press, 1981); and Grant McCracken, *Culture and Consumption: New Approaches to the Symbolic Character of Consumer Goods and Activities* (Bloomington: Indiana University Press, 1988).

31. Naomi Klein, *No Logo: No Space, No Choice, No Jobs* (New York: Picador, 2002), 66.

32. Juliet Schor, *Born to Buy: The Commercialized Child and the New Consumer Culture* (New York: Scribner, 2004), 13.

33. Mandel and Heine, "Terror Management and Marketing."

34. GM's Saturn had a social networking web site called ImSaturn, which was eliminated when the brand was discontinued. FedEx maintains an employee web site called I am FedEx (www.iamfedex.com) as part of its CSR initiative.

35. Look-Look does suggest this in its presentation, but it also seems to suggest a reduction in consumerism, which is simply not the case. See www.whatteenswant.com/whatteens/images/pdf/Look-LookTheConsciousBrand-2.pdf (accessed July 17, 2011).

36. See Robert D. Putnam, *Bowling Alone: The Collapse and Revival of American Community* (New York: Simon & Schuster, 2001).

37. Albert M. Muniz Jr. and Thomas C. O'Guinn, "Brand Community," *Journal of Consumer Research* 27, no. 4 (March 2001): 412–32.

38. Heidi Hatfield Edwards and Peggy J. Kreshel, "An Audience Interpretation of Corporation Communication in a Cause-Related Corporate Outreach Event: The Avon Breast Cancer 3-Day Walk," *Journalism Communication Monographs* 10, no. 2 (2008): 175–244.

39. Samantha King, *Pink Ribbons, Inc: Breast Cancer and the Politics of Philanthropy.* (Minneapolis: University of Minnesota Press, 2008), 52.

40. www.goodguide.com (accessed July 17, 2011). In addition to its consumer applications, the site may ultimately become an Internet-age version of the Good Housekeeping Seal, allowing companies to use its GoodGuide rating on their products. See Claire Cain Miller, "On Web and iPhone, a Tool to Aid Careful Shopping," *New York Times*, June 15, 2009, B4, www.nytimes.com/2009/06/15/technology/internet/15guide.html (accessed July 25, 2011).

41. National Conference on Citizenship, "The Emerging Generation: Opportunities with the Millennials," August 27, 2009, www.ncoc.net/2gp73 (accessed October 3, 2011).

42. Kate Zernike, "Generation OMG," *New York Times*, March 8, 2009, www.nytimes.com/2009/03/08/weekinreview/08zernike.html (accessed July 25, 2011).

43. http://trendwatching.com/trends/generationg (accessed July 17, 2011).

44. A screen grab from early June 2010 containing the retraction is available at www.mouseprint.org/2010/06/07/dawn-1-bottle-1-to-save-wildlife (accessed July 17, 2011).

45. Carrick Mollencamp, "Americans Pledge Millions, but Cash Flow Takes Weeks," *Wall Street Journal,* January 16, 2010, http://online.wsj.com/article/SB10001424052748704381604575005412610261000.html (accessed July 25, 2011).

46. Cone Trend Tracker, March 10, 2010, www.coneinc.com/stuff/contentmgr/files/0/a15fa8db491fa7480e129c545fea7b11/files/2010_cone_nonprofit_marketing_trend_tracker_release_and_fact_sheet.pdf (accessed July 25, 2011).

2. HOW CORPORATIONS CO-OPT CARING: STRATEGIC PHILANTHROPY, CAUSE-RELATED MARKETING, AND CORPORATE SOCIAL RESPONSIBILITY

1. This was not Hamburger Helper's first cause-marketing campaign. In 2006 and 2007, it ran a "My Hometown Helper" campaign that invited local communities to submit essays explaining why they deserved to get a portion of the $133,000 General Mills was doling out to improve local communities. General Mills must see these campaigns as connected, because the web site (myhometownhelp.com) now reroutes to "Show Your Helping Hand." From a marketing perspective, I can understand why the company would want to tie in with Beyoncé, but in terms of a fit between brand and cause, the earlier campaign was more appropriate. See Nina Lentini, "General Mills Program Links Hamburger Helper to 'Helping Hand,'" August 6, 2007, www .mediapost.com/publications/?fa=Articles.showArticle&art_aid=65198 (accessed July 2, 2010).

2. The connections among charity, celebrity, and publicity are examined more fully in chapter 3, as is the proliferation of oversized charity partners like Feeding America.

3. This information is hidden in Show Your Helping Hand's FAQs, something I discovered only after numerous e-mails and finally a phone conversation with someone at General Mills.

4. Americans didn't line up to lend a helping hand, at least not with this promotion. Consumer participation was so low that the company provided increased incentives: "To encourage you to continue participating in helping the hungry, Show Your Helping Hand™ will offer you a $1 coupon off of the purchase of 3 boxes of Hamburger Helper® if you donate $5 to Feeding America. Simply *click here* to participate." While this suggests the campaign was failing in terms of participation, it is unknown at this point whether it helped to generate product sales.

5. Poulomi Saha and Tobias Wedd, "Brave Branding," *Ethical Corporation,* March 2006, 10–11.

6. *PRWeek*/Barkley Cause Survey, "New Study Reveals: Men Really Do Have a Heart," press release, November 3, 2010, www.prnewswire.com/ news-releases/new-study-reveals-men-really-do-have-a-heart-106647888.html (accessed July 26, 2011).

7. Patrice Tanaka, interview, April 12, 2010.

8. Daniel Yankelovich, *Profit with Honor: The New Stage of Market Capitalism* (New Haven, CT: Yale University Press, 2007), 13. Yankelovich uses the term "stewardship ethics," which combines CSR with profits. "Stewardship" is a popular term within the CSR movement.

9. George Cheney, Juliet Roper, and Steve May, "Overview," in *The Debate over Corporate Social Responsibility,* ed. id. (New York: Oxford University Press, 2007), 3–12.

10. Sophia A. Muirhead, *Corporate Contributions: The View from 50 Years* (New York: The Conference Board, 1999), 35.

11. Ibid., 36.

12. By 1993, we began to see the first declines in giving since the Great Depression. Bad enough. More disturbing is that although companies' profits

continued to increase, they did not increase their level of giving as a percentage of pretax profits. "CEOs are no longer willing to serve as the champion of the giving function," according to Craig Smith, "New Corporate Philanthropy," *Harvard Business Review* 72, no. 3 (May–June 1994): 113.

13. Muirhead, *Corporate Contributions,* 41.

14. Michael Jay Polonsky and Greg Wood, "Can the Overcommercialization of Cause-Related Marketing Harm Society?" *Journal of Macromarketing* 21, no. 1 (2001): 8–22.

15. Joe Nocera, "The Paradoxes of Businesses As Do-Gooders," *New York Times,* November 11, 2006, C1.

16. See further www.nikebiz.com/responsibility.

17. "Sponsorship Spending Receded for the First Time in 2009," IEG press release, January 26, 2010, www.sponsorship.com/About-IEG/Press-Room/Sponsorship-Spending-Receded-for-the-First-Time-in.aspx (accessed July 18, 2011).

18. Amassing consumer information and its trade-offs brings up the larger issue of privacy and surveillance, which is beyond the scope of this book. However, on mass customization, database marketing, and the Internet, see Mark Andrejevic, *iSpy: Surveillance and Power in the Interactive Era* (Lawrence: University Press of Kansas, 2007).

19. Scott M. Smith and David S. Alcorne, "Cause Marketing: A New Direction in Marketing of Corporate Responsibility," *Journal of Consumer Marketing* 8, no. 3 (1991): 19–35.

20. Cone, Inc., "Cone Releases First Cause Consumer Behavior Study," press release, October 1, 2008, www.coneinc.com/content1188 (accessed March 17, 2009).

21. Aradhna Krishna and Uday Rahan, "Cause Marketing: Spillover Effects of Cause-Related Products in a Product Portfolio," *Management Science* 55, no. 9 (2009): 1469–85.

22. (RED) products are supposed to be priced the same as their non-(RED) equivalents. For example, a (RED) nano is the same price as a blue one. However, there is no equivalent to a (Red) T-shirt if you assume the brand has value. (RED) is reviewed in more detail in chapter 3.

23. Autism Speaks 2008 Annual Report, www.autismspeaks.org/docs/Autism_Speaks_Annual_Report_2008.pdf (accessed October 3, 2011); the 2009 lighters—the ones unassociated with the charity—were recalled as dangerous, see CPSC, "Zippo Recalls Candle Lighters Due to Burn Hazard," January 27, 2010, www.cpsc.gov/cpscpub/prerel/prhtml10/10124.html (accessed October 3, 2011).

24. Dirk Olin and Jay Whitehead, "CR: How Fast It's Growing, How Much It's Spending, and How Far It's Going: An Unprecedented Gauge of the Market, with NYSE Euronext," *CR Magazine,* March–April 2010, www.thecro.com/files/CRBestPractices.pdf (accessed July 18, 2011).

25. Juliet Schor, *Plentitude: The New Economics of True Wealth* (New York: Penguin Press, 2010), 18.

26. Andrew W. Savitz and Karl Weber, *The Triple Bottom Line: How Today's Best-Run Companies Are Achieving Economic, Social and Environmental Success—and How You Can Too* (San Francisco: Jossey-Bass, 2006).

27. William McDonough and Michael Braungart, *Cradle to Cradle: Remaking the Way We Make Things* (New York: North Point Press, 2002).

28. Minette E. Drumwright and Patrick E. Murphy, "Corporate Societal Marketing," in *Handbook of Marketing and Society,* ed. Paul N. Bloom and Gregory T. Gundlach (Thousand Oaks, CA: Sage, 2001)

29. Chad Boettcher, interview, April 2009.

30. Joe Nocera, "Green Logo, but BP Is Old Oil," *New York Times,* August 12, 2006.

31. Melanie Trottman and Guy Chazan, "BP to pay $50.6 Million for Texas Safety Lapses," *Wall Street Journal,* August 13, 2010.

32. By the 1960s, most corporations, including giants like Coca-Cola and General Motors, had their own foundations, according to Craig Smith, "New Corporate Philanthropy."

33. Dan Osheyack, class discussion/interview, March 31, 2010.

34. See www.signaturetheatre.org/tixini.htm (accessed July 26, 2011).

35. Quoted at 15belowproject.org/moreinfo/index.php/about (accessed September 29, 2011).

36. Laura E. Tesler and Ruth E. Malone, "Ethical Conduct in Public and Private Arenas: Corporate Philanthropy, Lobbying, and Public Health Policy," *American Journal of Public Health* 98, no. 12 (2008): 2123–32. Available at http://ajph.aphapublications.org/cgi/reprint/98/12/2123.pdf (accessed July 19, 2011).

37. From Philip Morris documents quoted at http://legacy.library.ucsf.edu/tid/dly97d00 and http://legacy.library.ucsf.edu/tid/rze45c00 (both accessed July 26, 2011).

38. http://disneyparks.disney.go.com/blog/2010/02/record-breaking-canned-food-sculpture-unveiled-at-walt-disney-world (accessed July 26, 2011).

39. Ken Wheaton, "Consumers Will Connect the Dots between Brands," *Advertising Age,* December 3, 2007, 16. See also Duffy, "Empowerment through Endorsement?"

40. Hamish Pringle and Marjorie Thompson, *Brand Spirit: How Cause Marketing Builds Brands* (Hoboken, NJ: John Wiley, 1999), 129–32. "Change for Good" ran until 2010 when the campaign became "Flying Start" (www.britishairways.com/travel/flying-start/public/en_gb) and the partner became Comic Relief (www.comicrelief.com), a UK-based charity that "strives to create a just world free from poverty" (both accessed July 20, 2011).

41. KPMG, "Sustainability, Corporate Social Responsibility through an Audit Committee Lens (February 4, 2010), www.kpmg.com/LU/en/IssuesAndInsights/Articlespublications/Pages/Sustainabilitycorporatesocialresponsibilitythroughanauditcommitteelens.aspx (accessed August 10, 2010).

42. Packaged Facts, "Ethical Food and Beverage, Personal Care and Household Products in the U.S." (New York: Packaged Facts, 2009), 311.

43. The Clorox Company Foundation (www.cloroxcsr.com/cc-foundation), created in 1980, donates approximately 2 percent of net sales to social and environmental issues.

44. See 3M's sustainability time line at http://solutions.3m.com/wps/portal/3M/en_US/3M-Sustainability/Global/VisionHistory/Timeline (accessed July 26, 2011). In 1975, 3M launched its "Pollution Prevention Pays" initiative.

By 2005, it had reduced pollutants by 2.6 billion pounds, with company savings of $1 billion. See David Lubin and Daniel Esty, "The Big Idea: The Sustainability Imperative," *Harvard Business Review,* May 2010, 44–50. Note that in December 2010, the attorney general of Minnesota filed a lawsuit against 3M for polluting the state's water supply with chemicals called perfluorochemicals, or PFCs, over the past fifty years. There are mixed opinions as to whether 3M did what it could or should do to rectify this situation. Some Minnesota municipalities are seeking compensation from 3M to cover costs to provide clean water to their communities. Jim Anderson, "East-Metro Cities Choose Divergent Paths in 3M Lawsuit," *Star Tribune,* July 30, 2011, http://m.star tribune.com/business/?id=126466168 (accessed September 5, 2011).

45. Patricia Aburdene, *Megatrends 2010: The Rise of Conscious Capitalism* (Charlottesville, VA: Hampton Roads Publishing, 2007), 35.

46. Packaged Facts, "Ethical . . . Products in the U.S." (cited n. 42 above), 5.

47. Tim McCollum, interview, April 7, 2010.

48. See www.lifeisgood.com and "Life is good: Words of Wisdom from the Brothers Behind the T-Shirts," www.wholeliving.com/article/good-vibrations (both accessed July 26, 2011).

49. John Rooks, interview, August 17, 2010.

50. See www.hoovers.com/chipotle/–ID__106335–/freeuk-co-factsheet.xhtml and http://money.cnn.com/magazines/fortune/fortunefastestgrowing/2010/snap shots/60.html (both accessed September 29, 2011).

51. There has been some controversy regarding Dean Foods and two of its dairy farms that produce milk under the Horizon label, much of this coming from the watchdog group The Cornucopia Institute (www.cornucopia .org/dairysurvey/FarmID_134.html [accessed September 29, 2011]). Hoover's states: "Ninety percent of its milk supply is contracted through some 500 certified organic family farms across the US, while the other 10% is produced at Horizon's two company-owned farms in Idaho and Maryland." (www.hoovers .com/company/Horizon_Organic_Dairy/rhsccyi-1.html?CM_PLA=Free&CM_ CAT=Google&CM_ITE=Factsheet&CM_VEN=Biz_Dev). Cornucopia claims the number of organic family farms is "at least half," implying far less than 90 percent, though that percentage is not verified.

52. Ellen Feeney, WhiteWave vice president of responsible livelihood, interview, August 31, 2010.

53. Paul H. Ray, "The Emerging Culture," *American Demographics,* 19, no. 2 (February 1997): 56.

54. David Vogel, *The Market for Virtue: The Potential and Limits of Corporate Social Responsibility* (Washington, DC: Brookings Institution Press, 2005).

55. Pamela Cohen, interview, June 15, 2010.

56. Interbrand, Best Global Brands 2010, www.interbrand.com/en/best-global-brands/Best-Global-Brands-2010.aspx (accessed July 26, 2011).

57. Vogel, *Market for Virtue,* 163.

3. THE BIRTH OF THE HYPERCHARITY AND THE RISE OF "CHARITAINMENT"

1. A few other celebrities did print ads for Gap free of charge, some of which say, "Can a T-shirt change the world? This one can." Bono specifically mentions

that Steven Spielberg did an ad for Gap, noting that he hadn't done advertising for any product prior to this. These were unpaid sponsorships.

2. Charities that bring in multiple brand partners have been called "umbrella charities." This is not an adequate description of what these organizations are because it merely suggests bringing many groups together under a charity. Another term that has been used to describe cases where a purchase leads to charitable donations is "embedded giving," but it is not widely accepted and is not usually associated with multiple corporate sponsors.

3. Hard Rock also ran a "Pinktober" tenth anniversary promotion, with Melissa Etheridge as the spokesperson.

4. See http://globalrace.info-komen.org/site/PageServer?pagename=hq_gr_ aboutkomen (accessed July 26, 2011).

5. Samantha King paraphrased from Kris Frieswick, "Sick of Pink," *Boston Globe,* October 4, 2009, www.boston.com/bostonglobe/magazine/articles/ 2009/10/04/sick_of_pink/?page=1 (accessed March 30, 2010).

6. These campaigns are in addition to sponsoring "Race for the Cure," a five-kilometer run/walk that is a major fund-raising and promotional event for the Komen Breast Cancer Foundation.

7. Carol Cone quoted in Emily Bryson York, "How Feeding America Became the Go-to Cause for Marketers: Rebranding Catapults Charity Onto Partners' and Celebrities' A-List," *Advertising Age,* May 3, 2010, http://adage.com/ article?article_id=143647 (accessed December 9, 2010).

8. What is confusing about Lee National Denim Day (www.denimday.com) is that its marketing materials say "Wear denim in exchange for a $5 donation to the Women's Cancer Programs of EIF," but wearing jeans has nothing to do with releasing money for the cause. After all, who would be checking this? Rather, like Avon, teams are created to raise money for the cause in addition to personal donations or product purchase.

9. Clifford Marks, "Charity Brawl: Nonprofits Aren't So Generous When a Name's at Stake," *Wall Street Journal,* August 5, 2010.

10. Frieswick, "Sick of Pink."

11. Terry Long, Ann M. Taubenheim, Jennifer Wayman, Sarah Temple, and Beth Ann Ruoff, "The Heart Truth: Using the Power of Branding and Social Marketing to Increase Awareness of Heart Disease in Women," *Social Marketing Quarterly* 14, no. 3 (2008): 3–29.

12. At shopheart.org, a site supporting the American Heart Association (AHA) and the "Go Red" campaign, you can buy earrings, umbrellas, T-shirts, bags, even golf balls, and, of course, pins, among other items. There is nothing on the site that tells you how much of the purchase price goes to the organization or how the funds will be used. However, I did call and was told that "all proceeds" go to the organization. Surprisingly, the person I talked with said that I was the first person in three years that had ever asked that question.

13. National Heart Blood and Lung Institute, *The Heart Truth,* www.nhlbi .nih.gov/educational/hearttruth/index.htm (accessed July 26, 2011).

14. CBSNews.com, "Coke Fit to be the Face of Heart Health?" (February 16, 2010),www.cbsnews.com/stories/2010/02/16/health/main6213763.shtml (accessed July 26, 2011).

15. CSPI also had issues with Hanover pretzels and Sara Lee being sponsors of this program.

16. For a full list of sponsors and their contributions, see the NHLBI web site, www.nhlbi.nih.gov/educational/hearttruth/partners/corporate-partners .htm (accessed July 26, 2011).

17. Quoted in Long et al., "The Heart Truth," 7.

18. Leading causes of death in American women, 2007. www.nhlbi.nih.gov/ educational/hearttruth/downloads/html/infographic-dressgraph/infographic dressgraph.htm (accessed July 26, 2011). The first two figures are from the CDC and the last two from the American Cancer Society.

19. NHLBI, "Women's Fear of Heart Disease Has Almost Doubled in Three Years, but Breast Cancer Remains Most Feared Disease," www.nhlbi .nih.gov/educational/hearttruth/about/fear-doubled.htm (accessed July 26, 2011).

20. Philip Kotler and Nancy Lee, *Corporate Social Responsibility: Doing the Most Good for Your Company and Your Cause* (Hoboken, NJ: Wiley, 2005), outlines six different types of social initiatives: cause promotion (companies donate money or products to help promote the cause), cause-related marketing (donations are tied to sales of a product), corporate social marketing (social behavior change is sought), corporate philanthropy (donations are made directly to the cause), community volunteering (employees or other stakeholders are encouraged to volunteer), and socially responsible business practices (discretionary practices that support social causes). Most marketers don't think in terms of fine-tuning differences in promotions in this way, and most do some combination of all of these. Social marketing, however, has a specific social end that the others do not.

21. (RED) has been the focus of much criticism from academics. See, e.g., Kathleen Kuehn, "Compassionate Consumption: Healing Africa through Gap's (RED) Campaign," *Democratic Communiqué*, 23, no. 2 (2010): 23–40, and Sarah Banet-Weiser and Charlotte Lapsansky, "RED Is the New Black: Brand Culture, Consumer Citizenship and Political Possibility," *International Journal of Communication* 2 (2008): 1248–68.

22. Ben Arnoldy, "Buy a Red T-shirt to Fight AIDS. But Does It Really Help?" *Christian Science Monitor,* March 12, 2007

23. www.bugaboo.com/learn/bugaboo-red (accessed July 26, 2011).

24. Sarah Dadush, "Profiting in (RED): The Need for Enhanced Transparency in Cause-Related Marketing," *New York University Journal of International Law and Politics* 42, no. 4 (2010): 1269–1336.

25. Michal Strahilevitz and John G. Myers, "Donations to Charity as Purchase Incentives: How Well They Work May Depend on What You Are Trying to Sell," *Journal of Consumer Research* 24, no. 1 (1998): 434–46.

26. The Persuaders LLC is not legally required, as a limited liability company, to make its books public.

27. Dadush, "Profiting in (RED)," 1293.

28. See http://theglobalfund.org/en/about/donors/public (accessed September 30, 2011) and Ron Nixon, "Bottom Line for (RED)," *New York Times,* February 6, 2008.

29. (RED)'s CEO, Susan Smith Ellis, responded to criticism of the art auction as follows: "When we have an offer of help to raise awareness and funds under the (RED) banner from friends, stars and non-celebrities alike, at bake sales, walkathons, and yes, art auctions, we will gladly accept that support to help prevent 4,400 people from dying every day from a preventable and treatable disease"; http://philanthropyaction.com/nc/the_global_fund_not_seeing_red (accessed July 26, 2011).

30. Bobby Shriver, "CEO: Red's Raised Lots of Green," *Advertising Age,* March 12, 2007.

31. Paul Vallely, "The Big Question: Does the RED Campaign Help Big Western Brands More Than Africa?" *The Independent,* March 9, 2007.

32. Yoplait's "Save Lids to Save Lives" is another good example. "Yoplait has placed a cap of $1.5 million in donations to the Susan G. Komen Breast Cancer Foundation," according to Mintel (www.mintel.com). "Yoplait spends far more than $1.5 million on the related advertisements promoting the Save Lids to Save Lives foundation. As such, the donation may be viewed internally as just a part of the ad expense."

33. "Inspi(RED) Marketing or (RED)wash?" (2008), http://lifeworth.com/lifeworth2008/2009/05/inspired-marketing-or-redwash (accessed July 26, 2011).

34. Michael Gerson, "A New Social Gospel," *Newsweek,* November 13, 2006, www.newsweek.com/2006/11/12/a-new-social-gospel.html (accessed July 26, 2011).

35. Jeane MacIntosh, "Poor Idea, Bono: Nonprofit Mails $wag to 'Help' Hungry," *New York Post,* September 20, 2010.

36. Emily Bryson York, "How Feeding America Became the Go-to Cause for Marketers," *Advertising Age,* May 3, 2010.

37. The "Pound For Pound Challenge" is a partnership among *The Biggest Loser,* Feeding America, General Mills, Subway, 24 Hour Fitness, and the Kroger Co. to help Feeding America deliver millions of pounds of groceries to local food banks across the United States.

38. Mintel (www.mintel.com) cause-marketing report. Of note is that there are no educational hypercharities either. This is likely due to the localized nature of teaching our children.

39. WWF's eleven corporate sponsors include Bank of America, CVS, and Barnes & Noble, with different cause campaigns attached to each company (see www.worldwildlife.org/how/goodstuff/item8160.html [accessed July 26, 2011]). The Nature Conservancy's web site lists more than thirty corporate sponsors, including Home Depot, Disney, and Tom's of Maine. As at WWF's web site, you can click on marketing partners' names at www.nature.org/joinanddonate/corporatepartnerships/about (accessed July 26, 2011) to see a full explanation of each relationship between the Nature Conservancy and the company. Many of these are long-standing, multi-year relationships.

40. "To be perfectly honest, it's not about us," 1% for the Planet's web site says. "It's about businesses recognizing that industry and ecology are inherently connected. It's about realizing the positive effects of connecting businesses, consumers and nonprofits through philanthropy. And it's about understanding that the true cost of doing business can be mitigated by a simple pledge to the

planet" (www.onepercentfortheplanet.org/en/aboutus/history.php [accessed July 26, 2011]).

41. Boston Consulting Group, "Capturing the Green Advantage for Consumer Companies," BCG report, January 2009, www.bcg.com/documents/file15407.pdf (accessed July 26, 2011).

42. Andrea Doyle, "Trials and Tribulations in the Cult of Celebrity," *O'Dwyer's PR Report,* December 2008, 8.

43. Indystar staff, September 30, 2010, "Ochocinco Cereal Boxes Surprisingly Spicy," www.indy.com/posts/ochocinco-cereal-boxes-surprisingly-spicy (accessed October 3, 2011).

44. Laura M. Holson, "Charity Fixer to the Stars," *New York Times,* December 5, 2010.

45. Other campaigns are vague and confusing. For example, the Entertainment Industry Foundation (EIF)'s "Create the Good" campaign is a confusing use of celebrity talent. Big-name stars do print ads telling readers to go to createthegood.org and www.iparticipation.org. Both sites send people to databases for local volunteering, which makes this befuddling and ineffective.

46. James Poniewozik, "The Year of Charitainment," *Time,* December 19, 2005.

47. Laurie Ouellette, "Reality TV Gives Back: On the Civic Functions of Reality Entertainment," *Journal of Popular Film and Television* 38, no. 2 (2010).

48. Reality series are tailor-made for product placement. This began when the producer of *Survivor,* Mark Burnam, needed to fund the then-unknown show. CBS wouldn't pay the license fee he wanted. Instead, it agreed that in lieu of an upfront payment, it would split the money from advertising sales if Burnam presold sponsorships to the program, and so he did. Because of this twist of fate, promoting things like Scope mouthwash or Oreos or Ziplock bags in the middle of a reality series is now commonplace.

49. www.pfpchallenge.com (accessed July 26, 2011).

50. *Celebrity Apprentice,* May 16, 2010.

51. Campbell Robertson, "In Iraq, Colbert Does His Shtick for the Troops," *New York Times,* June 7, 2009; www.nytimes.com/2009/06/08/arts/television/08colb.html (accessed July 25, 2011).

4. THE CONSEQUENCES OF CO-OPTING COMPASSION

1. See, e.g., Michael Jay Polonsky and Greg Wood, "Can the Overcommercialization of Cause-Related Marketing Harm Society?" *Journal of Macromarketing* 21, no. 1 (2001): 8–22. See also Peggy S. Bronn and Albana B. Vrioni, "Corporate Social Responsibility and Cause-Related Marketing: An Overview," *International Journal of Advertising* 20 (2001): 207–22, for a discussion of consumer skepticism. For more information from a business perspective, see Adam Werbach, *Strategy for Sustainability: A Business Manifesto* (Boston, MA: Harvard Business Press, 2009); Jeffrey Hollender and Stephen Fenichell, *What Matters Most: How a Small Group of Pioneers Is Teaching Social Responsibility to Big Business, and Why Business Is Listening* (New York: Basic Books, 2004); and Daniel C. Esty, *Green to Gold: How Smart Companies Use Environmental*

Strategy to Innovate, Create Value, and Build Competitive Advantage (New Haven, CT: Yale University Press, 2006).

2. Angela M. Eikenberry, "The Hidden Costs of Cause Marketing," *Stanford Social Innovation Review,* Summer 2009, 51–55, www.ssireview.org/articles/ entry/the_hidden_costs_of_cause_marketing (accessed July 22, 2011).

3. Holly Hall, "Charitable Giving Fell 3.2% Last Year, Report Finds," *Chronicle of Philanthropy,* June 8, 2010, http://philanthropy.com/article/Charitable-Giving-Fell-32-/65825 (accessed October 7, 2010).

4. Wendy Smith quoted in Stephanie Strom, "New Fame for the Everyday Donor," *New York Times,* November 12, 2009. With much ballyhoo and prompting by Warren Buffet and Bill and Melinda Gates, forty billionaires have pledged to donate half of their wealth to charity, an amount estimated as high as $600 billion. These "megagifts," however, raise concerns about giving considerable power to a handful of wealthy people who will be in the position to set the social agenda. One critic suggests that the wealthy should rather pay their taxes "'on time and in full,' stop lobbying against tax regulations and provide better wages for employees" (Anda Adams, Justin van Fleet, and Rebecca Winthrop, "Billionaire Pledges: The Innovative Financing We Need?" www .brookings.edu/opinions/2010/0820_philanthropy_winthrop.aspx [accessed July 27, 2011]). This is an important issue, but one too far afield for me to address here.

5. "Change Does Begin at Home," *Conservation,* www.conservationmagazine .org/2010/06/change-does-begin-at-home (accessed July 27, 2011), and Thomas Dietz et al., "Household Actions Can Provide a Behavioral Wedge to Rapidly Reduce U.S. Carbon Emissions," *Proceedings of the National Academy of Sciences* 106, no. 44 (2009): 18452–56. See www.pnas.org/content/106/44/18452/ T1.expansion.html (accessed October 1, 2011) for the full list of household actions to reduce emissions.

6. See Derrick Jensen, "Taking Shorter Showers Doesn't Cut It: Why Personal Change Does Not Equal Political Change," *Onion Magazine,* July–August 2009.

7. Other examples include an episode of *Project Runway* where the contestants created couture from environmentally friendly textiles and an episode of *Dance Your Ass Off* where the costume designers "recycled" outfits from previous episodes. Universal has added an annual "Green Week" in November.

8. Daniel B. Wood, "California Advances Grocery Store Plastic Bag Ban," *Christian Science Monitor,* June 3, 2010, www.csmonitor.com/USA/2010/0603/ California-advances-grocery-store-plastic-bag-ban (accessed July 22, 2011).

9. Joel Berg, *All You Can Eat: How Hungry Is America?* (New York: Seven Stories Press, 2008), quoted in Keith Goetzman, "Giving When It Hurts," *Utne Reader,* March–April 2009, www.utne.com/Politics/Giving-Rethinking-charity-in-the-economic-crisis.aspx (accessed July 27, 2011).

10. Jensen, "Taking Shorter Showers Doesn't Cut It."

11. Celia W. Dugger, "As Donors Focus on AIDS, Child Illnesses Languish," *New York Times,* October 30, 2009, A10. As the Columbia University economist Jeffrey Sachs is quoted as saying in this article, it is wrongheaded to think that we need to make "a terrible and tragic choice" between AIDS and these other tragedies. Both can be addressed.

12. See Alan R. Andreasen, *Ethics in Social Marketing* (Washington, DC: Georgetown University Press, 2001).

13. "While a few [Upromise] participants pledge as much as 10 percent of the purchasing price, most donate one percent. Thus, in order to earn $1,000 for college, relatives and friends must purchase $100,000 of goods and services, while providing the participating companies with a great deal of valuable demographic information," Inger Stole notes in "'Cause-Related Marketing': Why Social Change and Corporate Profits Don't Mix," PR Watch, July 14, 2006, www.prwatch.org/node/4965 (accessed July 22, 2011).

14. Amanda B. Bower and Stacy Landreth Grau, "Explicit Donations and Inferred Endorsements: Do Corporate Social Responsibility Initiatives Suggest a Nonprofit Organization Endorsement?" *Journal of Advertising* 38, no. 3 (Fall 2009): 113–26.

15. The American Cancer Society based its decision to license this product on the Food and Drug Administration's approval of the product. See Matthew Berglind and Cheryl Nakata,"Cause-Related Marketing: More Bang than Buck?" *Business Horizons* 48 (2005): 443–53.

16. www.goodhousekeeping.com/product-testing/history/green-good-house keeping-seal-faqs (accessed July 27, 2011).

17. The Consumers Union, known for producing *Consumer Reports,* has created a web site (www.greenerchoices.org) that evaluates the meaning of 150 labels used to sell groceries, including terms such as "100% biocompatible" and "water based."

18. Johann Hari, "The Big Business of Conservation: Corruption Has Destroyed America's Mainstream Environmental Groups," *Utne Reader,* July–August 2010, excerpted from *The Nation*, March 22, 2010, www .utne.com/Environment/Big-Business-of-Conservation-Corruption-Environ-mental-Groups.aspx?utm_content=07.06.10+Environment&utm_campaign =Emerging+Ideas-Every+Day&utm_source=iPost&utm_medium=email (accessed July 27, 2011).

19. Bower and Grau, "Explicit Donations and Inferred Endorsements," 118.

20. An independent not-for-profit company, the Carbon Trust, developed the United Kingdom's standards for greenhouse gas (GHG) emissions and created labeling for products that meet GHG emissions-reduction standards. See www .carbontrust.co.uk (accessed July 22, 2011). Packaged Facts, "Ethical Food and Beverage, Personal Care and Household Products in the U.S." (2009), 37; purchasable at www.packagedfacts.com.

21. Karen Flaherty and William Diamond, "The Impact of Consumer Mental Budgeting on the Effectiveness of Cause-Related Marketing," *American Marketing Association Conference Proceedings* 10 (1999): 151–52; Donald R. Lichtenstein, Minette E. Drumwright, and Bridgette M. Braig, "The Effect of Corporate Social Responsibility on Consumer Donations to Corporate-Supported Nonprofits," *Journal of Marketing* 68, no. 4 (2004): 16–32.

22. Berglind and Nakata, "Cause-Related Marketing," 451.

23. Alan R. Andreasen, "Profits for Nonprofits: Find a Corporate Partner," *Harvard Business Review,* November 1, 1996, raises additional concerns for nonprofits who hitch their wagon to the consumer marketplace. They may be

caused to change their funding activities to appeal or attract corporate sponsors, or they may be negatively affected by scandals associated with their corporate partners, and simply relying on corporate funding has inherent problems, because the firm is tied to the whims of the market.

24. Natalie Zmuda and Emily Bryson York, "Cause Effect: Brands Rush to Save World One Deed at a Time," *Advertising Age* 81, no. 9 (March 10, 2010): 1, 22.

25. ABC News, "Billions of Dollars in Donations Post-Katrina, Yet Very Little Relief," August 3, 2006, http://blogs.abcnews.com/theblotter/2006/08/billions_of_dol.html (accessed July 27, 2011).

26. "Wyclef Jean's Funny Money: Earthquake Aid Pours into Charity That Has Enriched Singer," The Smoking Gun, January 6, 2010, www.thesmokinggun.com/documents/crime/wyclef-jean-charitys-funny-money (accessed July 27, 2011)

27. See David Roodman's Microfinance Open Book Blog, October 2, 2009, http://blogs.cgdev.org/open_book/2009/10/kiva-is-not-quite-what-it-seems.php (accessed July 22, 2011).

28. This list is culled from Polonsky and Wood, "Can the Overcommercialization of Cause-Related Marketing Harm Society?" and Berglind and Nakata, "Cause-Related Marketing."

29. Robert J. Shiller in "Mind over Money" (*Nova* transcript), April 27, 2010; www.pbs.org/wgbh/nova/transcripts/3707_money.html (accessed July 22, 2011).

30. Elizabeth Martinez and Arnoldo Garcia, "What Is Neoliberalism: A Brief Definition for Activists," www.corpwatch.org/article.php?id=376 (accessed July 22, 2011).

31. Inger Stole, "Philanthropy as Public Relations: A Critical Perspective on Cause Marketing," *International Journal of Communication* 2 (2008): 20–40.

32. For in-depth discussions of the relationships among jobs, corporations, and taxes, see Naomi Klein, *No Logo: Taking Aim at the Brand Bullies* (New York: Picador, 1999); Greg LeRoy, *The Great American Jobs Scam: Corporate Tax Dodging and the Myth of Job Creation* (San Francisco: Berrett-Koehler, 2005).

33. Goetzman, "Giving When It Hurts."

34. Ibid.

35. "Role of 'Citizen Consumer' to Tackle Social Issues Rises, as Expectation of Government to Lead Declines," www.edelman.com/news/2010/Edelman goodpurposeUSpressrelease.pdf (accessed October 1, 2011).

36. Susanna K. Ripken, "Corporations Are People Too: A Multi-Dimensional Approach to the Corporate Personhood Puzzle," *Fordham Journal of Corporate & Financial Law* 15, no. 1 (2009): 97–177.

37. *Citizens United v. Federal Election Commission*, 558 U.S. 08-205 (2010).

38. Waggener Edstrom Worldwide, "Eighty-Six Percent of Consumers Believe Profitable Businesses Can Address Social Issues, but Want Efforts to Be in Keeping with Core Business Strategy" (press release, 2009).

39. Dan Pallotta, *Uncharitable: How Restraints on Nonprofits Undermine Their Potential* (Lebanon, NH: Tufts University Press, 2008), xii.

40. See Amy Feldman, "Philanthropy: Rethinking How to Give: A Growing Movement to Review and Rate Charities on Their Real World Results May Give Donors a Better Idea Where They Can Do the Most Good," *Businessweek*, January 21, 2010. Other sources for rating charities include GiveWell, Philanthropedia, GreatNonprofits, GuideStar, Root Cause, and Partners for Change Initiative.

41. For more information about these companies, see their web sites: http://bbmg.com, www.thesoapgroup.com, and www.whatonearthisgoingon.com/index.html.

42. There are also associations like Business for Social Responsibility (www.bsr.org), which created standards for business practices, faith-based groups like the Interfaith Center on Corporate Responsibility (ICCR), and www.CorporateRegister.com, which tracks reportage of corporate social responsibility.

43. See http://justcauseit.com/about (accessed July 27, 2011).

44. John A. Byrne, "The Promise of Reinvention," *Fast Company*, August 1, 2003, www.fastcompany.com/magazine/73/edlet.html (accessed October 1, 2011).

45. www.strategyforsustainability.com/do-one-thing (accessed July 27, 2011).

46. Packaged Facts, "Ethical Food and Beverage, Personal Care and Household Products in the U.S." (2009), 13; purchasable at www.packagedfacts.com.

47. Ilana DeBare, "The World According to Tom's of Maine," *San Francisco Chronicle*, October 10, 2007.

48. Samuel Fromartz, "Honest Tea Founder Talks on Coke Deal" (February 11, 2008), www.chewswise.com/chews/2008/02/interview-seth.html (accessed July 27, 2011).

49. "Patagonia's Journey to Sustainability," *LOHAS Weekly Newsletter*, July 1, 2001, www.lohas.com/articles/67666.html (accessed December 10, 2010).

50. www.bcorporation.net/about (accessed July 23, 2011).

51. Fary Haber, "Md. 'Becoming the Delaware of Benefit Corporations,'" *Baltimore Business Journal*, October 5, 2010, www.bizjournals.com/baltimore/stories/2010/10/04/daily18.html?surround=etf&ana=e_article (accessed July 27, 2011). Other states will or are expected to implement similar legislation. Vermont instituted a b corporation law in May 2011, and New York, New Jersey, Pennsylvania, Virginia, and Michigan are in various stages of introducing this type of legislation.

52. Stephanie Ryan, B Corp (www.bcorporation.net/team), e-mail to the author, November 24, 2010.

53. Josée Johnston, "The Citizen-Consumer Hybrid: Ideological Tensions in the Case of Whole Foods Market," *Theory and Society* 37, no. 3 (2008): 229–70. For historical discussion of citizen-consumers, see Greg Dickinson, "Selling Democracy: Consumer Culture in the Wake of September 11," *Southern Communication Journal* 70, no. 4 (2005): 271–84, and for an in-depth critique of ethical consumption, see Jo Littler, *Radical Consumption: Shopping for Change in Contemporary Culture* (New York: Open University Press/McGraw-Hill Education, 2009).

54. Robert D. Putnam, *Bowling Alone: The Collapse and Revival of American Community* (New York: Simon & Schuster, 2000).

55. Anand Giridharadas, "Boycotts Minus the Pain," *New York Times* October 11, 2009.

56. See also Toby Miller, *The Well-Tempered Self: Citizenship, Culture and the Postmodern Subject* (Baltimore: Johns Hopkins University Press, 1993); for a feminist interpretation, see Josée Johnston, and Judith Taylor, "Feminist Consumerism and Fat Activism: A Comparative Study of Grassroots Activism and the Dove Real Beauty Campaign," *Signs: Journal of Women in Culture and Society* 33, no. 4 (2008): 941–66.

57. Michael Schudson, "Citizens, Consumers, and the Good Society," *Annals of the American Academy of Political and Social Science,* 611, no. 1 (May 2007): 236–49.

58. Lawrence B. Glickman, "Boycott Mania: As Business Ethics Fall, Consumer Activism Rises," *Boston Globe,* July 31, 2005; www.commondreams .org/cgi-bin/print.cgi?file=/headlineso5/0731-03.htm (accessed July 23, 2011).

59. Michael J. Barone, Anthony D. Miyazaki, and Kimberly A. Taylor, "The Influence of Cause-Related Marketing on Consumer Choice: Does One Good Turn Deserve Another?" *Journal of the Academy of Marketing Science* 28, no. 2 (2000): 248–62.

60. In 2007, the top reason customers gave for buying a Prius was "it makes a statement about me"—much as wearing a Livestrong bracelet does, according to Micheline Maynard, "Say 'Hybrid' and Many People Will Hear 'Prius,'" *New York Times,* July 4, 2007, www.nytimes.com/2007/07/04/business/04hybrid .html (accessed October 1, 2011).

61. Aradhna Krishna and Uday Rahan, "Cause Marketing: Spillover Effects of Cause-Related Products in a Product Portfolio," *Management Science* 55, no. 9 (2009): 1469–85.

62. Josée Johnston, "The Citizen-Consumer Hybrid: Ideological Tensions and the Case of Whole Foods Market," *Theory and Society* 37 (2008): 229–70.

63. Margee Hume, "Compassion without Action: Examining the Young Consumers Consumption and Attitude to Sustainable Consumption," *Journal of World Business* 45, no. 4 (October 2010): 385–94.

64. Anand Giridharadas, "Expressing Convictions at the Mall," *New York Times,* October 9, 2009.

65. See *The Politics and Pleasures of Consuming Differently,* ed. Kate Soper, Martin H. Ryle, and Lyn Thomas (New York: Palgrave Macmillan, 2009).

66. Jensen, "Taking Shorter Showers Doesn't Cut It."

5. SHOPPING IS NOT PHILANTHROPY. PERIOD.

1. See Stephanie Soechtig's 2009 documentary *Tapped,* www.tappedthe-movie.com (accessed July 23, 2011); Krisy Gashler, "Thirst for Bottled Water Unleashes Flood of Environmental Concerns," *USA Today,* June 7, 2008. The industry no longer tracks by bottles but by liters, which in 2010 totaled more than 32.7 million ("Bottled Water Industry Profile: United States," *Bottled Water Industry: United States,* April 2011). For an investigative report about Fiji and its questionable marketing and sourcing practices, see Anna Lenzer,

"Fiji Water: Spin the Bottle," *Mother Jones*, September–October 2009, http://motherjones.com/politics/2009/09/fiji-spin-bottle?page=1 (accessed July 27, 2011).

2. Yian Q. Mui, "Bottled Water Boom Appears Tapped Out," *Washington Post*, August 13, 2009; Lempert Report/Consumer Insight, Inc., "Cold Shoulders for Bottled Waters," Facts, Figures & The Future, March 2009, http://app .subscribermail.com/dspcd.cfm?ec=fe74634530874e5a88f7f53c33025f7a& email=0 (accessed July 27, 2011).

3. David A. Lubin and Daniel C. Esty, "The Sustainability Imperative," *Harvard Business Review*, May 2010, 44–50. Coca-Cola has also pledged "water neutrality," an effort to reduce environmental effects by replenishing watersheds to the extent that it extracts. This is supposed to be functional by 2020, but seems mostly window dressing at this point.

4. Other examples include Tumai water and Give brand.

5. Aneel Kamani, "The Case Against Corporate Social Responsibility," *Wall Street Journal*, August 23, 2010, argues that private companies are free to pursue social concerns but public companies are not, because their first responsibility is to their shareholders.

6. Lubin and Esty, "Sustainability Imperative," 48.

7. Packaged Facts, "Ethical Food and Beverage, Personal Care and Household Products in the U.S." (New York: Packaged Facts, 2009), 191.

8. Another McDonald's ad demonstrating this mixed messaging was "Bee Good to the Planet," which obviously has an environmental message and was tied into Jerry Seinfeld's *Bee Movie*. The mechanism of the campaign was for kids to go online and pledge to "Bee Good to the Planet" at HappyMeal.com. It is hard to see this as anything but hypocritical when there is a throwaway plastic toy in every Happy Meal produced, as well as concerns around paper waste and beef production. It also entices kids to go online and interact with a web site that promotes consumption of nutrient-lacking food—action identified as a key contributor to obesity.

9. Matthew Berglind and Cheryl Nakata, "Cause-Related Marketing: More Bang than Buck?" *Business Horizons* 48 (2005): 443–53, here 452.

10. Starbucks commercial: www.youtube.com/user/starbucks?blend=1&ob =4#p/u/124/kkC5qYHolno (accessed July 23, 2011).

11. Angela M. Eikenberry, "The Hidden Costs of Cause Marketing," *Stanford Social Innovation Review*, Summer 2009, 51–55, here 54.

12. Heidi Hatfield Edwards and Peggy J. Kreshel, "An Audience Interpretation of Corporation Communication in a Cause-Related Corporate Outreach Event: The Avon Breast Cancer 3-Day Walk," *Journalism Communication Monographs* 10, no. 2 (2008): 208–9.

13. Camille Sweeney, "The Latest in Fitness: Millions for Charity," *New York Times*, July 7, 2005.

14. The nexus of charity, fitness, and consumerism is fully embodied in plus-3network.com, where people connect with corporate sponsors and causes while tracking their training progress, leading to charitable giving. This is a social networking site for charity, a topic covered more fully in chapter 7.

15. http://trendwatching.com/trends/generationg (accessed July 27, 2011).

16. Melanie Eversley, "Giving Is Good, but Wise Giving Helps Even More," *USA Today,* April 13, 2010, www.usatoday.com/news/sharing/2010-04-12-how-to-help_N.htm (accessed October 3, 2011).

17. *O, The Oprah Magazine,* April 2009, "The Green O List: Nine Organic, Sustainable, Natural, Green Things We Think Are Great, Just In Time for Earth Day," www.oprah.com/omagazine/O-Magazines-April-2009-Green-O-List (accessed July 27, 2011).

18. Joyce Wadler, "Green, but Still Feeling Guilty," *New York Times,* September 29, 2010; www.nytimes.com/2010/09/30/garden/30guilt.html (accessed July 23, 2011).

19. Bennett Gordon, "Money Can Make You Less Happy," *Utne Reader,* May 27, 2009, www.utne.com/Mind-Body/Money-Can-Make-You-Less-Happy .aspx (accessed October 3, 2011).

20. Sut Jhally, "Advertising at the Edge of the Apocalypse" (2000), in *Critical Studies in Media Commercialism,* ed. Robin Anderson and Lance Strate (Oxford, England: Oxford University Press), 27–39).

21. Coca-Cola demonstrates its lack of commitment to real change at almost every turn. When Pepsi Refresh was launched around the time of the Super Bowl in 2010, Coca-Cola also jumped on the social bandwagon. However, Coke's was with a very self-serving element. Instead of crowdsourcing good ideas, Coca-Cola donated a dollar to Boys and Girls Clubs of America every time someone went to the Coca-Cola Facebook page and shared a virtual Coke gift. Stuart Elliott, "Pepsi Invites the Public to Do Good," *New York Times,* February 1, 2010, B6.

22. Stacy Malkan, "Not so Pretty in Pink: Marketing Toxic Makeup to Young Girls," *Utne Reader,* January–February 2009; www.utne.com/Envi ronment/Not-So-Pretty-in-Pink-Marketing-Toxic-Makeup-to-Young-Girls .aspx?page=3 (accessed July 23, 2011). See also the Environmental Working Group's Skin Deep database, www.cosmeticsdatabase.com.

23. Peggy Orenstein, "Think about Pink," *New York Times Magazine,* November 14, 2010. See also Barbara Ehrenreich, *Bright-Sided: How the Relentless Promotion of Positive Thinking Has Undermined America* (New York: Metropolitan Books, 2009) on the happiness industry, including a discussion of the author's bout with breast cancer and how the emphasis on pink ribbons deflects feminism and encourages deference to medical authority.

24. TerraChoice, http://sinsofgreenwashing.org/findings/greenwashing-report-2009/ (accessed July 24, 2011).

25. Traci Watson, "'Green' Claims by Marketers Go Unchecked," *USA Today,* June 21, 2009. For a crowdsourcing site that rates advertising for its greenwashing claims, see http://greenwashingindex.com.

26. Jon Gingerich, "FTC Cracks Down on 'Green' Advertising Claims," *O'Dwyer's PR Report,* November 2010, 12.

27. Ken Peattie and Sue Peattie, "Social Marketing: A Pathway to Consumption Reduction?" *Journal of Business Research* 62, no. 2 (2009): 260–68.

28. Alan Andreasen, *Social Marketing in the 21st Century* (Thousand Oaks, CA: Sage Publications, 2005), 58.

29. See www.ppu.org.uk/chidren/advertising_toys_eu.html (accessed July 24, 2011) for this and other examples.

30. Andreasen, *Social Marketing*, 132.

6. CAN COMPANIES MAKE A DIFFERENCE?

1. On LOHAS, see www.lohas.com and chapter 1 above.

2. "The Future of 'Me,' 'We' and You," Faith Popcorn presentation at LOHAS Forum. June 24, 2010.

3. David A. Lubin and Daniel C. Esty, "The Sustainability Imperative," *Harvard Business Review*, May 2010, 47.

4. Steve French and Gwynne Rogers, NMI presentation at LOHAS Forum, June 2010, Boulder, CO.

5. Shelton Group presentation, LOHAS Forum, June 2010, Boulder, CO.

6. L'Oréal bought the Body Shop in 2006. This was, in part, to help reduce criticism from environmental activists and reverse its reputation as a selfish corporation. The Body Shop acquisition came with credentials in environmental retailing, fair trade, social responsibility, and multicultural marketing. The Body Shop remains a stand-alone entity within L'Oréal and continues its pro-social practices, for example, animal-cruelty-free products, fair trade, sustainable product sourcing, recycled packaging, and social programs, particularly initiatives that raise awareness of violence against women around the world. Ben & Jerry's, while also a wholly owned subsidiary, has had a rocky relationship with its corporate parent, the Anglo-Dutch conglomerate Unilever, which made cutbacks early on, but has retained many of the pro-social programs that existed during Ben & Jerry's independence.

7. newmansownfoundation.org/giving (accessed October 2, 2011).

8. www.corporatephilanthropy.org/membership/members.html (accessed July 27, 2011).

9. "General Newman's Own Questions," www.newmansown.com/genQA .aspx#q1a (accessed July 27, 2011).

10. James Eberhard quoted in Stephanie Schomer, "The Recovery Business," *Fast Company*, July–August 2010, 51.

11. www.metowestyle.com (accessed July 24, 2011).

12. www.clifbar.com/soul/who_we_are (accessed July 24, 2011).

13. Margaret Heffernan, "Eileen Fisher: Entrepreneur," *More*, April 2009.

14. MAC Cosmetics has other CSR initiatives, such as cruelty-free products and "Back to Mac," a recycling program that gives free lipstick to customers who return six empty packages from other products.

15. www.macaidsfund.org/#/glam/howitworks (accessed July 24, 2011).

16. http://photoproject.ecomagination.com (accessed July 24, 2011).

17. Paul Hawken, *The Ecology of Commerce: A Declaration of Sustainability* (New York: Harper Business, 1993, 2010). "Ray Anderson—Interface Carpets," www.youtube.com/watch?v=OUG4JXE6K4A (accessed July 24, 2011).

18. Ray Anderson died in late 2011 while this book was in preparation.

19. www.interfaceglobal.com/Sustainability/Our-Journey/Vision.aspx (accessed July 24, 2011).

20. www.interfaceglobal.com/Company/Leadership-Team/Ray-Watch/Meet-Ray.aspx (accessed July 24, 2011).

21. Walmart made a commitment in 2008 to increase its offerings of local fruits and vegetables. It claimed in a press release to be "the nation's largest purchaser of local produce" ("Walmart Commits to America's Farmers as Produce Aisles Go Local," July 1, 2008, http://walmartstores.com/pressroom/news/8414 .aspx [accessed July 27, 2011]). Its move into organic produce caused it to take off exponentially and enter the mainstream. However, environmentalists reacted negatively because most of this "local" produce comes from industrial farms, and while some of it is sold locally, it may also be shipped to stores throughout the United States.

22. Marc Gunther, "The Green Machine," *Fortune Magazine,* July 31, 2006, http://money.cnn.com/magazines/fortune/fortune_archive/2006/08/07/8382593 (accessed July 27, 2011).

23. Lubin and Esty, "Sustainability Imperative," 48.

24. Julie Schmit, "Going Greener: Wal-Mart Plans New Solar Power Initiative," *USA Today,* September 20, 2010.

25. Keith Johnson, "Tagged: Wal-Mart's Big Push for Eco-Labels," *Wall Street Journal,* July 16, 2009, http://blogs.wsj.com/environmentalcapital/2009/07/15/tagged-wal-marts-big-push-for-eco-labels (accessed July 27, 2011).

26. Joel Makower, "The State of Green Business 2009: Green Moves Up, and Down, the Chain of Command," February 11, 2009; www.greenbiz.com/news/2009/02/11/state-green-business-2009-green-moves-and-down-chain-command (accessed July 24, 2011).

27. Hamilton Nolan, "Life at Wal-Mart: The Workers Speak, Vol. 1," Gawker, October 15, 2010, gawker.com/5664893/life-at-walmart-the-workers-speak-vol-1 (accessed October 2, 2011).

28. Stephanie Rosenbloom, "At Wal-Mart, Labeling to Reflect Green Intent," *New York Times,* July 15, 2009, www.nytimes.com/2009/07/16/business/energy-environment/16walmart.html (accessed July 24, 2011).

29. "James Hansen and Heather Rogers Discuss Real Solutions to Climate Change," talk at CUNY Graduate Center, April 30, 2010.

30. Bob Gilbreath, phone interview by the author, July 1, 2010.

31. David Ignatius, "A New Way to Look at the Problem of Global Poverty," *Ottawa Citizen,* July 10, 2005, A10.

32. C.K. Prahalad, *The Fortune at the Bottom of the Pyramid: Eradicating Poverty through Profits.* 2005. Upper Saddle River, NJ: Pearson Education, 2009.

33. www.dlightdesign.com/home_global.php (accessed July 24, 2011).

34. Lisa Friedman, "Bringing Clean Light to Poor Nations and Moving Beyond Charity," *New York Times,* October 20, 2010.

35. Marci Alboher, "A Social Solution without Going the Nonprofit Route," *New York Times,* March 5, 2009, B5.

7. WE ARE NOT CONSUMERS

1. Tom LaForge, global director, human and cultural insights, Coca-Cola Company, presentation at the LOHAS Forum, Boulder, CO, June 2010.

2. In her book *SuperCorp: How Vanguard Companies Create Innovation, Profits, Growth, and Social Good* (New York: Crown Business, 2009), Rosabeth Moss Kanter of the Harvard Business School looks at large multinationals that are realigning their operations around a strong sense of purpose that guides innovation, what she calls "bringing society in." She concludes that connecting production to purpose is a trend corporations avoid to their detriment. "Companies that do *not* operate this way will not only lose the advantages of innovation, motivation, and public support, they will also have trouble being coherent and finding business opportunities," Kanter told Sean Silverthorne (Q&A with Rosabeth Moss Kanter, October 5, 2009, http://hbswk.hbs.edu/item/6295.html [accessed July 27, 2011]). She is not alone in thinking this. There is growing (although still controversial) evidence linking a concern for social interests with increased stockholder payoffs. Joshua D. Margolis and James P. Walsh conducted a meta-analysis of studies over thirty years that sought to link financial performance to some measure of social performance. They found a positive relationship in 42 of 80 studies (53%). Social performance led to better financial performance. However, the results were not unequivocal. They also found a reverse causation in nineteen studies, giving rise to the argument that a concern for society may come about only *after* good financial performance allows it to happen. See Margolis and Walsh, *People and Profits? The Search for a Link between a Company's Social and Financial Performance* (Mahwah, NJ: Lawrence Erlbaum Associates, 2001); id., "Misery Loves Companies: Rethinking Social Initiatives by Business," *Administrative Science Quarterly* 48 (June 2003): 268–305.

3. Monica Emerich, *The Gospel of Sustainability: Media, Market and LOHAS* (Urbana: University of Illinois Press, 2011).

4. Steve Jobs put an open letter to consumers on Apple's web site explaining its sustainability initiatives, because he felt compelled by customers to do so. The company continues, however, to balk at producing a sustainability report as its competitors do.

5. Noopur Agarwal, class presentation and interview, April 27, 2011.

6. At 35 percent, the U.S. corporate tax rate is the highest in the developed world. Companies avoid paying this high rate by moving operations overseas, particularly to Switzerland and Ireland, where the tax rates are significantly lower. It has been reported that approximately $1.2 trillion in American corporate profits remain overseas so as to avoid paying U.S. taxes. In addition, loopholes enable companies to get around the tax rate, enabling them to pay rates as low as 3.6 percent ("The New Tax Havens," *60 Minutes*, www.cbsnews.com/video/watch/?id=7360932n [acccessed October 2, 2011]). Repairing this system will require some combination of reducing the corporate tax rate—some have suggested a flat rate of 20 percent—and closing up the loopholes.

7. These figures are from 2006. The low rating may have spurred them to improve. In the past two years, the foundation has moved from a one-star to a three-star rating.

8. Elizabeth Royte, "Book Release: The Story of Stuff," www.elle.com/Pop-Culture/Movies-TV-Music-Books/Book-Release-The-Story-of-Stuff (accessed July 27, 2011). See also Paul Hawken, *Blessed Unrest: How the Largest Social*

Movement in History Is Restoring Grace, Justice, and Beauty to The World (New York: Penguin Books, 2007), and *The Ecology of Commerce: A Declaration of Sustainability* (New York: Harper Business, 1993, 2010).

9. Also see Aid Watch (http://aidwatchers.com), a blog run by William Easterly, a professor of economics at New York University and author of *The White Man's Burden: Why the West's Efforts to Aid the Rest Have Done so Much Ill and So Little Good* (2006). This site is no longer updated and may be too academic for some, but it offers smart insights and interesting debates.

10. http://poverty.com, managed by the Berkman Center for Internet & Society at Harvard University and the United Nations World Food Program, is a sister site to www.freerice.com. Poverty.com presents in straightforward detail how widespread hunger is around the world, as well as how the problems of hunger might be solved.

11. Laura Hahn, "FreeRice: A Game That Fights Hunger," www.goodhouse keeping.com/family/teens/free-rice-game (accessed July 27, 2011).

12. "Get the Vibe: SocialVibe.com Empowers Consumers to Get Sponsored, Do Good," press release, May 14, 2008, www.businesswire.com/news/home/20080514006582/en/Vibe-SocialVibe.com-Empowers-Consumers-Sponsored-Good (accessed July 27, 2011).

13. Kiva is not the only site for this. MicroPlace, a division of PayPal, is another.

14. The most publicized version of this is the "One Laptop per Child" (OLPC) program (http://one.laptop.org), based in part on Nicholas Negroponte's book *Being Digital* (New York: Knopf, 1985). Originally, if you bought a laptop for your child, OLPC donated a computer to a child in the developing world. However, the program was ended because of disappointing sales, owing to a combination of the recession and the increased availability of inexpensive netbooks. Now OLPC has a donation-based funding system.

15. George Alvarez, interview, December 16, 2010, New York.

16. Suzanne Shelton, CEO of the Shelton Group, presentation at the LOHAS Forum, Boulder, CO, June 2010.

17. Tim Showalter-Loch is now the Search Institute's vice president of strategic partnerships; www.search-institute.org/tim-showalter-loch (accessed October 2, 2011).

18. Bob Gilbreath, "Takeaways from the Cause Marketing Forum," www.marketingwithmeaning.com/2010/06/11/takeaways-from-the-cause-marketing-forum-cmf10 (accessed July 27, 2011).

19. Clive Thompson, "Nothing Grows Forever: Meet the Economists Who Are Rewriting the Gospel of Consumption," *Utne Reader,* November–December 2010.

20. Douglas Rushkoff quoted in Aaron Heinrich, "Can Consumer Culture Save the World?" *Just Cause,* June 1, 2009; http://justcauseit.com/articles/can-consumer-culture-save-world (accessed July 25, 2011).

21. Laura Daily, "Livin' La Vida Local: What You Buy Can Change Your Town for the Better," *AARP Magazine,* September–October 2010.

22. George Ritzer, *The McDonaldization of Society: An Investigation into the Changing Character of Contemporary Social Life* (Newbury Park, CA: Pine Forge Press, 1993).

23. Steve French and Gwynne Rogers, Natural Marketing Institute, presentation at the LOHAS Forum, Boulder, CO, June 2010.

24. Jonah Sachs, and Susan Finkelpearl, "From Selling Soap to Selling Sustainability: Social Marketing," in *State of the World, 2010: Transforming Cultures: From Consumerism to Sustainability: A Worldwatch Institute Report on Progress toward a Sustainable Society,* ed. Linda Starke and Lisa Mastny (New York: Norton, 2010).

Index

TEXT
10/13 Sabon

DISPLAY
Sabon, Din

COMPOSITOR
Toppan Best-set Premedia Limited

INDEXER
Leonard S. Rosenbaum

PRINTER AND BINDER
Maple-Vail Book Manufacturing Group